Caring for Preschool Children, 2nd Ed.

A Competency-Based Training Program

Volume II

Derry G. Koralek

Diane Trister Dodge

Peter J. Pizzolongo

Washington, DC

Published by

Teaching Strategies, Inc.
P.O. Box 42243
Washington, DC 20015

Distributed by

Gryphon House Inc.
P.O. Box 207
Beltsville, MD 20704

ISBN: 1-879537-26-5 (Volume II)

Library of Congress Card Catalog Number: 96-61070

Acknowledgments

Caring for Preschool Children has a long history and therefore we have many individuals to acknowledge and thank. The primary basis for this publication is a training program developed by the authors for the U.S. Navy and the U.S. Army Child Development Services Programs. Carolee Callen, then Head of the Navy Child Development Services Branch, originally conceived of the idea of a standardized, self-instructional training program for child care staff. In 1986 the Navy contracted with Creative Associates International, Inc., a Washington, DC-based consulting firm where the authors then worked, to develop a comprehensive training program. M.-A. Lucas, Chief of Child Development Services in the U.S. Army, funded an adaptation of the training program to support CDA training in Army child development centers. We are indebted to these two individuals, their Headquarters staff, and the staff at Army and Navy child development centers who reviewed all drafts of the materials developed under this contract and provided us with constructive and helpful suggestions that greatly improved the program.

During the development of this training program, in its original format for military child care settings and as revised by Teaching Strategies in 1989, several early childhood educators worked with us and provided expert advice. In particular, we want to thank Dr. Jenni Klein, whose considerable knowledge and vast practical experience made her contributions exceptionally valuable. Dr. Joan Lombardi reviewed the training materials from the perspective of the Child Development Associate (CDA) Standards and showed us where changes and additions were needed. On individual modules, we are grateful for the contributions of Laura Colker, Marilyn Goldhammer, Dr. Trudy Hamby, Bonnie Kittredge, Cynthia Prather, and Lillian Sugarman.

Since 1989, *Caring for Preschool Children* has been implemented in early childhood programs across the country and used as the text for college courses. It served as the basis for two new sets of materials—*Caring for Children in Family Child Care* and *Caring for Children in School-Age Programs*. Our experiences in developing the new materials led us to the decision to update this original work and publish a second edition.

We are especially grateful to Emily Kohn who edited the manuscript; Debra Al-Salám who served as production manager; Jennifer Barrett O'Connell who created the art work for our new cover and the graphics in each module; Ayesha Khwaja Husain who designed the cover and layout of the book and also assisted with production; and to Larry Bram who kept us all on track.

And finally, we want to acknowledge the many early childhood educators we have worked with over the years from whom we have learned a great deal. We have undoubtedly adapted and expanded on many of their excellent ideas; this training program is richer as a result.

It is our hope that this second edition of *Caring for Preschool Children* will have a positive impact on the quality of early childhood programs by giving staff developers and teachers a practical and comprehensive tool to support their important work.

Contents

Module 7: *Creative*

Overview

Promoting children's creativity involves:

- Arranging the environment to encourage exploration and experimentation
- Offering a variety of materials and activities that promote self-expression
- Interacting with children in ways that encourage and respect original ideas and expressions

---

Children who are creative are willing to try new ways of doing things. They see the possibility of playing a game or using an art material in more than one way. They are curious about how things work and why things happen as they do. They are willing to take risks. When they try something new and it doesn't work, they learn from their mistakes and try another approach.

The definitions of creativity are many and varied. Some say it is the **process** of creating, others say it is the **product** of creative efforts. According to Teresa Amabile, a social psychologist who has studied children's creativity, anything a child does or says can be considered creative if it meets two criteria.[1]

There are many ways to define creativity.

- The idea or activity must be **novel** or substantially different from some thing the child has seen or heard before.

- The idea or activity must be **appropriate** or useful in achieving a goal, and appealing or meaningful to the child in some way.

Thus, the cook who follows a recipe exactly is not using creativity; the cook who experiments with new ingredients is.

In defining creativity, it is also helpful to consider what it is **not**. Creativity is not the same as high intelligence. Many people of average intelligence are highly creative. Creativity is not the same as talent. Many talented people are skilled performers; however, they are not all creative. Creativity is not the same as being eccentric. Creative people often do things in different ways; however, this does not mean that something is wrong with them.

Everyone is born with the ability to be creative. Some children are more creative than others, and children express their creativity in different ways. Most preschool children are eager learners, naturally imaginative, and creative. They learn as they interact with people and objects in their environment. As children develop their motor and language skills, their play with one another becomes more inventive.

Children are naturally creative.

---

[1] Teresa Amabile, *Recognizing Children's Creativity* (NY: Crown Publishers, Inc., 1989), p. 25.

They make plans and carry them through. Their ideas may not always work and their answers may not always be "right." However, when children find that their ideas and creations are appreciated and valued, they gain confidence in their abilities.

Adults can nurture children's creativity.

The supportive relationships between children and adults are the foundation for nurturing creativity. When children feel secure, they are likely to explore and express themselves. Teachers encourage children's creativity by planning a daily schedule that allows children plenty of time to explore and play at their own pace. They organize the environment to encourage children to explore and experiment, and offer a variety of interesting, open-ended materials and activities. In addition, teachers promote creativity when they show respect for children's original ideas, thoughts, and expressions.

Listed on the following pages are three sets of examples showing how teachers demonstrate their competence in promoting children's creativity. Following each set of examples is a short reading and two questions to answer. When you have finished this section, compare your answers with those on the answer sheets at the end of the module. If your answers are different, discuss them with your trainer. There can be more than one good answer.

Arranging the Environment to Encourage Exploration and Experimentation

Display and store materials on low, open shelves so children can easily select and replace what they need without adult assistance.

"I see you found the new zoo animals in the block area. It looks like you're building a fence to separate the lions from the bears."

Set up the environment so children can spread out, explore, and be messy.

"Kyle and Tim, would you like me to help you move this big box into the library area so you can do your puppet show for an audience?"

Provide sufficient space to save creations that cannot be completed in one day so children can continue to make, use, and expand them.

"We'll save the store you and André made so you can play in it tomorrow."

Help children display their own creative work attractively and respectfully.

"Carlos, where would you like to hang your weaving project?"

Display interesting pictures and objects at a child's height on the wall and invite children to explore them.

"Jim, the dancing feather-fans your grandmother brought us are hanging on the wall in the music area. You and the others can get them when you want to use them."

Adapt the schedule, when appropriate, so children's creative work is not interrupted.

"Dion is still working hard on his painting. Let's start story time without him. He can join us when he's done."

Before the children arrive, Ms. Williams adds shoe boxes, oatmeal boxes, and wrapping-paper tubes to the art area. She makes sure there is plenty of school glue, paper fasteners, pipe cleaners, and twist ties, and puts some dryer lint she brought from home in the basket with the cotton balls, and yarn. She covers the empty table with butcher paper. Soon Kira arrives and retrieves her unfinished house from the shelf where it was stored. Ms. Williams asks, "What materials do you need?" Kira says, "I still have to make my puppy. I need some soft stuff." Ms. Williams shows Kira the cotton balls, dryer lint, and yarn, and says, "Yes, puppies have very soft fur."

1. How did Ms. Williams arrange the environment to encourage exploration and experimentation?

2. How do open-ended materials promote children's creativity?

Offering a Variety of Materials and Activities That Promote Self-Expression

Provide books, CDs or tapes, props, and art materials in response to children's current interests.

"Charnelle, I noticed you watching the birds at our feeder yesterday. Here's a book about birds. Maybe you can find some of our birds."

Offer a variety of materials, props, and objects that reflect the cultures and ethnic groups of all the children in the class.

"Indrani, your mom brought us some beautiful fabric and one of her saris from India. You can show your friend how to put on a sari."

Encourage children to use their imaginations through activities such as storytelling.

"The dragon ate three tons of mashed potatoes, two boxes of hot dogs, and a carrot. What do you think he ate next?"

Avoid using coloring books, product patterns, and dittos.

"The children can make anything they want with our woodworking supplies. We have wood scraps, nails and screws, glue, clamps, tools, and, of course, safety goggles."

Offer "messy" open-ended activities such as finger painting, bubble blowing, and water, sand, and mud play.

"Terrence, the designs you made on Aseem's face make him look really scary. Aseem, do you want to see yourself in the mirror?"

Provide materials children can use in many different ways such as blocks, musical instruments, art supplies, and dress-up clothes.

"Jacci and Anna, you're each using a different technique for rolling your clay. Jacci is using all her fingers and Anna is using her fists."

Ms. Vaughn, Emily, Maggie, and Tomás are making banana bread. As Maggie and Emily stir the flour, bananas, and eggs together, Ms. Vaughn asks, "What else do you want to put in this banana bread?" "Pineapple," says Maggie. "I like raisins," says Tomás. "Me, too," says Emily. "Let's add some raisins." "You all have some good ideas about what to put in, says Ms. Vaughn. "How about adding raisins this time and next time we can try another idea?" The children agree to add raisins this time. Maggie opens the jar of raisins and pours some in a measuring cup.

1. **Why are cooking activities good opportunities to promote creativity?**

2. **How did Ms. Vaughn encourage self-expression?**

Interacting With Children in Ways That Encourage and Respect Original Ideas and Expressions

Encourage children to express their ideas and feelings.

"That's an interesting idea, Paula. Bananas and pears might make a tasty fruit smoothie."

Extend children's dramatic play by assuming a "pretend" role.

"I need a haircut. Do I need an appointment or is this a 'walk-in' barber shop?"

Comment on children's creative thinking.

"Wow! You made a tunnel in the wet sand for your truck! How did you do that?"

Respect the creative process as well as the creative product.

"Lenny, you experimented by finger painting with your hands and then with your elbows."

Call attention to sensory experiences.

"How do the soap suds feel on your hands?"

Ask open-ended questions that encourage children to solve problems and think about things in new ways.

"Raoul, you're right, our tomato plants are falling over. How can we fix them?"

Accept and value each child's unique creative expression.

"After our field trip to the pet store, Jeremy made some snakes out of clay and Oanh Le painted a colorful picture of tropical fish."

When it's almost time to clean up, Ms. Kim walks over to the block area where Brian, Carlos, and Sabrina have been working. "That is the biggest house I ever saw," she says. "You must have worked hard building that." All three children ask, "Please, please, can we leave it up?" Ms. Kim smiles and says, "Yes, you may, but your building needs some protection. How can you let everyone else know that you are saving your building?" Carlos replies, "We can make a sign.'" "That's a good idea," says Ms. Kim. There are some markers, paper, and tape on the shelf." While helping Carlos make the sign, Ms. Kim continues, "Do you have any ideas about how we could remember this house for a long time?" "Take a picture!" says Sabrina. Ms. Kim laughs, "You children have lots of good ideas. Would you like to be in the picture, too? I'll go get the camera."

1. How did Ms. Kim encourage and respect the children's original ideas?

2. How did Ms. Kim's interactions with the children promote their creativity?

Your Own Creativity

Creative people are innovative and resourceful. They can take an idea, a plan, or an object and adapt it to make something new. Although some people are more creative than others, everyone has creative abilities they use on the job and at home. As adults, we sometimes confuse creativity with talent. Artists and musicians can be creative people—but so can cooks, plumbers, and teachers. However, you don't have to be able to paint a picture or write a book to be creative. Thinking of new ways to involve parents in planning a field trip, making up a song to sing at the end of the day, or rearranging your room to create an area for dancing and movement activities are all examples of ways you use your creativity.

Understanding your own creativity and how you approach problems and new situations will help you become sensitive to creativity in children. Think about the satisfaction you feel when you solve a problem while cooking, gardening, talking with a friend, or planning new activities. That feeling is similar to the pride children feel when they have figured something out for themselves. Here are some exercises you can do to help stimulate your own creative thinking.

Think of a time you felt really creative. What were you doing? What made it possible for you to be creative?

How many different ways could children use a collection of bottle caps?

Describe something you did with children that was creative.

Recognizing your creative abilities will enable you to help children develop their own creativity. Watching children gain self-confidence and enthusiastically explore their world can give you much satisfaction.

When you have finished this overview section, you should complete the pre-training assessment. Refer to the glossary at the end of the module if you need definitions of the terms used.

Pre-Training Assessment

Listed below are the skills teachers use to promote children's creativity. Think about whether you do these things regularly, sometimes, or not enough. Place a check in one of the boxes on the right for each skill listed. Then discuss your answers with your trainer.

Arranging the Environment to Encourage Exploration and Experimentation

I Do This:	Regularly	Sometimes	Not Enough
1. Display and store materials on low open shelves so children can easily select and replace what they need without adult assistance.	☐	☐	☐
2. Set up the environment so children can spread out, explore, and be messy.	☐	☐	☐
3. Provide sufficient space to save creations that cannot be completed in one day so children can continue to make, use, and possibly expand them.	☐	☐	☐
4. Help children display their own creative work attractively and respectfully.	☐	☐	☐
5. Display interesting pictures and objects at a child's height on the wall and invite children to explore and enjoy them.	☐	☐	☐
6. Adapt the schedule, when appropriate, so children's creative work is not interrupted.	☐	☐	☐

Offering a Variety of Materials and Activities That Promote Self-Expression

	I Do This: Regularly	Sometimes	Not Enough
7. Provide books, CDs or tapes, props, and art materials in response to children's current interests.	☐	☐	☐
8. Offer a variety of materials, props, and real things that reflect the cultures and ethnic groups of all the children in the class.	☐	☐	☐
9. Encourage children to use their imaginations through activities such as storytelling.	☐	☐	☐
10. Avoid using coloring books, product patterns, and dittos.	☐	☐	☐
11. Offer "messy" open-ended activities such as water, sand and mud play, finger painting, face painting, and bubble blowing.	☐	☐	☐
12. Provide materials children can use in many different ways such as blocks, musical instruments, art supplies, and dress-up clothes.	☐	☐	☐

Interacting With Children in Ways That Encourage and Respect Original Ideas and Expressions

13. Encourage children to express their ideas and feelings.	☐	☐	☐
14. Extend children's dramatic play by assuming a "pretend" role.	☐	☐	☐
15. Comment on children's creative thinking.	☐	☐	☐
16. Respect the creative process as well as the creative product.	☐	☐	☐
17. Call attention to sensory experiences.	☐	☐	☐

Interacting With Children in Ways That Encourage and Respect Original Ideas and Expressions

(continued)

I Do This:	Regularly	Sometimes	Not Enough
18. Ask questions that encourage children to solve problems and think about things in new ways.	☐	☐	☐
19. Accept and value each child's unique creative expression.	☐	☐	☐

Review your responses, then list three to five skills you would like to improve or topics you would like to learn more about. When you finish this module, you can list examples of your new or improved knowledge and skills.

Begin the learning activities for Module 7, Creative.

Learning Activities

I. Using Your Knowledge of Child Development to Encourage Creativity

---

In this activity you will learn to:

- Recognize some typical behaviors of preschool children
- Use what you know about children to encourage their creativity

---

Many experts on creativity believe children are most creative during the preschool years. Preschoolers have vivid imaginations. They tend to be very curious and adapt at solving problems that arise from their explorations.

Physical development during the preschool years affects children's ability to express themselves in several ways. Because the rate of growth slows down, children in this age group don't tire as quickly as toddlers do. They can stay involved in an activity for long periods of time, if they are interested and engaged. Preschool children also have much greater control over the large muscles used to run, jump, climb, throw, and carry. Their small muscle skills and eye-hand coordination are becoming more refined. This increasing control over small muscles allows children to hold and use a variety of materials and equipment such as brushes, markers, crayons, and other drawing tools; scissors; rhythm instruments; sand, water, and dramatic play props; a computer keyboard and mouse; beads and strings; and so on.

Along with children's greatly expanding physical skills comes rapid intellectual development. As they move, dig, build, lift, climb, handle, taste, fill, empty, and manipulate, they begin to gather and use information about objects and events in their environment: "These things are different; these look and taste the same; when you put this color with that color, it looks different." Preschool children are natural scientists. Their curiosity leads them to ask many "Why?" questions. When you encourage children to make their own discoveries (what happens when you mix two colors of paint, for example), they construct their own knowledge of math and science concepts. Language growth is also rapid as children learn new words and use them to describe what they are seeing and experiencing. They make up stories, give titles to their paintings, have conversations with teachers and each other, and ask many, many questions.

Preschoolers tend to be very creative.

Children can manipulate tools and materials as their small muscle skills become more refined.

Children can gather and use information from the environment as their intellectual development grows.

Many children use creativity in combination with social skills.

Preschool children also use their creativity in combination with their growing social skills. Children may invent new ways to share or take turns with a favorite play material. Some children use creative problem-solving skills to negotiate with others: "If you let me play, too, we can use more puppets and put on a bigger show."

Many preschool children use dramatic play as an outlet for their creativity. They invent complicated roles and scenarios and think of innovative ways to use props and wear dress-up clothes. Frequently, dramatic play themes carry over from one day to the next. Teachers can respond by providing new materials or by offering indirect suggestions that extend the play or move it in a slightly different direction: "Those muffins look really tasty. I wish this bakery had a place to sit down while I eat."

Preschool children are more interested in the process of creating than they are in the products or end results.

Preschool children enjoy the process of creating. They explore materials, ideas, and techniques rather than focusing on the end result or product. Teachers should avoid commenting on what a child has made. A wrong guess can be embarrassing or hurtful to the child. The teacher's goal is to encourage the child to be aware of how a painting was made, what colors were used, if it should be displayed, and so on. "Tell me about your picture," is always an appropriate comment.

Preschool children find opportunities to be creative in almost every activity, routine, and interest area. Their creativity extends far beyond the art and music activities typically thought of as "creative" times. Alert, observant teachers have ongoing opportunities throughout the day to encourage children to express themselves, solve problems, and carry out unique plans and ideas.

Applying Your Knowledge

In this learning activity you complete a three-day log describing the words and actions you use to encourage children's creativity. Focus on the small things you do each day to help children explore, solve problems, express their feelings, extend their play, use materials in new ways, and try new ideas. Review the example that follows. Then use the blank form to record your words and actions.

Encouraging Children's Creativity
(Example)

Dates: *March 20 - 22*

What Happened	How Did Your Response Encourage Creativity?
I was helping a group of children make playdough. Curt asked, "How can I make mine purple?" I said, "This morning you painted with purple paint." He said, "That's right. I mixed red and blue," and reached for the food coloring. I watched him knead drops of red and blue food coloring into the dough. It took a long time to get it to the right shade of purple. I said, "That's purple, all right." What other colors would you like to make?"	*I encouraged Curt to solve his problem without my direct assistance. I didn't intervene when he was taking a long time to color the dough. Instead I gave him plenty of time to carry out his plan. I asked him what other colors he would like to make to encourage him to apply what he knew about making different colors of paint to coloring dough.*
Janine and Hayley were making roads in the sand table. Their arm motions were quite vigorous, so some of the sand spilled on the floor. When they were finished with their work, I showed them where to get the broom and dustpan so they could clean up the sand.	*I allowed the children to express their creativity without telling them that they had to be more careful. I allowed them to work without interruption. When they were finished, I showed them how to clean up after themselves.*

Encouraging Children's Creativity

Dates: _____

What Happened	How Did Your Response Encourage Creativity?

II. Providing an Environment That Supports Creativity

> **In this activity you will learn to:**
>
> - Provide a variety of materials children can actively explore and use in different ways
> - Assess the environment and make changes, if needed, to ensure it encourages creativity

Children can experience the challenge and joy of discovery when the environment is arranged to support active exploration and the supply of materials is interesting and varied. One of the easiest ways to promote children's creativity is to provide open-ended materials—items children can use in a variety of ways. Because they tend to trigger the imagination, open-ended materials are interesting to children of different ages and stages of development. For example, given a box of recycled materials, children might:

Children can use open-ended materials in a variety of ways.

- make collages;

- sort and classify the items;

- make mobiles;

- decorate masks;

- use them in experiments; and

- turn them into dramatic play props.

Because children express their creativity in many different ways, it is important to include open-ended materials that invite discovery in all interest areas. Here are some examples of children engaged in creative work in different areas of the environment.

Materials in all interest areas can encourage children's creativity.

Eduardo and Nikki are **outdoors** measuring the height of the marigold seedlings. Some plants are much taller than the others. Mr. Collins asks, "What do you think is making some plants grow faster than the others?"

Ron is in the **library area** "writing" and "illustrating" a book. He tells Ms. West that he'd like to make a "real" book. She shows him some cardboard to use for a cover and demonstrates using a hole punch and a shoe lace to bind the pages together.

Rhonda and Janine are setting up a bakery in the **dramatic play area**. They display their playdough cakes and cookies on some shelves made from shoe boxes. Ms. Lanier stops by to purchase a birthday cake.

Brianna and Abdullah are in the **table toy area** making designs with a set of small colored, wooden cubes. Ms. Brunetti comments on their choice of materials, "Brianna, you are using red and blue blocks for your design. Abdullah, your design includes all the colors."

J. J. is using a drawing program on the **computer.** He is learning how to make circles, squares, and triangles to use in his design. Ms. Whitcomb asks, "How do you put a triangle inside a circle?"

Carley and Shoshana are in the **cooking area.** They are having a discussion about which ingredients to put in the trail mix. Mr. Bent asks, "What could you do so you both can make the kind of trail mix you like best?"

Module 3, Learning Environment, includes a checklist of materials for indoor interest areas and for the outdoor area. Refer to these checklists for more examples of open-ended materials.

Coloring books, dittos, and craft kits do not encourage creativity.

Many teachers wonder if it is a good idea to offer coloring books, dittos, or product patterns as part of their environment. The answer is simple: **No, it is not a good idea.**[2]

First of all, it is very difficult for young children to color within the lines of a ditto or coloring book figure. In addition, these types of experiences are not creative. They deny children opportunities to experiment, use their imaginations, and express their individuality as they can with open-ended materials.

What should you do if parents want their children to use these materials? Take the time to explain to parents why these structured materials don't help children grow and learn.

By sharing with parents your approach to encouraging creativity, you can offer them the reassurances they need. It doesn't take long to convince parents that their child's green and purple version of a pumpkin is more of a treasure than a perfectly round orange pumpkin that a teacher cut out and labeled with the child's name.

Applying Your Knowledge

In this learning activity you review characteristics of an environment that encourages children's creativity. As you read each one, think about whether your classroom environment meets these characteristics regularly, sometimes, or not enough. Mark one of the boxes on the right for each item listed and give a brief explanation for your "rating." An example is provided for the first one.

---

[2] Adapted with permission from Diane Trister Dodge and Laura J. Colker, *The Creative Curriculum® for Family Child Care* (Washington, DC: Teaching Strategies, 1991), p. 139.

Does Your Environment Encourage Creativity?

I Do This:	Regularly	Sometimes	Not Enough

1. A display of children's work greets visitors to the room. **[X]** [ ] [ ]

   We hang (at children's eye-level) children's pictures and photos of children doing creative activities on a bulletin board outside our room.

2. There are examples of creative "products"—drawings, paintings, photographs, books, sculptures, recipes, and inventions. [ ] [ ] [ ]

3. The daily schedule includes long child-choice times, during which children can select what they want to do, what they want to use, and with whom. [ ] [ ] [ ]

4. There is space to store works-in progress on the top of cabinets or shelves. [ ] [ ] [ ]

5. Materials from indoors are brought outdoors so children can use them in a different setting. [ ] [ ] [ ]

	I Do This:	Regularly	Sometimes	Not Enough
6. The interest areas reflect children's families, cultures, skills, and interests, and are rotated when children seem ready for new experiences.		☐	☐	☐
7. The environment can be rearranged when children need more room for movement or dancing.		☐	☐	☐
8. There is room to spread out and be messy. Cleaning supplies such as sponges, paper towels, and brooms are stored within children's reach.		☐	☐	☐
9. All interest areas are stocked with a variety of open-ended materials children can use in many ways.		☐	☐	☐

Use the space below to record any changes you would like to make.

Share the assessment results with your colleagues and plan ways to improve your environment.

III. Promoting Creativity Through Interactions With Children

In this activity you will learn to:

- Listen to and talk with children in ways that respect and encourage their efforts and accomplishments
- Ask open-ended questions that help children learn to think and solve problems

Your daily interactions with children can help them gain confidence in their abilities to create and learn. When you respond thoughtfully to questions, ask open-ended questions that encourage thinking and problem solving, and comment on what children are doing during the creative process, you support their creativity.

The ways in which you respond to preschool children can convey the message that you value and support their creativity. What you say, how you ask and answer questions, and the ways in which you encourage learning through discovery all nurture creativity in children. Careful listening to what a child has to say and recognizing each child as an individual are crucial. Your enthusiasm for children's efforts and successes will greatly support their creativity. These practices also help children develop positive attitudes about sticking to a task and learning from mistakes. When these attitudes are encouraged during the preschool years, they are likely to have lasting effects on the child's entire development. An example showing how a teacher nurtures creativity follows.

> Ms. Williams watches Alex finger painting on a tray. She sees him using both hands to make large circles. He gets some paint on the elbow of one sleeve, which has started to slip down. She pushes up his sleeve gently, and says, "Alex, tell me about those enormous circles you are making. You seem to be enjoying that paint!" Alex smiles and says, "First, I made some big circles. Now, I'm going to make small ones." Ms. Williams continues watching for a while. When Alex appears to be finished with his creation she asks, "Would you like some paper to make a print of your circles?" "No, thanks," says Alex as he smooshes the circles with his hand. "That's enough circles. It's time to make some squiggly lines." Ms. Williams gets up to see what the other children are doing. "Let me know if you'd like to show me your squiggles," she says.

Teachers' thoughtful responses to children's questions and actions can support children's creativity.

Ms. Williams showed Alex that she valued and supported his creativity in several ways. She commented on the process Alex used in his finger painting. She didn't ask, "What are you making?" nor did she point out the paint on his sleeve. Ms. Williams knows that it is important to be patient about children's messes. She gently pushed up his sleeve for him rather than interrupt the creative process. She suggested paper to preserve the creation, accepted Alex's lack of interest in making a print, and offered to come back to see his "squiggles."

Teachers can ask open-ended questions to encourage children to explore and experiment.

Another way for teachers to encourage preschool children to think creatively is to ask open-ended questions. These are questions with many possible answers. In the following example, Mr. D'Souza asks open-ended questions to help David and Juana find a way to play with the same doll.

Mr. D'Souza: "How could you both play with the doll?"

Juana: "I should get it first because I'm older."

David: "I could have the doll and Juana could have the carriage."

Mr. D'Souza: "What could you do with the doll together?"

David: "We could give her a bath."

Juana: "I'll wash her hair and then you can give her a bottle. Okay?"

Mr. D'Souza's open-ended questions helped the children think of a way to solve the problem for themselves. His approach allowed the children to use creative thinking to arrive at a solution that both could agree with. As a result, the children felt competent, learned a problem-solving strategy they can use in the future, and practiced an important social skill, compromising.

Try asking these open-ended questions to encourage creative thinking.

Here are some questions that encourage creative thinking.

- What do you think about. . . ?

- Why do you think this happened?

- What would happen if. . . ?

- How do you think this works?

- What else can we use this for?

- How did you. . . ?

- What else is like this?

- How could you. . . ?

- Is there another way to do this?

- What's similar about these?

- What if we added this?

- In what ways are these different?

- What if we take this away?

(See Module 5, Cognitive, to learn more about asking open-ended questions.)

Applying Your Knowledge

In this learning activity you review a list of teaching practices that encourage children's creativity. As you read each one, think about whether you and your colleagues use similar practices regularly, sometimes, or not enough. Mark one of the boxes on the right for each item listed and give a brief explanation for your "rating."

Do Your Interactions With Children Encourage Creativity?

	I Do This:	Regularly	Sometimes	Not Enough
1.	We comment on the techniques children use during the creative process rather than focusing on end results or products.	☐	☐	☐
2.	We ask open-ended questions to help children think and solve problems.	☐	☐	☐
3.	We show that we value each child's individual characteristics. We help children appreciate their own uniqueness and that of others.	☐	☐	☐
4.	We accept children's messes and mistakes.	☐	☐	☐
5.	We encourage children to make and carry out their own plans rather than telling them the "best" way to do things.	☐	☐	☐
6.	We identify and try to reduce potential sources of stress and anxiety.	☐	☐	☐

	I Do This:	Regularly	Sometimes	Not Enough
7. We make sure children have pleasant and supportive experiences each day.		☐	☐	☐
8. We respond to children's requests for assistance.		☐	☐	☐
9. We observe children and intervene when appropriate to help them carry out their plans.		☐	☐	☐
10. We show enthusiasm for children's efforts and accomplishments.		☐	☐	☐

Use the space below to record any changes you would like to make.

Discuss the results of this learning activity with your colleagues. Encourage each other to continue using teaching practices that promote children's creativity.

IV. Encouraging Self-Expression Through Music and Movement Experiences

---

In this activity you will learn to:

* Recognize how music and movement experiences foster creativity in children
* Encourage children to express themselves through a variety of music and movement experiences

---

Children naturally connect music with moving their bodies.

You don't have to be talented to provide music and movement experiences for preschoolers. Most children love to sing, frequently repeating their favorite songs over and over. They aren't concerned with the quality of their voices or the teacher's ability to sing; they experience the enthusiasm and pure enjoyment of playing with sounds and moving their bodies. Because children naturally connect movement with music, listening to music invites them to explore what their bodies can do and to become aware of their bodies in space.

From a very early age, children respond to music. Infants smile when adults sing to them. They begin to move their bodies when they hear music, and they respond to toys that make a noise. Soon, they hum, sing, and make up chants. As their coordination increases, children begin moving to music. They sway, dance, bounce up and down, clap their hands, and stamp their feet.

Preschool children are becoming aware of rhythm and can use simple rhythm instruments. They like to move, walk, or jump when someone claps rhythmically or plays an instrument. They invent new ways to move their bodies and use props such as scarves, streamers, and hula hoops.

Listening to Sounds and Music

You can provide many opportunities throughout the day for children to listen to various sounds and different types of music. Children develop their listening skills when you make them aware of sounds in their environment, play background music, or offer special listening activities.

Encourage children to listen to the sounds that are all around us.

You can encourage children to become aware of familiar sounds: the ringing of the telephone, the rain banging on the window, the wind blowing leaves on trees. Preschoolers enjoy guessing games in which they close their eyes and listen to sounds. You might play music that includes sounds that children can identify. Try pointing out sounds during walks: "Do you hear the birds singing?" "The wind sounds like a howling dog." "Our shoes make different sounds on the sidewalk than they do on grass."

Teachers can introduce children to different musical styles, including children's songs, classical, jazz, marches, musical plays, instrumentals, and traditional music from a variety of cultures. Many public libraries have a wide selection of children's CDs and tapes as well as other types of music that children will enjoy. Ask parents what kinds of songs or music their children like to listen to at home and try to incorporate these preferences into music experiences in your room.

Each type of music may have a different effect on children's moods. Classical music or quiet children's songs can be relaxing at naptime, while a march or a jazz piece can prompt dancing or parading around the room.

You can help older preschoolers learn to pay attention and concentrate by encouraging them to listen with you for a few minutes. Sometimes a child will stop to listen to a favorite song or to a melody that is particularly appealing. Younger children might not be able to sit still and listen to music for very long, but they could enjoy listening while they do something else. For example, try playing music in the art area. Ask the children who are painting or drawing to do so to the music.

"What does the music make you think of?"

"What different colors do you think of as you listen?"

"Does this music make you feel like painting quickly or slowly?"

Remember: play music selectively. When music is on all the time, it becomes background noise rather than something to listen to, experience, and enjoy.

Help children enjoy and respond to different kinds of music in different ways.

Use various strategies to focus children's attention on the music.

Singing with Children

Some teachers schedule singing times every day or several times a week. Others enjoy singing during frequent informal sessions. Here are some suggestions for singing with preschool children.

Make a list of all the simple songs the children know. Keep the list handy to remind you of songs they like to sing. As children learn new songs, add them to the list.

Sing songs during transitions. For example, sing while getting ready for lunch or during clean-up. When children have to wait for a short time, reduce the frustration by singing.

Make specific songs a part of familiar routines. You can tie special songs to daily routines, such as starting the day or cleaning up. Some children gain a sense of security from knowing that certain events will always occur in the same way. They will quickly point out if you forget to include regular songs in their regular places.

Play singing games. Encourage everyone to sing while they play games such as "London Bridge" and "The Farmer in the Dell."

Act out story songs. You can make props for some songs, such as "The Old Woman Who Swallowed a Fly", so children can sing and act at the same time.

Make audiotapes of the children singing alone or in a group. Most children enjoy hearing their own voices on tape. You can share the tapes with family members.

Sing the same song in different ways. Try singing the same song with and without instruments, loudly, softly, in a whisper, quickly, slowly, sitting, standing, marching, or hopping.

Make up new songs with the children. They can be short and simple.

"How are you?" "I'm fine, I'm fine."

"What are we making?" "Ice cream!"

Keep in mind what preschool children are like. Remember that they typically.

enjoy repeating songs they like;

prefer quick, lively songs to slow ones;

like funny songs and nonsense songs;

improve their ability to carry a tune with careful listening and practice; and

do not always understand that some songs are appropriate for specific events; for example, they want to sing "Jingle Bells" in May or "Good Morning" before going home.

Try these suggestions when introducing a new song.

Learning a new song should be a pleasant experience for children. If children don't pick the song up easily, come back to it later. If the song seems too difficult, pick one with a simpler tune and lyrics. These tips may help you introduce new songs.

- Help children recognize the difference between a speaking and a singing voice. First, say the words to a song in your speaking voice; then sing them.

- Make a tape of yourself singing the new song. Children can learn the song by listening to the tape. They would probably rather hear your voice than that of a professional singer.

- Tell a story about the new song, using a flannel board if you like. "Once there was a girl named Mary. She had a little lamb . . ."

- Repeat the words for the song several times; break up the phrases if they are too long for preschoolers to remember.

- Sing the song several times, encouraging children to join you.

- Let the children sing the song several times if they like.

Playing With Rhythm Instruments

Most children love to make their own music. They even use their bodies as their first rhythm instruments. Start clapping and invite children to join you: "Let me hear you clap. How softly can you clap? How loudly can you clap? Can you clap slowly like this? Can you clap really fast?"

Preschool children also enjoy making music with simple rhythm instruments. A basic set of rhythm instruments includes the following:

drums	cymbals
xylophones	rhythm sticks
hand bells	tambourines
clackers	sandpaper blocks
maracas/shakers	triangles

Preschool children also enjoy using harmonicas, xylophones, hand bells, kazoos, and an electronic keyboard.

Because the primary purpose of instruments is to produce interesting and varied sounds, children don't need expensive professional instruments. Here are some ideas for making simple instruments:

Drums: Glue lids to cylindrical oatmeal boxes, or cover ice cream containers (donated by a local store). Use dowels as drum sticks.

Cymbals: Flatten aluminum pie plates, make holes, then attach noise makers such as thread spools or large buttons with string.

Shakers: Fill boxes or plastic containers with pebbles or beans. Tape the lids shut so the contents won't fall out.

Kazoos: Use a rubber band to attach a piece of waxed paper around the end of a cardboard tube from a roll of paper towels or toilet paper.

Sand blocks: Use thumb tacks to fasten coarse sandpaper to small blocks of soft wood, and screw-on cabinet knobs to make a handle on each block.

Hand and wrist bells: Sew bells on a piece of wide elastic, then sew the ends of the elastic together.

Children can produce interesting and varied sounds using homemade instruments.

When you first introduce rhythm instruments, give each child the same kind. As you expose children to a greater variety of instruments, provide duplicates to minimize conflicts over sharing. Allow plenty of time for children to explore the instruments. Name each instrument and make up a song about the name. Invite children to take turns demonstrating the sounds they can make with their instruments. Ask open-ended questions: What sounds does the instrument make? How can you make different sounds? How can you make the sounds louder or softer?

Preschool children enjoy marching in a band or having a parade.

To form a marching band, have each child select an instrument and move around the room playing the instrument to different types of music. Try a march, then something slower. Put the instruments down and have the children clap or stamp their feet to the beat. You can march backward, in a circle, or following a pattern made by laying rope on the floor. A variation on a marching band is to have a parade. Children can make flags or banners and carry them as they walk or march around the playground or through the halls. Teachers can use these activities as opportunities to talk about how people in different cultures use marches and parades to celebrate special days such as Thanksgiving Day, Cinco de Mayo, Mardi Gras, the Fourth of July, and so on.

Encouraging Creative Movement

Music and movement tend to go hand in hand. Many children automatically respond to music by moving the way the music makes them feel. They also enjoy experimenting with moving their bodies in different ways. You can encourage their creativity by asking questions such as:

"What can your feet do?"

"How can you move your arms?"

"How can you move just your hands?"

You can also invite children to:

"Bend from your waist."

"Wiggle your fingers."

"Stamp your feet as loudly as you can."

"Tiptoe in place."

You can expand children's enjoyment of moving to music and stimulate their imaginations by adding open-ended props. It's fun to use streamers, light-weight fabric, sheets, scarves, feathers, balloons, capes, ribbons, and hula hoops while moving and dancing to music. There is no right or wrong way to use these props, so children can decide what they want to do with them.

Another simple movement activity that encourages children's creativity is imitating how animals walk and move, with or without musical accompaniment. Children can crawl like a snake, waddle like a duck, kick like a mule, slither like a snake, or jump like a kangaroo. Or, you can tap into children's vivid imaginations by suggesting that they pretend to be the wind, the rain, snow, or thunder (especially on windy, rainy, or snowy days), or asking how they think a car moves, or a truck, a rocking chair, or a weathervane.

Applying Your Knowledge

In this learning activity you meet with a colleague to discuss your responses to the questions posed on the previous pages. Together you will decide how to improve your approach to using music and movement experiences as opportunities to enhance children's self-expression. Then, you will select a strategy to implement, try it out, and reflect on what happened. Begin by reviewing the example that follows.

Do Your Music and Movement Experiences Promote Creativity?

(Example)

How could you improve your approach to listening to music and sounds?

Because we play background music all day long, nobody really pays attention to it. From now on we want to be more selective about what we play, and when.

How could you improve your approach to singing with children?

There isn't really anything we want to change, except to expand our repertoire of songs.

How could you improve your approach to using rhythm instruments?

Our set of rhythm instruments is missing several items and this often causes problems, so we don't use the instruments very often. We will order new instruments or make some ourselves.

How could you improve your approach to creative movement?

This is a favorite activity in our room. We have lots of props and a wide variety of music the children enjoy listening to for movement activity.

Select one of the strategies you listed above and try it out for a week or more. Then answer the questions that follow.

Strategy: *Making rhythm instruments.*

How did you implement your strategy?

We sent home a notice asking parents to collect materials we could use to make instruments. We collected or purchased additional materials. Then, we set up the materials along with a book of instructions in the staff lounge. We had fun making instruments during breaks and planning times. Finally, we introduced the new instruments to a small group of children.

How did the children respond?

They were excited about using the new instruments. All the children tried all of the instruments. Then each child returned to the instrument he or she found most interesting

What other changes would you like to make?

We don't plan to make any more changes for now. We will continue introducing new instruments to small groups of children. We'll also observe how children use the instruments independently. If our observations indicate the need for further changes, we'll discuss what to do next.

Do Your Music and Movement Experiences Promote Creativity?

How could you improve your approach to listening to music and sounds?

How could you improve your approach to singing with children?

How could you improve your approach to using rhythm instruments?

How could you improve your approach to creative movement?

Select one of the strategies you listed above and try it out for a week or more. Then answer the questions that follow.

Strategy:

How did you implement your strategy?

How did the children respond?

What other changes would you like to make?

Discuss this activity with your trainer. Work with your colleagues to implement the other strategies you came up with in this activity.

V. Offering Art Experiences That Invite Exploration and Experimentation

In this activity you will learn to:

- Provide a variety of open-ended materials and activities that encourage children to express themselves through art
- Offer materials and experiences that respond to children's individual skills and interests

Art experiences should be relaxed comfortable times when children can move at their own pace.

Art is an important part of any program serving preschool children. For many children, art is a relaxing activity that stimulates all their senses as they paint, draw, glue things together, or pound a lump of clay. Art activities encourage children to use their imaginations and create something of their own. They can make choices and try out their own ideas without thinking that there has to be a right or wrong result. The daily schedule should include long periods of time during which children can decide what they want to do, gather the materials they need, and carry out their plans.

As noted in Learning Activity I, most preschool children tend to be more interested in the process of art than they are in the products. They want to discover what will happen if they use the side of a crayon to make scribbles, or if they finger paint with their fists or elbows. The youngest preschoolers simply enjoy the physical experience of scribbling with a crayon or squeezing playdough through their fingers. As they develop small muscle skills and coordination, they are pleased to find out that they can control the marks the crayon makes on the paper or determine the width of a playdough "snake." As they learn to use a variety of media, they like experimenting with colors, brush strokes, textures, and combinations of shapes. Older preschoolers begin to care about the products, and may become critical of their own work. Ask children who make drawings to tell you about their creations. Listen carefully to what they are telling you; these early pictures are a form of communication.

Materials in the art area should be set up within children's reach so that they can use them without adult assistance. Typically, the following activities are available every day:

painting: easels, paint, brushes, large pieces of paper, clothesline and pins for hanging pictures to dry;

drawing: crayons, markers, chalk, and paper in several sizes;

making collages: paste, school glue, paper, cardboard, scissors, a variety of natural and recycled materials, magazines to cut or tear, scraps of paper from other projects;

using playdough and clay: airtight containers holding clay or playdough and a variety of tools and utensils.

Some art experiences require a teacher's supervision or leadership. Children may need help using tools or materials safely, or they may need a simple step-by-step explanation of a process. Also, some activities have the potential to be very messy. In these instances, teachers have to communicate to children that it's all right to be messy if the messes are a necessary part of the creative process. Some examples of art activities supervised or led by teachers include:

- finger painting on paper, cookie sheets, or a table covered with vinyl;

- weaving with paper, cloth strips, or yarn;

- making puppets;

- painting murals;

- making three-dimensional sculptures using wood scraps, recycled items, and school glue or nails; and

- making prints using paint and objects such as Styrofoam packing material, lengths of string, or pieces of sponge cut in a variety of shapes.

If the children are enjoying an activity you can offer it for several days and add new materials to expand their explorations. The goal is to provide a balance of experiences: those which children can choose and do independently and those which teachers plan in advance. Several popular and effective preschool art experiences are described below: drawing, painting, creating collages and assemblages, and using clay and playdough.

Drawing and Painting

All young children go through the same stages as they develop drawing and painting skills. Ask children who make drawings to tell you about their creations. Listen carefully to what they are telling you; these early pictures are a form of communication. Teachers need to understand and recognize the stages of artistic development so that they can:

- provide appropriate materials and art experiences; and

- respond to children's work in ways that promote creativity.

The following chart summarizes the stages children pass through as they develop drawing and painting skills.

Developmental Stages of Children's Art[3]

Stage	What Children Do	What It Looks Like
Early scribbles	Make random marks in many directions. Enjoy physical motions.	
Later scribbles	Make circles, lines, or zigzags. May cover whole paper. Control use of a drawing tool.	
Basic shapes	Recognize shapes such as circles, rectangles, and crosses and repeat them.	
Drawing mandalas	Combine designs—crosses with circles or rectangles.	
Drawing suns	Draw circles or ovals with lines at the edges or marks in the middle. Adults think they look like suns or human faces.	
Drawing humans	Combine shapes and lines to make a figure that represents a person.	
Drawing animals and trees	Combine the same shapes and lines to draw animals and trees. Animals have ears on top of circle. Later animals are no longer upright. Trees begin as rectangles with a circle on top.	
Making pictorial drawings	Combine shapes and figures they have mastered. Size and color may not be realistic. Objects on the same page may not be related and may be free floating.	

[3] Based on Rhonda Kellogg, *Analyzing Children's Art* (Palo Alto, CA: National Press Books, 1970).

Children move through the same stages in painting as they do in drawing. At first, children are interested only in how it feels to paint. They love the way the brush slides across the paper and usually are not very interested in the color that results. This is why many first paintings look the same; they are generally a brownish-purplish color that results when the child brushes layer upon layer of color onto the paper, often using every inch of available space.

First-time painters may need help learning how to hold the brush or how to wipe the brush on the jar so that paint doesn't form globs on the paper. It's best to put small amounts of paint in the jar; children find it easier to control where the paint goes when there is not too much of it. Also, brushes tend to last longer when the paint level goes no higher than the bristles. Teachers should assist children who request help, while at the same time allowing all children to experiment and learn through trial and error.

Most four- and five-year-olds enjoy a wide range of colors. They mix colors together and add white paint to create pastels. They like using colors such as purple and black as well as the primary colors. And they may still enjoy mixing every color available to create those brownish-purplish colors that adults find hard to name!

Gradually, children become more purposeful in their painting. They ask for specific colors to use and want to place things on the paper in specific ways. They may be concerned with drips that disrupt what they are trying to do. Eventually, they reach the stage where they plan what they want to paint.

You can provide children with a wealth of experiences by simply changing what they paint on, the paint itself, or the paper. The list below suggests a variety of art experiences young children will enjoy.

- Using different types of paper

  colored construction paper

  sandpaper

  wrapping paper

  wallpaper samples

  Styrofoam packing pieces (on tables instead of easels)

  shapes such as circles, squares, or long strips.

- Using a variety of techniques

  blow painting—using a straw to blow a glob of paint across the paper

  spatter painting—using a toothbrush and screen to paint stencils of leaves, feathers, shells, and so on

For most children, the feel of the brush on the paper is as interesting as the color that results.

Some children may need help learning painting skills.

Experienced painters plan what they want to paint.

Changing paper, paint, and tools can give children a variety of painting experiences.

crayon-resist painting—painting with diluted paint over crayon designs

folded painting—placing globs of paint on a piece of paper, folding it, then unfolding it

- Using different textures

    paper and brushes

    sawdust, sand, salt, and tempera paint in separate containers

    experimenting with the effects of different substances on paint and paper—for example, adding a substance to the paint beforehand; sprinkling it on the paper and painting over it

- Experiencing different colors

    using finger or tempera paint in primary colors

    experimenting with white paint

    adding white paint to create pastels

    discovering what happens when specific colors are mixed

- Working with different painting tools

rollers	plastic squeeze bottles
whisk brooms	sponges cut into shapes
straw	stamps
marbles	string

Many children enjoy finger painting.

Preschool children find finger painting a particularly appealing art experience. Whenever possible, allow children to finger paint directly on a Formica tabletop so they have ample room to experiment with paint and fingers. If you want to spend the money, you can purchase glossy paper, especially designed for finger painting. Children can also finger paint on a large piece of plastic or vinyl stretched across a table and taped in place, on cookie sheets, or on cafeteria-type trays.

Collages and Assemblages

Collages are made by pasting all kinds of things on a flat surface. An assemblage is a three-dimensional piece made by fastening a variety of objects together. Assemblages and collages offer wonderful opportunities for creative expression.

Children can use a variety of materials to make original collages. These materials may include fabric scraps, ribbon, wood scraps, Styrofoam, feathers, magazine pictures, and buttons. Children paste the selected items on cardboard, heavy corrugated paper, construction paper, or posterboard. Computer paper will work for collages made with paper scraps.

After the children have had experience in making collages, they can use scissors to cut pieces of paper or thin materials (such as wallpaper samples or ribbon) to the size and shape they want.

Children make imaginative assemblages by putting together a variety of three-dimensional items in unusual ways. To make assemblages, children need items such as:

- a framework for the structure: blocks of wood, shoe boxes, plastic containers, berry boxes;

- materials to extend the framework: tile pieces, Styrofoam, wooden clothespins, dowels;

- things for fastening items to the structure: toothpicks, wire, wooden dowels, straws, paper fasteners, yarn, nails, pipe cleaners, school glue, and tape;

- things used to poke into or attach: cork, fabric, paper, Styrofoam balls, sponge fragments; and

- things with interesting shapes and textures (from your collection of recycled materials).

Making assemblages can encourage growth and development in many ways. The invitation to experiment reinforces natural curiosity. Thinking of what to put with what leads to growth of planning and organizational skills. Learning that a big piece of cork is too heavy for one toothpick to hold up is a science discovery. Trying different ways to make an assemblage stand up is practice in solving problems. Looking around at other people's work is part of learning to appreciate unique approaches to creative self-expression.

Exploring Playdough and Clay

Given a clump of playdough for the first time, most children will smell it, taste it, poke it with a finger, pinch it, squeeze it between their fingers, push it around the table, and pound it with their hands. Children need plenty of time to explore this material, experience its texture, and find out what it can do.

Children can use dough directly on a table top. As they become familiar with this material, children enjoy using props such as wooden spoons, wooden mallets, rolling pins, and cookie cutters. Make sure you have duplicates of the most popular items. (See Module 3, Learning Environment, for more examples of playdough props.)

Making playdough is an excellent creative experience.

Children have as much fun making playdough as they do using it. When they make their own dough, they can vary the texture, amount, and color. The chart on the following pages includes two popular playdough recipes. Store the finished playdough in the refrigerator in sealed plastic bags, large plastic containers, or coffee tins lined with plastic.

Clay provides a different kind of experience.

There are two types of clay that match the developmental skills of preschool children: soft modeling clay, which does not harden and dry out, and clay that can be baked or left to harden by itself. If possible, provide both types of clay in your art area. Children enjoy manipulating soft clay and might use it to make balls, snakes, or different shapes. Soft clay is also fun to use with rolling pins, cookie cutters, and tongue depressors. Clay that hardens is a good choice for children who want to save their work. Once the clay hardens, children can paint their creations.

Display individual containers of clay and playdough and an assortment of props to use with them on low, open shelves where children can reach them. Children can decide which material they want to work with and choose some props.

The chart that follows describes materials children can use for a variety of art experiences.

Suggested Art Materials for a Preschool Room

Item	Comments
Paper and cardboard	*Provide a variety of papers—tissue, construction, wrapping, sandpaper—so children can experiment with texture, color, and absorbency. A local newspaper or printer may give away end rolls of newsprint. Stores may donate outdated wallpaper and fabric sample books. Offices may save their scrap paper for your class. When you purchase paper, buy large sizes (at least 12" x 18") so that children can make bold movements.*
Brushes	*Offer a variety of sizes. Young children find one-inch brushes with thick handles about 5" or 6" in length easiest to use.*
Other painting tools	*Provide sponges, cotton balls, paper towels, marbles, ink stamps, feathers, leaves, tongue depressors, straws, strings, eye droppers, and anything else you or the children think of.*
Easels	*Hang a piece of plastic on the wall and tape or clip paper on the plastic, or build simple easels.*
Paint	*Use liquid tempera paint because, although expensive, it lasts a long time and produces vibrant colors. Powdered tempera is much cheaper, but it must be mixed to the right consistency. Add a few drops of alcohol or wintergreen to mixed tempera to keep it from going sour. Add a few soap flakes to improve the consistency and to make the paint easier to wash out of clothes.*
Finger paint	*Make finger paint by combining 1 C liquid starch with 6 C water, 1/2 C soap flakes, and a few drops of food coloring. Or, you can mix 3 T sugar with 1/2 C cornstarch in a sauce pan, then add 2 C cold water. Cover the mixture and cook it over low heat until it thickens. Add food coloring after the paint cools.*
Building materials—any size scraps	*Offer linoleum, masonite, metal pieces, nails, tiles, wallboard, wire, wire mesh, wood scraps, large tapestry materials, and wooden dowels.*
Crayons and other drawing materials	*Provide large, good-quality crayons that produce even, vibrant, color. (Less expensive crayons use more wax and have less color.) For variety, offer white and colored chalk, pens, pencils, and washable markers. To make soap crayons for water play, mix 1/8 C water with 1 C soap flakes and add food coloring. Pour the mixture into plastic ice cube trays or popsicle molds. Remove when hardened.*
Playdough	*Commercial varieties can be harmful if swallowed and are difficult to remove from carpets. To make playdough, combine and knead 2 C flour, 1 C salt, 2 T oil, 1 C water, and a few drops of food coloring. To make a smoother playdough, add 1T cream of tartar to the above ingredients and heat the mixture in a pan, stirring constantly, until the dough pulls away from the sides of the pan and forms a lump. Then knead the dough. Store in plastic bags or containers in the refrigerator.*

Item	Comments
Clay	*For dough that will harden, mix and knead 2 C corn starch, 1 C baking soda, 1 C water, and food coloring. The recipe for modeling clay is 1 C salt, 1 1/2 C flour, 1/2 C warm water, 2 T oil, and food coloring.*
Tools for playdough and clay	*Provide thick, short dowels, rolling pins, cookie cutters, gadgets that make impressions such as meat tenderizer.*
Paste or glue	*Offer white paste and school glue. Both are inexpensive and adequate. You may need a specific kind of glue for some projects and activities.*
Scissors	*Invest in good-quality scissors with blunt ends. Provide left-handed scissors as needed.*
Natural items	*Collect acorns, feathers, flowers, pine cones, seashells, seeds, stones, pebbles, and so on for collages or decorating.*
Sewing items	*Have on hand beads, braids, buttons, cotton balls, ribbons, shoelaces, snaps, hooks and eyes, and yarn on felt or fabric. Large plastic sewing needles, thick yarn and plastic canvas are available at craft or variety stores.*
Fabrics	*Offer a variety of colors and textures. Save (or ask parents or a fabric store to save) burlap, canvas, denim, felt, fake fur, lace, leather, oilcloth, and terry cloth scraps of all sizes.*
Household items	*Provide items such as aluminum foil, bottle tops, plastic wrap, parchment, corks, egg cartons, clean bleach bottles, empty food and beverage containers, boxes, Styrofoam packaging, cans, doilies, spray bottles, string, and toothpicks.*
Other "artsy" items	*Use your own imagination; try glitter, confetti, broken appliance parts, pipe cleaners, wooden beads, stamp pads and stamps, marbles, shredded paper, old business cards, hangers, and wires. Some communities have recycling centers where you can purchase interesting "junk" for a nominal charge.*
Clean-up items	*Maintain a good supply of mops, sponges, brooms, and towels so all the children can participate in clean-up. Store toxic cleaning products in locked cabinets.*

Applying Your Knowledge

In this learning activity you observe a child participating in art experiences over a period of three days. Based on your observations, you select, plan, and implement an art activity to match this child's skills and interests. Review the examples that follow, then begin the activity.

Observing a Child and Planning an Art Activity
(Example)

Child: *Ronnie*　　　　　**Age:** *4 years*　　　　　**Dates:** *October 7- 9*

Art Experiences	Time	What Happened
Day One		
Drawing with markers on paper	*10 minutes*	*Ronnie used blue and red markers to make circles and spirals. He left his paper on the table.*
Easel painting outside	*20 minutes*	*He used a wide-bristled brush and red paint. He made a circle and long vertical lines. He switched to black paint and made horizontal lines and dots. He finished by using red again. He took down his paper and asked me to hang it up to dry.*

Planning an Art Activity

Activity: *Sponge painting*　　　　　**Date:** *March 12*

Setting: *In the art area after the children wake up from naps.*　　**Number of children at one time:** *Four*

Why did you plan this activity?

Ronnie seems to like the feeling of painting. I think he'd like to experiment with a different tool—a sponge instead of a brush to make dots or other marks.

What materials are needed?

Three pie pans to hold tempera paint; sponges cut up into small pieces; large pieces of paper.

What did the children do?

Three children came and had fun making sponge paintings. Then Ronnie came over. He used the sponge to make lines on his paper. Then he smeared them all together.

What did you do and say to encourage children's creativity?

I set up the materials and waited to see if any children would choose the activity. When they asked what to do, I explained without telling them exactly what to do. I asked Ronnie if he would like to try using the sponge like he uses the brush. He tried it but went back to making lines. I stepped back to let him fully explore the new tools.

Observing a Child and Planning an Art Activity

Child: _____ **Age:** _____ **Dates:** _____

Art Experiences	Time	What Happened
Day One		
Day Two		
Day Three		

Planning an Art Activity

Activity: _____ **Date:** _____

Setting: _____ **Number of children at one time:** ____

Why did you plan this activity?

What materials are needed?

What did the children do?

What did you do and say to encourage children's creativity?

Discuss this activity with your trainer.

Summarizing Your Progress

You have now completed all the learning activities for this module. Whether you are an experienced teacher or new to the profession, this module has probably helped you develop new skills for promoting children's creativity.

Before you go on, take a few minutes to review your responses to the pre-training assessment for this module. Summarize what you've learned, and list the skills you developed or improved.

If there are topics you would like to know more about, you will find recommended readings listed in the Orientation in Volume I.

Your final step in this module is to complete the knowledge and competency assessments. Let your trainer know when you are ready to schedule the assessments. After you have successfully completed them, you will be ready to start a new module. Congratulations on your progress so far, and good luck with your next module.

Answer Sheet

Arranging the Environment to Encourage Exploration and Experimentation

1. **How did Ms. Williams arrange the environment to encourage exploration and experimentation?**
   a. *She displayed an interesting variety of containers, fasteners, and miscellaneous materials on open shelves and in baskets so children could make selections and clean up without adult assistance.*

   b. *She covered a table and left it empty so children could spread out, explore, and be messy.*

   c. *She provided space to store unfinished projects so children could work on them the next day.*

2. **How do open-ended materials promote children's creativity?**
   a. *There is no right or wrong way to use the materials.*

   b. *They invite children to explore and experiment without any rules (e.g., connecting pieces, constructing houses or spaceships, making moving parts).*

   c. *They allow children to use their imaginations, make choices and decisions about how to use the materials, and express themselves in ways that are unique and relevant to their own lives.*

Offering a Variety of Materials and Activities That Promote Self-Expression

1. **Why are cooking activities such as baking banana bread good opportunities to promote creativity?**
   a. *Children feel proud of their accomplishments when they actively participate in making something "real."*

   b. *Children can express their own unique ideas by varying the recipe.*

2. **How did Ms. Vaughn encourage self-expression?**
   a. *She invited the children to express their ideas about special ingredients.*

   b. *She let the children know that all of their suggestions were valuable. She demonstrated respect by asking the children if they could use one idea now and the other the next time they bake banana bread.*

Interacting With Children in Ways That Encourage and Respect Original Ideas and Expressions

1. **How did Ms. Kim encourage and respect the children's original ideas?**
   a. *She commented on the size of their building.*

   b. *She allowed them to leave their house in place rather than dismantling it and putting the blocks away.*

2. **How did Ms. Kim's interactions with the children promote their creativity?**
   a. *She asked open-ended questions to help the children figure out a way to protect their building and to think of a way to remember it for a long time.*

   b. *She showed that she valued their ideas by telling Carlos where he could find materials to make a sign and by offering to get the camera and take a picture of the children and their building.*

Glossary

Creativity

The ability to develop something new-an idea or product-that is substantially different from anything the person has seen or heard before.

Open-ended materials

Materials (such as blocks, dramatic play props, and art supplies) that children can use in many different ways.

Open-ended question

A question that can be answered in a number of ways.

Problem solving

The process of thinking through a problem and coming up with one or several possible solutions.

Overview

> **Fostering children's self-esteem involves:**
> - Developing a positive and supportive relationship with each child
> - Helping children accept and appreciate themselves and others
> - Providing opportunities for children to be successful and feel competent

This module is about two closely related topics—how children gain a sense of self and how this understanding can lead to self-esteem. A sense of self is an awareness of one's identity. Your identity is made up of many variables: physical characteristics, likes and dislikes, strengths, interests, language, the foods you do or don't eat, experiences in your family, at school, and in the community, your expectations and values, what is expected of you, and whether you feel valued by others. Your identity and sense of self develops and changes throughout your life. Your physical appearance changes, you develop new skills and interests, you experience and learn from your successes and failures, and you establish relationships with new people.

Self-esteem evolves from a sense of self.

Self-esteem grows out of a sense of identity. Some people have mainly negative feelings about themselves. They might dislike the way they look, feel they have nothing in common with other family members, reject their ethnicity and culture, or think they are not capable of succeeding. Others are comfortable with themselves. They may still want to improve some aspect of their lives by, for example, beginning an exercise program or being more attentive to their families, but, overall they have a positive sense of self and feel valued by others.

From birth, children begin developing a sense of self. Some of their feelings towards themselves may be positive and some may be negative. These feelings will affect their entire adjustment to life—their ability to play, to relate to others, and to learn. These feelings are strongly influenced by their relationships with other people—such as family members, friends, and teachers.

Children develop self-esteem when they feel valued and experience success.

There has been much discussion among those who work with young children about the importance of self-esteem and what adults can do to foster children's positive feelings about themselves. Some popular practices designed to promote self-esteem may lead instead to over-indulgent self-love that is based solely on trivial things. For example, when children are asked to name something that makes them special, they may focus on relatively insignificant personal characteristics such as their long hair or new shoes. If this type of response is reinforced often enough, children may begin to believe that superficial traits make them special. The strategies recommended in this module focus on providing opportunities for children to experience the deep satisfaction that comes from mastering a new skill or helping another person. Children's sense of self grows from real accomplishments as they learn what they can do and receive encouragement for meaningful efforts and accomplishments.[1] Self-esteem gives children the confidence to tackle problems, attempt new challenges, help others, recover from setbacks, and learn from their mistakes.

Teachers can help children develop a positive sense of self.

As a teacher, you play an important role in helping children develop a sense of identity and self-esteem. By demonstrating respect—for each child as an individual, for the needs of the group, and for yourself and your colleagues—you convey the message that each person is valued. When you offer help in solving a problem, listen and respond to feelings, or comment on a new painting technique—you are fostering children's sense of self and self-esteem. Your support and encouragement help children develop confidence in their own abilities. Through your relationships with children, you help them learn to value themselves and others. By offering a variety of appropriate materials, activities, and experiences you provide opportunities for children to meet challenges and experience success.

Listed on the following pages are three sets of examples showing how teachers demonstrate their competence in fostering children's self-esteem. Following each set of examples is a short reading and two questions to answer. When you have finished this section, compare your answers with those on the answer sheet at the end of this module. If your answers are different, discuss them with your trainer. There can be more than one good answer.

---

[1] Based on William Damon, *Greater Expectations* (New York, NY: The Free Press, 1995).

Developing a Positive and Supportive Relationship with Each Child

Observe each child regularly to learn about individual needs, skills, abilities, interests, culture, and family experiences.

"Roger seems to be getting more used to his new baby sister. I saw him in the house corner saying to a doll, 'Don't cry. I'll get you a bottle.'"

Encourage children to talk about their feelings and take their concerns seriously.

"I know you want to play with the truck now. It's hard to wait. What would you like to do until it's your turn?"

Learn and use a few words in the home language of children whose first language is not English.

"Silvia, ¿puedes ayudárme buscar estós libros por favor?" (Can you help me look for those books?)

Know what each child can do and show that you think each child is special.

"James, the gerbil ran behind the shelves. You're good at getting him back in his cage. Could you help us?"

Offer verbal and gentle nonverbal contact—a hug, a touch, a smile—to show you care.

"Dion, you're the first to wake up from nap! How would you like to help me prepare the snack?"

Spend individual time with each child every day.

"I'm coming over to the block area right now to hear all about your building."

Ms. Kim passes the easels where Shawn is painting a picture. Shawn is smiling and seems very happy with his work. He steps back from the easel to look at his picture. Ms. Kim stops to talk with him. "Shawn, would you like some help hanging your picture?" "Okay," he answers. They each hold one side of the picture and hang it up on the line. Ms. Kim points to the picture and says, "I see you have used a lot of blue paint, and it looks like you used the side of the brush to make those marks. Last week I also noticed you using a lot of blue paint Blue seems to be one of your favorite colors." Shawn nods and says, "Yeah, I like blue. I'm going to paint another blue picture." He goes back to the easel to start another picture.

1. How did Ms. Kim work on building a positive and supportive relationship with Shawn?

2. How did Ms. Kim work on building Shawn's self-esteem?

Helping Children Accept and Appreciate Themselves and Others

Provide a variety of activities and materials that encourage all children to participate. Avoid making biased remarks concerning gender, disabilities, culture, ethnic background, or any other differences.

"Therese, tell Carlos that of course girls can build with blocks. Look at those pictures of construction workers. There are men and women."

Acknowledge children's efforts and accomplishments.

"Leila, I heard you use your words to ask the other children for a turn with the wagon."

Display pictures of children's families and offer home-like materials and activities to help children feel secure.

"Ms. Cane, the children had a great time trying your recipe for flat bread. If you have other recipes, you can send them with Dustin."

Show by what you say and do that you respect each child.

"Martha, I put a new book in the library on whales because you told me how much you like them."

Reinforce children's behavior when they share, cooperate, or help others.

"Marcus, I noticed you showing Krystina how to make a print of her finger painting You're the kind of person who likes to help others."

Make sure the environment and activities reflect the cultures of all children in the group and help children learn about and appreciate a wide variety of cultures and ethnic groups.

"Teresa, you're right Mardi Gras masks are like the ones people from other countries wear in their celebrations."

Jerry places a wooden block on the tower he is building. "Look, I did it!" he calls to Mr. Lopez. "That's a very tall tower you've built," says Mr. Lopez, bending down for a closer look. Jerry smiles proudly. Just then, Sandy walks by, swinging her arms. Crash! Jerry's tower tumbles to the floor. "No!" shouts Jerry. He lifts his arm to hit Sandy. "Jerry," Mr. Lopez says, reaching up to stop Jerry's swing. "Sandy hit your tower by accident, but I can't let you hit her." Tell Sandy how you feel." Jerry turns to Sandy and says, "Don't knock down my building! Be careful."

1. What feelings did Jerry appear to have about his block tower?

2. How did Mr. Lopez help Jerry learn to express his feelings in an appropriate way?

Providing Opportunities for Children to Be Successful and Feel Competent

Encourage children to do as much as possible for themselves, even if this takes a long time. Provide help only when asked or when a child is anxious.

"You climbed to the top of our climber by yourself. How do you like the view up there?"

Accept mistakes as a natural part of learning to do something new.

"Whoops! The paint spilled. Get a sponge from the sink so you can clean it up."

Provide a range of activities and materials that can be enjoyed by children with different interests, abilities, and skill levels.

Keep on hand playdough and utensils, a variety of puzzles, a range of picture books, and so on.

Help children learn how to solve their own problems.

"You both want to use the same puppet. How can we solve this problem? Who has an idea?"

Help children handle their feelings about separating from their families.

"It's hard to say good-bye to Grandma. She'll be back to get you just like she does every day."

Repeat activities so children can master skills and experience success.

"It's time to get ready for lunch, now, so we have to clean up. You can get the bean bags and basket out again later and continue your game."

Consider children's individual characteristics when setting up the environment, choosing materials, and planning activities.

"Now that we've rearranged the room we need to measure the traffic paths to make sure there's room for Frankie's wheelchair."

Ms. Williams observes Mark in the table toy area selecting a new truck puzzle that has 18 pieces. Ten minutes later, she notices that Mark is no longer at the puzzle table, but the puzzle pieces are all over the table. Ms. Williams finds Mark in the book corner and says, "Mark, it looks like that new truck puzzle was hard to do. If you come back to the puzzle table, we can work on the puzzle together. New puzzles with lots of pieces are hard to do at first. I bet after you try a couple of times you'll be able to do it alone." Mark and Ms. Williams return to the puzzle table. They talk about the puzzle pieces—where the wheels belong, the cab of the truck, the driver, and so on—until the entire puzzle is put together.

1. **Why did Ms. Williams encourage Mark to come back to complete the puzzle?**

2. **How did Ms. Williams support Mark's positive feelings about himself?**

Your Own Sense of Self

The more you know about yourself, the more you can help children develop a sense of self and self-esteem. Think about your likes, dislikes, learning style, opinions, and feelings. How do your past experiences—culture, home life, school experiences, successes, failures—affect your understanding of individual children? Do you sometimes make inaccurate assumptions about children whose characteristics and experiences differ from yours?

Here are some questions to help you reflect on your childhood experiences. As you answer them, think about how these experiences might influence your views and behaviors today.[2]

What messages did your family and community deliver concerning accepted behaviors? (For example, were children allowed to be noisy and physically active, could they look adults directly in the eye when being spoken to? Was it okay for boys to cry or girls to play "rough?")

What messages did you receive about using your talents? Were there different expectations and treatment of boys and girls? (For example, was it acceptable to be "smart," "athletic," or "artistic?")

How and when were you expected to express your ideas and feelings? (For example, were children encouraged to speak up? Was it all right to speak when others were speaking? Did everyone talk at the same time?)

[2] Adapted with permission from Diane Trister Dodge, Judy R. Jablon, and Toni S. Bickart, *Constructing Curriculum for the Primary Grades* (Washington, DC: Teaching Strategies, Inc., 1994), pp. 213-214.

How was your racial/ethnic identify described to you? Were any characteristics of your group identified as special? What messages did you receive about the characteristics of other ethnic groups?

What messages did you get from the media concerning different groups of people? How have those messages influenced your opinions and behaviors?

What messages did you receive from school, community, and peers about your family's socio-economic position? (For example, were certain behaviors expected of children based on where they lived or their parents' occupations?)

What types of exposure did you have to people with mental or physical disabilities? (For example, did you attend school with children with disabilities? What words were used to describe people with disabilities?)

We can choose to keep or change our beliefs and behaviors.

As you recalled your childhood experiences and what was valued in your home and community, you probably came to realize that your values have changed over time. You may see how your experiences (or lack of experiences) with people of diverse backgrounds have helped to shape your views and interactions with people today. With this awareness, you can make a conscious decision to keep those beliefs and behaviors that match your current experiences and change those that don't.

At times, you may want to question and challenge your attitudes and beliefs. You might ask yourself: "Why am I uncomfortable around people with disabilities? Why do I think they are different? Have I really ever known someone who had a disability?"

Some people find they frequently have the same strong reactions to certain situations. In these cases, it is important to reflect on what's causing your response. Here is an example.

> Ms. Trent gets really upset when girls won't join in outdoor activities. She believes that it is important for boys and girls to participate in all activities. She observes that Maya always looks like she wants to participate, but something seems to stop her from running, climbing, and riding. She wonders to herself, "Could Maya's behavior reflect a cultural expectation that I'm not aware of?" She discusses her observations with a colleague to get a fresh view and talks with Maya's family about their expectations for their child's behavior. This research helps Ms. Trent understand Maya's behavior. Her parents have told her to keep her clothes clean while at the program. Ms. Trent works with the family to reach a compromise that respects their values and allows Maya to benefit from the program's activities. Maya will wear play clothes to the program so she won't have to worry about keeping them clean.

Ms. Trent reflected on her own behavior. When we take time to think about the reasons for our behaviors, we become more skilled at understanding ourselves and why children may behave in certain ways.

Adults can help children understand that all people are alike and different in many ways.

With greater personal awareness, you will be able to help children accept and appreciate their own individual characteristics. You can help them identify with and feel positive about their own families, culture, ethnicity, and home language. With your support they will learn that there is a place for everyone in the group and that people are alike and different in many ways. How you interact and respond to children conveys your respect and acceptance of them. Respect and acceptance are what most children and adults ultimately want from others.

When you have finished this overview section, complete the pre-training assessment. Refer to the glossary at the end of the module if you need definitions of the terms used.

Pre-Training Assessment

Listed below are the skills teachers use to foster children's sense of self and self-esteem. Think about whether you do these things regularly, sometimes, or not enough. Place a check in one of the boxes on the right for each skill listed. Then discuss your answers with your trainer.

Developing a Positive and Supportive Relationship with Each Child

	I Do This: Regularly	Sometimes	Not Enough
1. Observe each child regularly to learn about individual needs, skills, abilities, interests, culture, and family experiences.	☐	☐	☐
2. Encourage children to talk about their feelings and take their concerns seriously.	☐	☐	☐
3. Learn and use words in the home language of children whose first language is not English.	☐	☐	☐
4. Know what each child can do and show that you think each child is special.	☐	☐	☐
5. Offer verbal and gentle nonverbal contact—a hug, a touch, a smile—to show you care.	☐	☐	☐
6. Spend individual time with each child every day.	☐	☐	☐

Helping Children Accept and Appreciate Themselves and Others

	I Do This: Regularly	Sometimes	Not Enough
7. Provide a variety of activities and materials that encourage all children to participate. Avoid making biased remarks concerning gender, disabilities, culture, ethnic background, or any other differences.	☐	☐	☐
8. Acknowledge children's efforts and accomplishments.	☐	☐	☐

Helping Children Accept and Appreciate Themselves and Others

(continued)

	I Do This: Regularly	Sometimes	Not Enough
9. Display pictures of their families and offer homelike materials and activities to help children feel secure.	☐	☐	☐
10. Show by what you say and do that you respect each child.	☐	☐	☐
11. Reinforce children's behavior when they share, cooperate, or help others.	☐	☐	☐
12. Make sure the environment and activities reflect the cultures of all children in the group, and help children learn about and appreciate a wide variety of cultures and ethnic groups.	☐	☐	☐

Providing Opportunities for Children to Be Successful and Feel Competent

	Regularly	Sometimes	Not Enough
13. Encourage children to do as much as possible for themselves, even if this takes a long time. Provide help only when asked or when a child is anxious.	☐	☐	☐
14. Accept mistakes as a natural part of learning to do something new.	☐	☐	☐
15. Provide a range of activities and materials that can be enjoyed by children with different interests, abilities, and skill levels.	☐	☐	☐
16. Help children learn how to solve their own problems.	☐	☐	☐
17. Help children handle their feelings about separating from their families.	☐	☐	☐

Providing Opportunities for Children to Be Successful and Feel Competent

(Continued)

	I Do This: Regularly	Sometimes	Not Enough
18. Repeat activities so children can master skills and experience success.	☐	☐	☐
19. Consider children's individual characteristics when setting up the environment, choosing materials, and planning activities.	☐	☐	☐

Review your responses, then list three to five skills you would like to improve or topics you would like to learn more about. When you finish this module, you can list examples of your new or improved knowledge and skills.

Begin the learning activities for Module 8, Self.

Learning Activities

I. Using Your Knowledge of Child Development to Foster Self-Esteem

> **In this activity you will learn to:**
>
> - Recognize some typical characteristics of preschool children
> - Use what you know about children to promote a positive sense of self

Socio-emotional development is the foundation for self-esteem. At every stage of life, children (and adults) must deal with age-specific challenges before they move on to the next stage. If these challenges are handled successfully, children's socio-emotional development is enhanced.

Psychologist Erik Erikson has outlined eight stages of socio-emotional development from infancy to old age. Erikson's first stage of development is **trust**. Infants develop a sense of trust when the adults who care for them respond quickly to their basic needs. Responsive adults help infants to trust their world and feel safe. Trust is essential as infants begin to explore the environment, try new activities, develop new skills, and interact with others. Establishing a sense of trust is essential to the development of autonomy, which generally occurs during the toddler years.

Infants and toddlers are building trust and autonomy.

Autonomy is about being independent, doing things for oneself, making decisions, and exploring the world. As toddlers assert their growing independence, they like to say "no" and insist on doing everything themselves. Autonomy is essential to the development of initiative, which generally occurs during the preschool years.

Initiative is the term Erikson uses to describe the preschool years. Three- to five-year-olds tend to be active, talkative, creative, and eager to learn and have new experiences.

Erikson's last four stages cover the school-age years, adolescence, maturity, and old age. They focus on industry, intimacy, the ability to reach out to others, and reflecting on one's life. Erikson's message is that socio-emotional development continues throughout our lives.

Preschool children seem to have endless energy. They can build, draw, mold, paint, climb, and swing with increasing skill. If you encourage them to explore, solve problems, and do things for themselves, they will show initiative. Their sense of self and their confidence in what they can do will grow as their knowledge and skills increase.

Preschool children are at the stage of initiative.

Most preschool children talk a lot. They usually know many words, and they can express their ideas verbally. They ask "why" and "what" and how" questions because they want to know more about their world.

Preschool children tend to be social. They play with other children and develop strong friendships. They notice how people are alike and different and are curious about these differences. Dramatic play is a favorite activity. By watching children play, you can learn a lot about what they know and how they view their experiences.

When activities are matched to children's abilities, they develop self-confidence.

Sometimes adults try to push children into academic learning too early. They teach letters and numbers so children will be "ready" for first grade. If preschool children are pushed to do things before they are ready, they may experience failure, and as a result, their self-esteem will suffer. Rather, teachers should offer children many opportunities to learn through play. Preschool children need activities that allow them to succeed easily and feel good about themselves. In this way they develop self-esteem.

Conversely, sometimes teachers aren't aware of how capable preschool children are. They may continue to help children eat, dress, and use the toilet even when children can do these things for themselves. It is important to let children do as much as possible for themselves, so that they become aware of their abilities and feel competent. Teachers can provide help when asked or when adult assistance would calm an anxious child and lead to success.

Applying Your Knowledge

The chart on the next two pages identifies some typical behaviors of children in the preschool years, ages three to five. Included are behaviors relevant to developing a positive sense of self. The right-hand column asks you to identify ways teachers can use this information to foster children's sense of self and self-esteem. Try to think of as many examples as you can. As you work through the module, you will learn new strategies and you can add them to the chart. You are not expected to think of all the examples at once. If you need help getting started, turn to the completed charts at the end of the module. By the time you complete this module, you will find you know many ways to foster children's self-esteem.

Using Your Knowledge of Child Development to Foster Self-Esteem

What Preschool Children Are Like	How Teachers Can Use This Information to Foster Self-Esteem
They are eager to please adults and may seek approval and attention.	*Join in children's play and work with them during clean-up. Offer specific, targeted encouragement for "real" efforts and accomplishments. Acknowledge children's requests for your approval and attention, even if you must ask them to wait for a few minutes until you are available. Help children learn to value their own skills and abilities.*
They may be fearful of such things as loud noises, monsters, the dark, animals, or some people.	
They can feed, dress, and do many things for themselves.	
They usually have mastered independent use of the toilet and can ask to use the bathroom (if it isn't in the room).	
They like to help during chores and routines.	
They like to play make-believe and act out roles.	
They can take turns and share, but they don't always want to.	

Using Your Knowledge of Child Development to Foster Self-Esteem

What Preschool Children Are Like	How Teachers Can Use This Information to Foster Self-Esteem
They can express feelings verbally using large vocabularies but may also stutter or use "baby talk."	
They have strong emotions.	
They may express feelings such as anger and jealousy by hitting or kicking.	
They have a great deal of physical energy.	
They like to try new things and to take risks.	
They know their names and ages and can identify with their own gender, family, culture, community, and ethnic group.	
They may have difficulty making the transition from home to school.	

When you have completed as much as you can do on the chart, discuss your answers with your trainer. As you proceed with the rest of the learning activities, you can refer back to the chart and add examples of ways teachers can promote children's sense of self and self-esteem.

II. Getting to Know Each Child

In this activity you will learn to:

- Recognize and understand children's individual characteristics
- Observe children carefully and regularly to get to know what makes each one unique

---

Each child is a unique human being. By getting to know children, you demonstrate respect and appreciation for their unique characteristics. When you plan a program that responds to children's individual characteristics—needs, interests, skills, temperament, culture, language—you help children learn to respect and value themselves. Self-respect and appreciation of one's individual characteristics and abilities are the essence of self-esteem.

Although most children pass through the same stages of development in the same order, each child develops according to an individual time line which can be faster or slower than the average for a specific age group.   In addition, children's development is uneven—a child may be more advanced than her age-mates in one area (for example, riding a tricycle before most of her classmates have mastered this skill) and less advanced in another (for example, developing classification skills after most of her peers).   It is important to use the stages of development as guidelines, while remembering that within any age group there can be great variation.

Your own experiences as a child, as a teacher, and perhaps as a parent can affect your expectations of children's behavior. For example, you may have strong memories of your own childhood and how you and your siblings felt and behaved in different situations. A child in your program may remind you of nieces or nephews, children you worked with in past years, or a childhood friend. In addition, if you are a person who usually prefers quiet activities you may find it hard to understand a child who is happiest when fully involved—physically, cognitively, and emotionally—in routines and activities. You will need to spend more time getting to know that child so you can respond in supportive ways.

To get beyond preconceived notions of how a child might feel or what he or she may need, it is important to get to know each child as an individual. Here are some examples of the ways in which children can differ:

Adaptability. Rico loves to try new foods. Amy prefers to fill up on familiar items instead. Tiffany adjusts easily when a sudden thunderstorm prevents the class from going on a planned nature walk, but Leona keeps asking when the rain will stop.

Your experiences can influence how you view children in the program.

It is important to learn what makes each child unique.

Activity Levels. Stuart is constantly moving. He runs more often than he walks, and he throws his whole body into every activity. Barney is usually content to play quietly while watching what's going on around him.

Regularity of Body Rhythms. Some children function most effectively when routines—eating meals and snacks, resting, using the bathroom—occur at the same time each day. Children who have less predictable body rhythms need flexible schedules for routines.

Intensity. Some children express their emotions quietly, others with great gusto. Lynn raises her voice and moves her body when she is excited or happy, while Tracy smiles and speaks in muted tones.

Distractibility. Deisy can focus on what she's doing without being distracted by a slamming door or other children's conversations and activities. She can fall asleep easily no matter what else is going on in the room. Gerard frequently leaves buildings, pictures, and puzzles unfinished and finds it hard to fall asleep unless his cot is in a protected corner of the room.

Persistence. T. J. can spend long periods of time building a block tower or learning something new, such as using an egg beater. Carrie needs encouragement to take on a new challenge or to stick with a difficult task.

The differences described above are neither good nor bad traits. They simply describe the different ways children (and adults) may respond to people and experiences in their lives. As you get to know each child, keep these characteristics in mind. You can use the information you collect as you plan and implement a program that responds to children as individuals.

Try these suggestions.

Here are several suggestions to help you get to know and understand each child.

Communicate frequently with children's families. Effective early childhood programs involve families as partners. Children's sense of self is rooted in their relationships with parents and other family members. Make it a point to share information with parents frequently. Ask them to keep you up-to-date about their child's experiences and activities at home and in the community.

Accept and respect individual differences without trying to change children. Children need to know that other people accept them in order to learn to value themselves. Feelings of self-worth allow children to accept and respect others.

Observe children frequently, especially those who are difficult for you to understand or with whom you find it hard to work. Record a child's behavior for five minutes, several times a day for a week. Review your observation notes and ask yourself what the child might be feeling and thinking. Look for patterns that give you insight into the child's behavior.

Be aware of your own style and preferences. Are you a person who likes a lot of physical contact? Do you prefer quiet times, or do you enjoy excitement? Are you slow to get angry? Are your feelings hurt easily? How does your own style affect your relationships with children?

Ask a colleague, your supervisor, or your trainer to observe a child whose behavior you do not understand or are having trouble handling. Compare and discuss the observation notes. Often a fresh perspective leads to greater awareness of the reasons for a child's behavior.

Building relationships with children is part of being a professional. You may enjoy being with some children more than with others, and find some children harder to get to know. Make it a point to spend individual time regularly with every child in the group. Challenge yourself to find something special about each child that may not have been obvious at first.

Applying Your Knowledge

In this learning activity you will learn more about the individual characteristics of two children by completing a five- to ten-minute observation of each child. (You might want to read Module 12, Program Management, Learning Activity I: Using a Systematic Approach to Observing and Recording.) Begin by reading the example below. Then select two children to observe indoors or outdoors as they engage in play or routines. During the observations, make quick notes about what the child does and says, who the child talks and plays with, and how his or her facial expressions change. After the observations, spend a few minutes adding any details you left out. Review your notes and think about what you learned about each child. Then answer the questions on the blank forms that follow.

Getting to Know a Child

(Example)

Child: *Cynthia*   **Age:** *4 years, 3 months*   **Date:** *January 10*

Setting: *House Corner*   **Time:** *10:45 a.m.*

Observation Notes

Cynthia is alone. She puts on the firefighter hat and raincoat. She says, "I have to make my lunch and eat it fast. I have to get to the fire station in a hurry." She gets pots from the shelf and puts them on the stove. She puts playdough pieces in the pots. She stands at the stove and sings a song:

Firefighter, Firefighter, put on your boots!

Firefighter, Firefighter, put on your coat.

She removes the pots from the stove, puts the playdough on plates, and sits at the table smiling. She pretends to eat, puts the dishes in the sink, and quickly walks to the block corner.

What do you think the child was feeling?

Cynthia smiled and sang as she played. She appears to be happy today. She feels good about cooking her lunch and being a firefighter.

What did you learn about the child that might affect her sense of self?

Cynthia seems to enjoy acting out roles. She may have been thinking about cooking for herself. She pretended she was a firefighter preparing to go to work. She is happy when she is busy. Also, she memorized a song.

How can you use this information to foster self-esteem?

Put additional firefighter props in the house corner and block area.

Sing the firefighter song with her

Mention during group time that Cynthia seems to like this song.

Talk with her during free play about things a firefighter does.

Include her in our next cooking project.

Watch to see when she might be ready to join other children in dramatic play.

Getting to Know a Child

Child #1: _____ **Age:** _____ **Date:** _____

Setting: _____ **Time:** _____

Observation Notes

What do you think the child was feeling?

What did you learn about the child that might affect his or her sense of self?

How can you use this information to foster self-esteem?

Getting to Know a Child

Child #2: _____ **Age:** _____ **Date:** _____

Setting: _____ **Time:** _____

Observation Notes

What do you think the child was feeling?

What did you learn about the child that might affect his or her sense of self?

How can you use this information to foster self-esteem?

Use your notes from both observations to answer the following questions.

How are these two children similar?

How are these two children different?

Based on your observation notes, what else would you like to know about these children?

There are numerous methods for continuing to get to know and understand children. You can conduct regular, systematic observations, use checklists, keep anecdotal records, and share and discuss information about the child's activities and experiences with parents and colleagues. In the next activity you will learn how to use what you know about the children to promote a sense of competence.

III. Responding to Each Child as an Individual

> **In this activity you will learn to:**
>
> - Plan an environment and activities that match children's interests and abilities
> - Interact with children in ways that build their sense of competence

Preschool children are developing physical, cognitive, and social skills they will use throughout their lives. Every day they are learning new skills, developing new interests, and gaining a greater understanding of their world. As children acquire new skills, they develop a sense of their own competence—what they are capable of doing—that contributes to self-esteem. You can help children feel capable by creating an appropriate environment, planning for individual abilities and interests, and tailoring your support to match individual needs. In a safe and accepting atmosphere, children can practice skills they already have and learn new ones.

The Environment

The indoor and outdoor environment includes a number of elements—furniture, equipment, interest areas, materials, the daily schedule. Teachers can help children feel competent by considering children's individual and developmental interests when planning for these elements. The more children can explore the environment, use materials, and do things on their own, the more they will be proud of themselves. Their self-esteem grows with their increasing independence and their sense of competence.

Materials should offer choices and encourage children to develop and use skills.

The inventory of materials in each classroom should offer a variety of interesting experiences without overwhelming children with too many choices. Too many materials can lead to confusion. Too few can cause disagreements or boredom. The key is to provide the right number of toys and other items that respond to children's skills and interests.

The furniture and equipment must be the right size, sturdy, safe, and age-appropriate. If these items are too small or too large for preschoolers, you will be constantly reminding children to be careful or to keep off. Children will not be challenged to learn new skills.

Interest areas should be stocked with toys and materials that match children's skill levels and are safe and in good repair. When items are too simple or too difficult, are broken, or have missing pieces, children are likely to become frustrated and may misuse them.

Sometimes adults expect too much from preschool children. When they see a child successfully complete a five-piece puzzle, they put out one with twenty-five pieces. When a child can paint at the easel with one color, they think he or she can handle five colors. Given toys and materials that are too difficult, children are likely to fail, which lowers their self-esteem. Therefore, consider children's skills and abilities when selecting materials. Provide materials that offer children challenges while also allowing them to experience success.

Everything should have a place in a preschool room. Displaying materials on low shelves labeled with pictures of the materials allows children to find and return the things they need. When children have access to materials, they feel independent because they don't have to rely on adults. They learn to make choices for themselves and to take care of their environment. The more children can explore the interest areas, make and carry out plans, and use their developing skills on their own, the more pride they will have in themselves.

Children feel independent and proud when they have access to play materials.

The daily schedule, including how routines are handled, can also contribute to promoting a sense of competence. A schedule with many opportunities for children to choose what they want to do—and with whom—encourages independence and decision making. An appropriate schedule includes long blocks of time during which children can carry out their plans and become fully involved in activities. Most preschool children participate in routines. They like doing "real" work and feel proud of their contributions to making the classroom run smoothly. Look at your approach to carrying out routines (such as preparing snack or getting ready to go outdoors) to make sure you are encouraging children to do as much as they can without your help. Also, remember to invite children to help with jobs such as washing paintbrushes or restocking the paper towel supply.

A well-planned schedule and routines encourage children's full involvement in the program.

You and your colleagues are the most important parts of the environment. Your knowledge of child development and each child's individual characteristics enables you to plan activities and provide materials that are at the right level—challenging but not overwhelming. The children who grow to trust you will be free to explore and learn, thereby building trust in themselves and their abilities.

Individual Abilities and Interests

Children in the preschool years have a wide range of interests and abilities. It is important to provide materials, equipment, and activities that represent this range. For example, you can set up the art area so one easel has only one or two colors of paint and wide brushes, while another has five colors and brushes in several widths. Puzzles and manipulatives can range from the simple to the complex. Books can include those that are mostly pictures as well as those with several sentences on every page.

Provide open-ended materials that respond to a wide range of interests and abilities.

One way to accommodate a range of abilities and interests is to provide open-ended materials. Open-ended materials are ones that can be used in various ways by children at different stages of development. As children develop new skills, they find new ways to successfully explore and use open-ended materials. Teachers can offer items to respond to children's interests and expand their play. For example, putting zoo animals in the block area might encourage children to build a zoo. Offering cake pans and aprons in the dramatic play area could lead children to create a bake shop.

It's important to include toys and materials that reflect children's homes, cultural backgrounds, languages, and individual interests. Children tend to feel secure and accepted when books, pictures, dolls, music, and other items reflect them and their backgrounds. They will see themselves reflected in the environment.

The activities you plan can also foster self-esteem. Getting to know children through observation and by talking with parents and colleagues helps you discover their special interests and abilities. When you plan an activity you know will interest a child or build on his or her skills, you are saying to that child, "You are important to me and I know you will like this."

The Right Level of Support

One of the hardest things to know is when to offer help to a child attempting something new and when to withdraw this support gradually so the child can manage independently. As a teacher, you use your knowledge of individual capabilities and limitations to provide the right kind of support and guidance as children approach new tasks.

Offer support in a way that matches children's needs and skills.

Observe children closely so you will know who needs support throughout the learning process, who needs words of encouragement, and who simply needs you to nod or smile at them as they try a new activity. If you intervene only when necessary, you help children acquire new skills in a way that builds their sense of competence.

In the following example, the teacher uses knowledge of each child to tailor her approach to providing support.

> Ms. Henry has ordered a new indoor climber to be delivered to her room. She knows that the children's reactions to the new equipment will be as varied as their abilities to climb and jump. Cheryl is very curious, but may be timid about trying the climber. To support her, Ms. Henry displays pictures of the climber and talks about how children can use it. Bonita and Dean are both risk-takers. They will be excited about the climber and may take too many chances. To meet their needs, Ms. Henry discusses safety limits and provides ongoing guidance to encourage their safe play. Marguerite and Lloyd may take a long time to adjust to the new climber. The group time discussion might make them more fearful. Ms. Henry plans to talk to these children individually so she can reassure them that they are capable of climbing safely. She will stay with them at the climber for as long as they need her support.

You and your colleagues probably spend much of your day doing things for children that they cannot do for themselves. It is important, however, to recognize when children are ready to help themselves and to provide opportunities for them to be successful and feel competent. For example, you might help three-year-old Sara climb up the slide while holding her hand; encourage four-year-old Andy to try a puzzle he's never done before; or put some sturdy plastic knives next to the peanut butter and crackers so all the children can make their own snacks. Children feel good about themselves when they can practice skills they already have and learn new skills in a safe and accepting atmosphere.

The children in your program will change a great deal during the year. In fact, they change each day as they develop physically, cognitively, and socially; learn new skills; and develop new interests. To promote children's sense of competence, observe them frequently and change the environment as well as your approach to offering support and guidance to reflect children's new abilities and interests.

Provide many opportunities for children to feel successful and competent.

Applying Your Knowledge

The previous activity focused on getting to know two children. In this activity you will continue observing the same two children and record what you learned. You will then use this information to help each child develop a sense of competence. Begin by reviewing your observation notes and responses to the questions posed in Learning Activity II. Then read the example that follows and complete a blank form for each of the two children.

Responding to Each Child as an Individual

(Example)

Child: *Cynthia*   **Age:** *4 years, 3 months*   **Dates:** *January 15—19*

What You Learned About This Child	How You Can Encourage Competence
What does this child like to do on arrival?	
Quiet activities. Looks at books or does simple puzzles.	*Read to her. Ask her parents for suggestions of types of books to match her interests. Point out more difficult puzzles.*
Who does this child play with? Who initiates the play—this child, or others?	
Kim and Joey. They ask her, then she joins in. All three are quiet children.	*Set up activities for the three of them, such as playing with new props in the block area.*
What skills has this child recently learned?	
She used to play alone. Now she plays and shares toys and props with one or two others.	*Comment on her play with other children. Provide new dress-up clothes to expand play.*
What are this child's self-help skills?	
She can button and zip and loves to help with chores. She's learning to twist her laces, trying to make a knot.	*Ask her to help others learn to zip and button. Suggest making knots on the lacing board. Ask her parents to help her practice lacing at home.*
What does this child like to do outdoors?	
She plays quietly in the sandbox, sometimes with Kim and Joey. She says she likes to ride a tricycle, but rarely asks for a turn.	*Comment on her group play in the sandbox. Help her learn how to use words to tell other children she wants to use the trike next.*
What does this child do very well?	
She remembers stories that we've read and can repeat them as she looks at books.	*Ask questions such as: "What do you think is going to happen next?" and "What if . . .?"*
What does this child do at the end of the day?	
She "reads" to Kim and Joey, who get tired and ask her to read to them.	*Ask her to "read" to a small group of children. Also, let her read or play alone.*

Responding to Each Child as an Individual

Child #1: _____ Age: _____ Dates: _____

What You Learned About This Child	How You Can Encourage Competence
What does this child like to do on arrival?	
Who does this child play with? Who initiates the play—this child, or others?	
What skills has this child recently learned?	
What are this child's self-help skills?	
What does this child like to do outdoors?	
What does this child do very well?	
What does this child do at the end of the day?	

Responding to Each Child as an Individual

Child #2: _____ **Age:** _____ **Dates:** _____

What You Learned About This Child	How You Can Encourage Competence
What does this child like to do on arrival?	
Who does this child play with? Who initiates the play—this child, or others?	
What skills has this child recently learned?	
What are this child's self-help skills?	
What does this child like to do outdoors?	
What does this child do very well?	
What does this child do at the end of the day?	

Discuss this activity with your colleagues. Plan ways to respond to each child through the environment, activities, and interactions.

IV. Helping Children Deal with Separation

In this activity you will learn to:

- Observe how individual children react to being separated from their families
- Communicate with children in ways that help them deal with separation
- Provide an environment that helps children deal with separation

Each day at your center begins with families and children saying goodbye to each other. This can evoke deep feelings in both adults and children. Consider how you feel when you must say goodbye to someone you love: Sad? Angry? Guilty? Afraid? Parents and children have these feelings too. It can be tempting to get separations over as quickly as possible.

Separation is a lifelong experience and an important part of growing up. It deserves the same careful planning as every other aspect of your program. When you help children deal with their feelings about separation, they learn they are capable of handling painful feelings. They also learn that you, someone they trust, will be there if they need help.

Although preschool children vary in their ability to deal with their feelings, most can understand and accept separation. At this age, children can create a mental picture of their absent parents. Also, they understand their teacher's explanation of where their parents have gone and when they will be back to pick them up. "Grandma went to her job at the airport. She'll see you at home tonight. Your dad will pick you up this afternoon after our outdoor play time."

Some preschool children have great difficulty separating from their parents. These difficulties may be expressed in different ways.

Children deal with separation in different ways.

- Vanessa stopped sucking her thumb last year but began again when she started coming to the center. Thumb-sucking helped cope with her feelings about missing her mother.

- Although Felipe seemed to adjust easily to his new life at the center, his mother reported that he had been wetting his bed at night. He expressed fears about separation in a familiar home setting rather than at the center.

- Four-year-old Cheryl has been dressing herself for more than a year. She has been coming to the center for three weeks. Her mother says that Cheryl tells her in the morning, "I can't get my clothes on today, so I can't go to school." Cheryl knows that she can't go to the center if she doesn't have clothes on.

- Peter brought his large teddy bear to the center today. He has been carrying it around all day. It's so big that it gets in the way of anything he tries to play with. But his need to feel connected with home and his parents is greater than his need to move freely.

Occasionally, children revert to behaviors more typical of infants or toddlers in reaction to being separated from their families. As the examples have shown, one child might suck her thumb; another might have toileting accidents. It's best to take these incidents in stride without paying undue attention to them. Instead, recognize the behaviors as signs that the child needs your help to handle strong feelings about separation.

Try these suggestions.

Here are some suggestions for helping children handle separation in ways that also foster a sense of competence and self-esteem.

Examine your own feelings about separation. What good and bad separation experiences do you remember from your childhood? How do your feel about parents saying goodbye and leaving their children with you for the day? How do your feelings influence your responses to parents and children? "When Brenda says she misses her Mom, it reminds me of how much I missed my parents when they went on trips without me."

Encourage activities that help children gain a sense of mastery over separation. Children often express their feelings about separation through dramatic play, art, and the books they choose to "read." Provide dress-up clothes and props such as hats, briefcases, and empty food containers. Children can use these items to role-play situations where people leave and come back, such as going to work and to the grocery store. These make-believe activities help children handle their fearful feelings. Give children lots of time for art, and read books such as *Goodnight Moon* and *The Runaway Bunny* by Margaret Wise Brown, or *Ira Sleeps Over* by E. Waber—three favorites.

Help children become aware of the daily schedule. A predictable and consistent order of events gives children a sense of security. When children understand the daily schedule, they are better able to determine when their parents will return to take them home. Make a picture version of the schedule using drawings and photographs. Explain the pictures: "Here we are waking up from our naps. Then we eat snack. Then we play outside for a while. When we come in it's almost time for your parents to come."

Encourage children to help during daily routines and activities. Children gain self-confidence as they pour juice, tie shoe laces, and select and replace their own materials. They also learn to cope with separation. They feel important and valued at the center, even though their parents are absent.

Make the environment as home-like as possible. Encourage parents to bring a child's special blanket or stuffed animal from home. Provide private spaces for children to store their possessions. Hang pictures of families to help children feel connected to their parents even when they are away. Use family recipes in cooking activities to make the center more home-like. Make a parent mailbox so children can "write" letters to their parents during the day.

Listen as children express their feelings. Sharing feelings makes them more manageable. Though you may not like to hear complaining or crying, when you listen, you show respect. You help children learn that you will be available to listen to their feelings.

Talk with children about their parents during the day. Look at family pictures. Encourage children to make pretend calls to their parents. Comments such as "did your mom put that bow in your hair?" or "tell me about helping your dad cook dinner" can help children feel connected to their families.

One of the most important ways you can help children cope with separation is to build strong partnerships with families. Get to know children's parents and plan ways to work together to support their children. Encourage parents to visit the center or participate in other ways. If parents trust and value the work you and your colleagues do, their children will sense this and feel more secure. "Delante was glad to see you at lunch time. He was sad for a little while when you left, but then we talked about what to have for lunch the next time you come. He says that your favorite food is pizza!"

Some parents may find it tempting to sneak out of the room while their child is looking the other way. Though it may seem the easiest thing to do, imagine how you would feel if the most important person in your life disappeared with no warning. Saying goodbye gives children the security of knowing they can count on their parents to let them know what is happening. Try to explain to parents how their children might be feeling. "I'm sure it's really hard to say goodbye to Tyler when he has tears rolling down his face. When you give him a hug and tell him you will see him soon, he may still feel sad, but he knows that you love him and will come back for him." Some families develop goodbye rituals with their children. The familiar actions of having a giant hug or blowing kisses to each other are reassuring and can give children a sense of control. It is easier to deal with open feelings than ones that are bottled up inside.

Building partnerships with families helps children cope with separation.

Help parents foster their child's trust by saying goodbye directly to the child.

Help parents understand confusing end-of-day behaviors.

Reunions are the other side of separating. Some days children run gleefully into their parents' arms because they are ready to go home. Other days they have ambivalent feelings. They may burst out in tears, have a tantrum about getting their coats on, or complain about something that happened in the day—an event they haven't mentioned earlier. Help parents understand that children sometimes save their deepest feelings for them—the people they trust the most.

Teachers' visits to the children's homes also can help children deal with separation. The teacher can see the child's home environment, how the child behaves in a different setting, how the adult family members interact with the child, the role of siblings, and so on. After a visit from their teacher, many children feel a greater connection between home and center and are more comfortable spending time at the center.

Applying Your Knowledge

In this learning activity you will identify the ways two children cope with separation. First, review the example that follows. Then choose two children in your care whom you think are very different from each other. Use what you have learned in this module and what you know about these children to complete the questions on the blank chart.

Helping Children Deal with Separation

(Example)

	Child/Age: *Tony, 3-1/2 years*	**Child/Age:** *George, 4 years*
How does this child say goodbye to his or her parents in the morning?	*He holds on to his mother for a few minutes. She helps him hang up his coat and sits with him in the book area until she leaves for work.*	*His father asks him what he's going to play with first. George usually says blocks," and takes his father to the block corner. His father watches for a few minutes and says goodbye.*
What kinds of make-believe does this child engage in?	*Usually scenes from home—cooking, cleaning, eating. Sometimes he plays grocery store—that's where his mother works.*	*He likes to be a police officer directing traffic. Sometimes he's a daddy in the house corner.*
How does this child use art materials to express feelings?	*He likes "soothing art"—he finger paints carefully and smoothly.*	*He's quick. He makes broad brush strokes up and down and side to side when he's feeling angry or sad.*
How do you know this child is thinking about his or her family?	*He points at the photo of his family. He pretends to call his parents on the phone. He strokes his stuffed bunny.*	*He doesn't talk about his family very much. When we talk about families at group time, he joins in.*
How does this child help with daily routines?	*He likes to sweep. He's very serious about his work.*	*Sweeping doesn't interest George—he gets bored before he's done. He does well stacking the cots after nap-time.*
How could you help this child deal with feelings about separation?	*Read to him after his mother leaves and at the end of the day. Encourage him to try water play when he seems sad.*	*Ask him about things he does with his parents and sisters. Use family pictures to talk about where they are when George is at the center.*

Helping Children Deal with Separation

	Child/Age:	Child/Age:
How does this child say goodbye to his or her parents in the morning?		
What kinds of make-believe does this child engage in?		
How does this child use art materials to express feelings?		
How do you know this child is thinking about his or her family?		
How does this child help with daily routines?		
How could you help this child deal with feelings about separation?		

Discuss your responses with your trainer and the parents of the two children.

V. Using Caring Words that Help Foster Self-Esteem

In this activity you will learn to:

- Listen carefully to children to find out what they are saying and feeling
- Talk to children in ways that demonstrate understanding and respect

Most preschool children can use words to express their thoughts and feelings. Some children are very good at using words; others need your help. As a teacher you provide a model for children. Children listen to what you say and try to understand your meaning. The words you use teach them a great deal about themselves. When those words are caring, they help a child feel valued and respected.

The words you use can show children that you respect them.

Talking with children in ways that build self-esteem requires two special skills. First, a teacher must listen carefully and determine what the child is really saying through words and/or actions—and what he or she is feeling. By looking at and listening to a child and thinking about your own experiences, you can often tell how the child feels. Second, a teacher must respond so that the child knows that he or she is understood and respected.

It is important to talk to children using the same courteous voice you use with your friends and family. Begin by giving the child your full attention. Stand near the child and establish eye contact. Listen and observe carefully so you can determine what he or she is really saying and feeling. An example follows.

Give your full attention to children and listen carefully to what they are saying.

> Ms. Ferraro watched and listened to four-year-old James, who was new to the center. James looked at the children's paintings hanging in the art area and said, "These sure are ugly pictures." Ms. Ferraro said, "We let children paint all kinds of pictures here. All children paint in their own way, and they can hang up their pictures if they want to. When you want to paint I'll help you find a smock and an empty easel."

Ms. Ferraro guessed that James was wondering about how his paintings would turn out. He was worried that his pictures would not be acceptable. He expressed his worry by calling the paintings on the wall ugly. In this situation Ms. Ferraro listened carefully to what James said and tried to figure out what he was feeling. Her response showed James that she respected his concern about being able to paint and understood his worried feelings.

If Ms. Ferraro had not developed skills in listening and talking with children, she might have said, "These pictures aren't ugly. It isn't nice to say that about the other children's work." This statement would have made James feel bad. It would have left him worried about this own painting ability.

Arrival time is an opportunity to say something special about each child.

When you greet children each morning, you set the tone for their day. By saying something special about each child, you show that you notice and care for each one. Your caring words are also important to the parents who bring their children to your room. Here are some examples of what you might say when greeting children and their parents.

- "You're the first to arrive today. You and I can spend some quiet time together. Would you like to choose a book to read?"

- "Raoul, I see you smiling this morning. Are you looking forward to playing in the loft again today while your daddy goes to work?"

- "Julia, is this your Grandpa Fred whom I heard so much about? I know you're really happy he came to visit."

Children may translate an adult's angry words into negative feelings about themselves.

Sometimes adults lose control, take out their anger on children, or fail to pay attention to a child's needs. These behaviors can make children question their own worth. They may think our words carry more meaning than we intend. When a child hears an angry or thoughtless statement: "Can't you sit still and listen?"—he or she may translate the words into a negative self-image—"I am a bad person because I can't sit still." Words that demonstrate respect and caring help foster a child's positive sense of self. "I can see you are having trouble sitting still. Would you like to do something else?" Children are very sensitive to adult opinions. Your "language environment" is as important as the physical environment.

Using caring words takes some practice. It may be a while before new ways of talking to children feel natural. You will be rewarded when the children you care for let you know how much better they feel because of your understanding and care.

Applying Your Knowledge

In this learning activity you read several examples of how to talk to children in different situations. Then you write down what you might say in typical situations to show respect for children. If possible, tape record or videotape yourself talking with children to learn more about how your interactions affect a child's positive sense of self.

Using Caring Words
(Example)

What do you say when a child calls another child or an adult a name, such as *fat* or *stupid*?

"We don't call people names here, Carol. We just use each other's real names. Kent is not stupid, and neither are you. He is playing in his own way, just like you do. Both ways are fine."

What do you say when a child knocks down something another child is building or tries to destroy another child's work?

"Scott, you have just knocked down the building that Monica worked so hard to build. It's okay to be angry but it's not okay to destroy someone else's work. Monica, you need to tell Scott how you feel. Scott, if you are angry at Monica about something, use your words, not your feet."

What do you say when a child hurts or bites another?

"Trish, it's okay to be angry with people, but I'm not going to let you hit or bite Paul. I'm not going to let him hurt you, either. You can tell him how you feel. Say, 'I'm angry with you, Paul. I don't like what you did.'"

What do you say when a child expresses a fear of monsters?

"There are no monsters here at the center or at home, only on television, in books, and in make-believe. They are not real so they can't hurt you. It's okay to be scared, but we won't let anything bad happen to you."

What do you say when a child makes fun of another child's work?

"Jerry, we let children paint all kinds of pictures and hang their pictures wherever they choose. When you finish yours, you can show me where you want it to be. Your picture is special because you made it, and Pamela's is special too, because she made it."

What do you say when a child is sad because his or her mother or father went to work and left him or her?

"Mommy has to go to work. It's hard when she leaves you. She goes to work to get money to buy clothes and food for you because she loves you and wants to take good care of you. After you wake up and have a snack, she'll be here to take you home."

What do you say when a child's parent is away traveling for work?

"Daddy did not go away because of anything you did wrong or because of anything you thought or said. Daddy's job needs him to be somewhere else for a while. He will not forget you while he is gone. He'll love you no matter where he is. He will come back as soon as he can."

What do you say when a child wants your attention and you are busy?

"Greg, I know you want me to watch you on the monkey bars, but right now I'm over in the tree house. If you wait five minutes I can come there, or you can come join us in the tree house."

What do you say when a child has a new sibling in the house and expresses jealousy?

"Sometimes it's hard to have to share Mommy and Daddy with a new baby. Maybe you think they love the baby more than you because they have to do all those things for the baby, like changing diapers. When you were a baby Mommy and Daddy did these same things for you. They still love you, too, as four-year-old Justin. You don't have to be like a baby for Mommy and Daddy to love you. I bet you feel good about being able to do so many things because you are four."

What do you say when a mother and father separate and one parent leaves the home?

"Daddy/Mommy did not leave home because of anything that you did wrong or because of anything you thought. Sometimes grown-ups have problems, too, and decide they can't live in the same house together. But you did not make it happen. Mommy and Daddy both love you, and they will both still take good care of you."

Using Caring Words

When a child doesn't want to go home:

When a child is upset or angry:

When a child has trouble doing a task:

When a child who can use the toilet wets his or her pants:

When (add your own here):

Share your words with your trainer. You could also display your caring words in your room to help you get used to using them.

See and Hear Your Interactions

If you were able to tape record or videotape yourself talking with children, listen to or view the recording to determine what you did well and what you would like to improve. You might want to review the tape with your trainer and discuss the children's verbal and nonverbal reactions to your communication.

Summarizing Your Progress

You have now completed all of the learning activities for this module. Whether you are an experienced teacher or a new one, this module has probably helped you develop new skills for fostering children's sense of self and self-esteem.

Before you go on to the next module, take a few minutes to summarize what you've learned.

- Turn back to Learning Activity I, Using Your Knowledge of Child Development to Foster Self-Esteem, and add to the chart specific examples of what you have learned about fostering self-esteem while you were working on this module. Read the sample responses on the completed chart at the end of this module.

- Next, review your responses to the pre-training assessment for this module. Write a summary of what you learned and list the skills you developed or improved.

If there are areas you would like to know more about, you will find recommended readings listed in the Orientation in Volume I.

Your final step in this module is to complete the knowledge and competency assessments. Let your trainer know when you are ready to schedule the assessments. After you have successfully completed them, you will be ready to start a new module. Congratulations on your progress so far, and good luck with your next module.

Answer Sheets

Developing a Positive and Supportive Relationship with Each Child

1   How did Ms. Kim work on building a positive and supportive relationship with Shawn?
    a. *She took time to talk with him on her way to the block corner.*

    b. *She stated that she liked the color blue without making judgments about his work.*

2. How did Ms. Kim work on building Shawn's self-esteem?
    a. *She gave him one-to-one attention while they hung his picture.*

    b. *She let him know that she remembered he had used blue paint last week, too.*

Helping Children Accept and Appreciate Themselves and Others

1. What feelings did Jerry appears to have about his block tower?
    a. *Pride*

    b. *Anger*

2. How did Mr. Lopez help Jerry learn to express his feelings in an appropriate way?
    a. *He expressed understanding at Jerry's anger.*

    b. *He held Jerry's arm while reminding Jerry to use words to express anger.*

Providing Opportunities for Children to Be Successful and Feel Competent

1. Why did Ms. Williams encourage Mark to come back to complete the puzzle?
    a. *She didn't want him to feel badly about not being able to finish the puzzle.*

    b. *She wanted him to feel good about working hard to complete a task.*

2. How did Ms. Williams support Mark's positive feelings about himself?
    a. *She helped him finish the puzzle.*

    b. *She said that after a few more times he could do it on his own.*

    c. *She stayed with him until the puzzle was finished.*

Using Your Knowledge of Child Development to Foster Self-Esteem

(p.67)

What Preschool Children Are Like	How Teachers Can Use This Information to Foster Self-Esteem
They are eager to please adults and may seek approval and attention.	*Join in children's play and work with them during clean-up. Offer specific, targeted encouragement for "real" efforts and accomplishments. Acknowledge children's requests for your approval and attention, even if you must ask them to wait for a few minutes until you are available. Help children learn to value their own skills and abilities.*
They may be fearful of such things as, loud noises, monsters, the dark, animals, or some people.	*Acknowledge fears and recognize that children feel them deeply. Reassure children by telling them you will keep them safe and won't let them be hurt. Encourage children to express their fears through talking, drawings, stories, pretend play, or other means. Let children know it's okay to be afraid.*
They can feed, dress, and do many things for themselves.	*Let children do as much as possible for themselves. Model ways to do things—such as zipping a coat—and allow plenty of time for a child to complete the task. Offer help only when asked, or when your assistance would calm an anxious child and lead to success.*
They usually have mastered independent use of the toilet and can ask to use the bathroom (if it isn't in the room).	*Set up a system so children can use the bathroom with little supervision, according to their own bodily needs. Make and post pictures to remind children to wash their hands. When needed, offer positive verbal reminders: "Wash your hands after using the toilet."*
They like to help during chores and routines.	*Work with your colleagues to develop plans for carrying out routines that allow children to participate according to their abilities. Invite children to help you with tasks such as moving furniture, wiping tables, or getting books ready to return to the library.*
They like to play make-believe and act out roles.	*Provide and rotate as needed a wide variety of props that respond to children's cultures, families, and interests. Extend and expand children's play by offering new props and by assuming a role and joining in the play. Follow a schedule with long blocks of time when children can choose what they want to do and with whom.*
They can take turns and share, but they don't always want to.	*Make positive comments when you see children sharing with each other, "Tosin heard you ask for more red paint, so he gave you some of his." Provide duplicates of popular materials so children don't have to wait to participate. Help children learn to negotiate with each other so they can share and take turns without getting into disagreements.*

Using Your Knowledge of Child Development to Foster Self-Esteem

(p. 68)

What Preschool Children Are Like	How Teachers Can Use This Information to Foster Self-Esteem
They can express feelings verbally using large vocabularies but may also stutter or use "baby talk."	*Allow children as much time as they need to express their ideas and feelings. Avoid stepping in to "speak" for them.*
They have strong emotions.	*Talk with children about their feelings. Help them understand the difference between feelings and actions. Reassure them that it is all right to have any and all of their feelings.*
They may express feelings such as anger and jealousy by hitting or kicking.	*Encourage children to use words rather than physical behaviors to tell each other what they want. If needed, help children express the words that identify their feelings. Provide outlets such as clay and playdough, water play, tearing paper, or moving to music that help children manage strong feelings.*
They have a great deal of physical energy.	*Provide indoor and outdoor opportunities for children to use their bodies. Recognize when children need to expend some energy and steer them to appropriate activities such as riding tricycles or dancing with streamers. Follow a schedule that limits the times children have to wait or sit still.*
They like to try new things and to take risks.	*Create an environment that allows children to take risks safely. For example, put mats under the climber so children won't be hurt if they fall. Offer new materials and activities regularly in response to growing skills and changing interests, and to expose children to new information and concepts.*
They are learning about what makes them the same or different from others. They know their names and ages, and learn to identify with their own gender, family, culture, community, and ethnic group.	*Provide books, props, pictures, and other materials that reflect children's cultures, ethnic groups, and communities in positive ways. Read books that show both genders, as well as people with a range of abilities engaged in a variety of activities, jobs, and roles. Talk with children about what makes each person, including themselves, a unique individual.*
They may have difficulty making the transition from home to school.	*Allow children to bring "security" items from home if these help them feel safe. (Children can store the items in their cubbies so they don't hinder participation.) Ask families to share photographs and post them in the room where children can see them. Suggest children "phone" their parents when they seem to be missing them. Reassure children by showing them on a picture schedule when their parents will return: "After we come in from outdoor play we get ready to go home. Next, parents pick up their children."*

Glossary

Autonomy

Independence; the stage (usually taking place in the toddler years) when children develop the ability to do things for themselves, make decisions, and control their own actions.

Environment

The complete makeup of the indoor and outdoor areas used by children; environment includes the space and how it is arranged and furnished, routines, materials and equipment, activities, and the children and adults who are present.

Initiative

Self-motivation; the stage (usually taking place during the preschool years) when children display high energy and use their skills to explore their world actively and accomplish tasks.

Observation

The act of systematically watching a child's behavior, movement, and body language to learn more about that child. The information gained from observation is used to plan a program that responds to the child's needs, strengths, interests, and other individual characteristics.

Sense of self

Understanding who you are; how you identify yourself in terms of culture, environment, physical attributes, preferences, skills, and experiences. A sense of self evolves throughout life as an individual's perceptions are revised in response to experiences and interactions with others.

Self-esteem

A sense of worth; a good feeling about oneself and one's abilities. Someone who feels connected to others, respected and valued, and able to do things successfully and independently is likely to have self-esteem.

Separation

The lifelong process of growing up and becoming independent from one's parents. Children often have strong feelings about separating from their families, and teachers can help children understand and express these feelings.

Temperament

The nature or disposition of a child; the way a child responds to and interacts with people, materials, and situations in his or her world.

Trust

Security; the stage (usually taking place in infancy) when children develop feelings of comfort and confidence because their needs are met promptly, consistently, and lovingly.

Module 9: *Social*

Overview

> **Promoting children's social development involves:**
>
> - Helping children learn to get along with others
> - Helping children understand and express their feelings and respect those of others
> - Providing an environment and experiences that help children develop social skills

Social development refers to children's increasing ability to get along with others and to enjoy the people in their lives. Social skills are evident when infants respond to the familiar voice or touch of a parent or caregiver, toddlers learn to play alongside others, and preschoolers play cooperatively with their friends. As children develop socially, they learn to share, cooperate, take turns, and negotiate with others. Although they may argue and disagree, most children really enjoy playing with others. They learn to cooperate so that play can continue. Children's social development is strengthened when they have secure relationships with their parents and teachers, when they have many opportunities to play with other children, and when they feel good about themselves.

Social skills are critical to a child's happiness and success in school and in life. Children who are unable to relate positively to others, or who do not know how to make and keep a friend, tend to be lonely and have low self-esteem. The preschool years are a critically important time to help children acquire positive social skills. Children who do not develop these skills in early childhood are likely to have problems when they enter school. They may act out in ways that interfere with their learning: becoming disruptive in the classroom; attacking their peers; failing to do their work; and eventually dropping out of school.

Social development is essential to children's success.

In recent years, American society has become increasingly characterized by high levels of violence. Most children experience violence on television and in the movies. Even more frightening are the increasing number of children who observe violence first hand in their communities and homes, or experience it as direct victims of aggressive behaviors. Because violence is glorified by the media, children receive mixed messages concerning the appropriateness of violent behaviors. They may take violence for granted, and just as they imitate other adult behaviors, they become aggressive towards each another. Many parents and educators are eager to play an active role in counteracting the trend towards violence. Teachers can assist by creating a safe environment for children and by teaching them positive social behaviors.

Teaching children pro-social skills helps to prevent violence and aggression.

Children who play well are more likely to have social skills.

The ability to play is one of the most important ways children develop social skills. Sara Smilansky, an early childhood researcher, has identified four kinds of play young children enjoy—functional play, constructive play, games with rules, and socio-dramatic play.[1] **Functional play** occurs when children explore and examine the properties of objects and materials and find out how things work. When preschoolers take apart an old radio, make designs with colored blocks, or bake bread, they are enjoying functional play. Through **constructive play,** children use materials—for example, blocks, Legos, or sand—to create a representation of something real or imagined. **Games with rules** include card and board games, many computer games, sports, or any type of play governed by a set of rules, that everyone understands and follows. Preschool children can learn simple games with rules—such as Candyland or Lotto—and enjoy group games led by the teacher.

Dramatic play is especially important for social development.

The fourth type of play is **socio-dramatic play.** Children pretend to be real or imaginary characters, try out different roles, and invent stories and situations to role play. For children to participate in socio-dramatic play, they have to be able to generate ideas, share what they know, listen to each other, compromise, and see somebody else's point of view. Through dramatic play, children can learn to control the ways they express their own feelings and emotions. They can role play being mean and nasty because it doesn't really count; it's only pretend. They can also deal with real fears, such as going to the dentist or moving to a new house. The social skills children develop through dramatic play can help them deal with many other situations in everyday life.

Children learn about acceptable behaviors through relationships with adults.

Through their relationships with adults, children learn acceptable social behaviors. As a teacher, you let children know that they are loved and accepted; you meet their needs as consistently and promptly as possible. This gives children a sense of security, which in turn allows them to appreciate, respect, and get along with other children and adults. In addition, you provide an environment where children can spend time alone or play with others. You also help children learn to respect the rights of others, so that everyone can enjoy the benefits of being part of a group. Finally, you help children understand their own feelings and show them acceptable ways to express themselves. (Because children's feelings about themselves affect how they develop socially, you may want to review Module 8, Self, while working on this module.)

Listed on the following pages are three sets of examples showing how teachers demonstrate their competence in promoting children's social development. Following each set of examples is a short reading and two questions to answer. When you have finished this section, compare your answers with those on the answer sheet at the end of the module. If your answers are different, discuss them with your trainer. There can be more than one good answer.

---

[1] Based on Sara Smilansky and Leah Shefatya, *Facilitating Play: A Medium for Promoting Cognitive, Socio-Emotional, and Academic Development in Young Children* (Gaithersburg, MD: Psychosocial and Educational Publications, 1990).

Helping Children Learn to Get Along with Others

Encourage children to help each other.	"Peter, if you ask him, I think Todd might help you carry the sawhorse outside."
Include large blocks of time in the daily schedule when children can choose to play with special friends.	"Diandria, I know you've been eager to make playdough. Who would you like to have help you?"
Model positive ways to interact with others.	"Ms. Kim, I have an extra pair of gloves you can wear when we go on our walk."
Help children find solutions to their conflicts.	"You both want to play with the helicopter. Let's think of different ways you could share it or take turns."
Assist children who have difficulty being accepted by the group.	"Roxanne, leave some space between your carpet square and André's. That way you can both listen to the story without getting in each other's way."

Ms. Frilles looks around the room to see what the children are doing. She sees Sally and Gina, two good friends, playing in the house corner. They are each waving their arms and look very angry. Ms. Frilles walks over to the girls so she can hear what they are saying. The children are playing restaurant, and both girls want to be the waitress. Ms. Frilles says to them, "I ate in a restaurant last week. There were so many customers they needed two servers." Then she steps back. The girls look at each other, then Sally says, "Let's sit the dolls in the chairs. Then we can both be waitresses." Ms. Frilles said, "That's good thinking, girls. You found a way to have fun together." As Ms. Frilles walks away she sees the two dolls sitting at a table in the "restaurant."

1.   **How did Ms. Frilles help the girls find a way to continue their play?**

2.   **How did Ms. Frilles help the girls feel good about solving their problem?**

Helping Children Understand and Express Their Feelings and Respect Those of Others

Share some of your own feelings when appropriate.	"I'm excited because my sister and her family are coming to visit us next week."
Accept children's feelings while helping them control their actions.	"I know you felt angry when John grabbed the truck. You can tell him you're angry, but I can't let you hurt him."
Help children understand how their peers are feeling.	"Karen is happy because you let her use the water wheel."
State what you think children are feeling when they are having trouble expressing their emotions.	"I wonder if you are having a bad day because you miss your mom a lot when she goes away on a trip."
Give children words they can use to express how they feel.	"When Michael teases you, it makes you feel unhappy so you cry. Tell Michael that you want him to stop teasing you."
Read and discuss stories that help children deal with their feelings about difficult situations.	"Can you think of a time when you had a 'terrible, horrible, no-good, very bad day'?" *(Alexander and the Terrible, Horrible, No-Good, Very Bad Day* by Judith Viorst)

Ms. Kim walks around the play yard to watch and listen to the children who are engaged in a variety of activities. Maddie and Peter are at the bottom of the ladder to the slide. Maddie begins to climb the ladder, then stops. Peter, who is next in line, tells her to hurry up, puts his hand on her back, and pushes her. Maddie turns around and pushes him back. Ms. Kim quickly walks over near the slide and says, "Maddie, I think you might be feeling a little scared about going down the slide, so you are taking your time climbing up the ladder. Peter, I think you might be feeling impatient because you want to have your turn on the slide. I can't let you push each other. What can we do about this problem?" Peter says, "Maddie, if you let me go first, I won't push you and you can take your time." Maddie steps down off the ladder so Peter can have his turn while she takes a little more time to conquer her fears. As Ms. Kim walks away, she turns back and hears Peter encouraging Maddie to come down the slide, "It's really fun, Maddie. You won't hurt yourself!"

1. **How did Ms. Kim let the children know that she understood and respected their feelings?**

2. **How did Ms. Kim help the children respect each other's feelings?**

Providing an Environment and Experiences That Help Children Develop Social Skills

Encourage children to work together during chores and routines.	"The plants in our garden are very dry. Juan and Patty, can you please water them?"
Establish and maintain rules and guidelines that help children learn social skills.	"Derek, there's only room for four children at the easels. What can you do while you are waiting?"
Extend children's dramatic play by activity participating.	"Dr. Jones, thank you for fixing my broken arm. I'll come back so you can take off the cast."
Encourage cooperation rather than competition.	"Let's help the block builders clean up so we can all go outside together."
Provide a variety of props that children can use for dramatic play.	When you put the old hair dryer in the house corner, Jackie and Kia started a beauty shop."
Provide duplicates of popular toys so children who have difficulty sharing can play together.	"Tasha, there's another tambourine on the shelf that you can use."
Provide materials and activities two or more children can enjoy together.	"Heather, why don't you ask Corinna if she wants to play Lotto with you?"

The children are getting ready to go outside. "Where's your other shoe?" Mr. Lopez asks Becky. "I lost it," she says. "I've looked everywhere." Jerry and Sukie, who are ready to go out, are standing by the door. "We have to find Becky's shoe before we go outside," Mr. Lopez explains. "Jerry and Sukie, will you two help Becky find her shoe? Then we can all get outside faster." They begin searching. "Here it is," they call. "It was under the pillows." Jerry holds up the shoe proudly and hands it to Mr. Lopez, who gives it to Becky so she can put it on. "Thank you both for helping," he says. "This bag of balls is very heavy. Who would like to help carry it?" The three children help Mr. Lopez lift the bag. "We are all ready now," he announces. "I like it when we work together to help each other."

1. **How did Mr. Lopez use a daily routine—getting ready to go outside—as an opportunity to help the children develop social skills?**

2. **What social skills did the children learn as they prepared to go outside?**

Your Own Social Development

Adults use social skills every day. When you yield to another car in traffic, share your lunch with a colleague who forgot hers, or wait for your turn to speak at a staff meeting, you are using social skills.

Sometimes you find yourself in situations where you need to adapt to a new group of people. Perhaps you just joined a reading group or began a new exercise class. In both of these situations you use social skills to get to know the other members and to adjust to the group's accepted ways of doing things.

Some adults find it very difficult to adjust to new situations. This difficulty may be due to characteristics of their temperament or personality. It's possible, though, that during childhood they didn't have many opportunities to get to know new people.

Young children learn how society expects them to behave by watching adults interact with each other as well as with children. When children see the important adults in their lives working cooperatively, sharing feelings and ideas, having friendly conversations, and enjoying each other's company, they learn important lessons. Sometimes teachers are so busy that they forget to say "please" or "thank you," and don't take time to enjoy the company of their colleagues. When teachers model social behaviors for children, everyone benefits. Teachers feel positive about their jobs and the people they work with, and the children can gain a more complete picture of their teachers. They see adults working out problems, sharing happy experiences, and cooperating with each other.

Think about how you and your colleagues model social skills. Give some examples below.

Sharing:

Cooperating:

Taking turns:

Solving problems:

Helping:

Appreciating each other:

Showing concern:

Positive relationships at work make your job more enjoyable and rewarding. The social skills you use and model promote your own mental health as well as children's learning.

When you finish this overview section, you should complete the pre-training assessment. Refer to the glossary at the end of this module if you need definitions for the terms that are used.

Pre-Training Assessment

Listed below are the skills that teachers use to promote the social development of preschool children. Think about whether you do these things regularly, sometimes, or not enough. Place a check in one of the boxes on the right for each skill listed. Then discuss your answers with your trainer.

Helping Children Learn to Get Along with Others

	I Do This:	**Regularly**	**Sometimes**	**Not Enough**
1.	Encourage children to help each other.	☐	☐	☐
2.	Include large blocks of time in the daily schedule when children can choose to play with special friends.	☐	☐	☐
3.	Model positive ways to interact with others.	☐	☐	☐
4.	Help children find solutions to their conflicts.	☐	☐	☐
5.	Assist children who have difficulty being accepted by the group.	☐	☐	☐

Helping Children Understand and Express Their Feelings and Respect Those of Others

6.	Share some of your own feelings when appropriate.	☐	☐	☐
7.	Accept children's feelings while helping them control their actions.	☐	☐	☐

Helping Children Understand and Express Their Feelings and Respect Those of Others

(continued)

	I Do This:	Regularly	Sometimes	Not Enough
8. Help children understand how their peers are feeling.		☐	☐	☐
9. State what you think children are feeling when they are having trouble expressing their emotions.		☐	☐	☐
10. Give children words they can use to express how they feel.		☐	☐	☐
11. Read and discuss stories that help children deal with their feelings about difficult situations.		☐	☐	☐

Providing an Environment and Experiences That Help Children Develop Social Skills

		Regularly	Sometimes	Not Enough
12. Encourage children to work together during chores and routines.		☐	☐	☐
13. Establish and maintain rules and guidelines that help children learn social skills.		☐	☐	☐
14. Extend children's dramatic play by actively participating.		☐	☐	☐
15. Encourage cooperation rather than competition.		☐	☐	☐
16. Provide a variety of props that children can use for dramatic play.		☐	☐	☐

Providing an Environment and Experiences That Help Children Develop Social Skills

(Continued)

	I Do This:	Regularly	Sometimes	Not Enough
17. Provide duplicates of popular toys so children who have difficulty sharing can play together.		☐	☐	☐
18. Provide materials and activities two or more children can enjoy together.		☐	☐	☐

Review your responses, then list three to five skills you would like to improve or topics you would like to learn more about. When you finish this module you will list examples of your new or improved knowledge and skills.

Begin the learning activities for Module 9, Social.

Learning Activities

I. Using Your Knowledge of Child Development to Promote Social Development

> **In this activity you will learn to:**
>
> - Recognize some typical characteristics of preschool children
> - Use what you know about children to promote their social development

A child's social development begins at birth. Young infants are entirely dependent on the adults who care for them. Through their interactions with the adults who diaper, feed, comfort, and talk to them, infants learn to trust their parents and caregivers. This trust is the foundation for social development.

Toddlers work hard to define themselves as separate and independent beings with minds of their own. When they run, climb, jump, test limits, and shout, "No! Me do!" they are saying, "This is me!" The experiences of being loved, cooperated with, and cared for help toddlers feel good about themselves and let them know what it means to love and care for another person.

By the time children enter the preschool years, most of them understand which behaviors are acceptable and which are not. Preschoolers are eager to be liked by their peers. They spend more time playing with their peers and are less dependent on adults. They learn from each other and frequently copy what they see others do. It's important to allow ample time each day for children to choose what they want to do and with whom.

Preschool children learn from playing and talking with their peers.

Preschool children use their rapidly developing language skills to engage in real conversations with each other—you are likely to hear all kinds of interesting discussions. If you listen carefully to these conversations, you will learn how children are getting along, what their interests are, whose ideas are listened to, and who needs help learning how to get others to listen. You can use this information to plan ways to meet individual needs.

The preschool years are also characterized by exclusion. You may notice that some children tend to be the excluders while others tend to be the ones left out. Forcing children to play with each other does not work, nor will it help them learn social skills. You can observe to see how often a child is excluded and coach the child by suggesting ways to become included in group play. You might provide a special prop to share or suggest a role to play.

A teacher can help a child learn how to become included in group play.

Play helps children develop in all areas.

Play is children's work. Because play helps children grow in all areas, it is one of the most important ways in which children develop social skills. Through play, children have fun, try out ideas, make friends, pretend, and learn about the world. They develop physical skills, learn how to think and solve problems, find out what they're good at, and develop a sense of competence and self-esteem. They learn to take turns, share favorite things, understand how a friend feels, and express their feelings in acceptable ways. In addition, play helps children try out adult roles and overcome their fears.

Children begin playing when they are infants. An infant may discover his or her toes and find that playing with them is fun. A parent or older sibling may play with an infant, rolling a ball back and forth. Older infants are keen observers and enjoy pretending and imitating adults.

Toddlers enjoy doing the same things again and again. This repetition is a way they master skills. A toddler may play alone with toys that are different from those that others in the group use. Although other children are nearby, the child may not talk to or move toward them. This is called **solitary play**. As children get older, they begin playing alongside each other, using the same kinds of toys and sometimes talking to each other. This is called **parallel play**. For example, two children sitting in a sand box, using shovels and chatting with one another are involved in parallel play. They are enjoying each other's company but are not yet ready to dig a hole in the sand together.

In the preschool years, children often engage in cooperative play.

Solitary and parallel play don't end once a child reaches the preschool years. During a typical day a child might work at the computer alone, do a puzzle while sitting next to other children, or join a group in make-believe play. However, preschool children tend to spend most of their time playing cooperatively in groups. During **cooperative play**, children organize their own activities, assign roles, make up rules, give out specific tasks, and often work toward a common goal. For example, a group of children may decide to build a town in the block corner. Through discussion and negotiation, they decide who will build the different structures—roads, houses, and stores. They resolve conflicts by compromising. The results, both the completed town and the process of working together, are more rewarding than building alone. Children at this level of play really enjoy working and playing together. Enjoying the company of other people is an important part of their social development.

Applying Your Knowledge

The chart on the next page identifies some typical behaviors of children in the preschool years, ages three to five. Included are behaviors relevant to social development. The right column asks you to identify ways teachers can use this information to promote children's social development. Try to think of as many examples as you can. As you work through the module you will learn new strategies and you can add them to the chart. You are not expected to think of all the examples at one time. If you need help getting started, turn to the completed chart at the end of this module. By the time you complete this module, you will find that you have learned many ways to promote social development.

Using Your Knowledge of Child Development to Promote Social Development

What Preschool Children Are Like	How Teachers Can Use This Information to Promote Social Development
They can help to make and follow a few simple rules.	*Involve children in making the rules for the classroom. Play simple games such as* Lotto *or* Go Fish *to help children learn to follow rules in play situations. Offer positive reminders: "Walk indoors, please" to help children follow rules.*
They are learning to share, cooperate, and take turns.	
They like to imitate adult activities.	
They carry on conversations with other children, in pairs and also in groups.	
They may exclude other children from their play.	
They are moving from parallel to cooperative play.	
They continue to need opportunities for solitary play.	

Using Your Knowledge of Child Development to Promote Social Development

What Preschool Children Are Like	How Teachers Can Use This Information to Promote Social Development
They ask many questions.	
They begin to develop friendships and may have a best friend.	
They gain greater awareness of the larger community.	
They engage in make-believe play alone and with others.	
They show pride in their own work, and they seek and value adult approval.	
They have strong emotions and feelings and are learning to use words to name them.	

When you have completed as much as you can do on the chart, discuss your answers with your trainer. As you proceed with the rest of the learning activities, you can refer back to the chart and add examples of ways to promote children's social development.

II. Promoting Children's Dramatic Play

In this activity you will learn to:

- Observe how preschool children learn and develop through dramatic play
- Provide props to expand children's play
- Interact with children in ways that help them become fully involved in play

What children do during dramatic play differs according to their age and stage of development. Young preschoolers typically spend a lot of time running away from monsters or imitating what they have seen first hand. At this age, children do a lot of collecting and gathering, packing suitcases, filling purses, planning trips. Sometimes the planning is all they have time for.

As they get older, preschoolers continue to be fascinated by super heroes and scary monsters. Their play expands to include creating safe places to hide so the monster can't get them. They like dress-up clothes and other props, and develop a wide variety of roles to play. As they begin to understand the difference between fantasy and reality, you may hear them say, "Let's pretend that . . . ."

The dramatic play of older preschool children is more involved. They develop complex sets of characters and situations and may pretend to be real people or fantasy figures from books or television. For many children, dramatic play becomes a means to practice doing something they fear, such as getting a shot at the doctor's or going on an airplane trip. Children also may use dramatic play to work through anxieties about situations in their lives, such as a new baby at home or a parent about to go on a business trip.

What children do during dramatic play changes as they get older.

Creating an Environment that Supports Dramatic Play

Dramatic play can take place in almost any setting: on the playground, in the house corner, at the woodworking bench, or on a neighborhood walk. It can occur spontaneously—two children at the water table may begin pouring "coffee" into cups and serving each other—or it can also be planned and organized. For example, after a parent visits the classroom to tell children about his job as a flight attendant, several children might decide to take a plane trip. They talk about who will be the pilot, navigator, passengers, and flight attendants; they decide where they will go and what will happen. They use social skills such as negotiation and cooperation to carry out their plans.

In some interest areas, the materials—sand, water, playdough, and finger paint—invite social interaction. Preschoolers are drawn to these materials and feel relaxed when they use them. As they play, they begin to share and talk to each other. When additional props are offered, children begin to pretend and make up play episodes with each other. A basket filled with rolling pins, cookie cutters, plastic knives, and cups and saucers to use with playdough can lead to dramatic play about cooking, baking, and serving.

Dramatic play also occurs in the block area. Young children need time to explore with blocks before they can create a setting for dramatic play. Props such as wooden and rubber animals, people, and cars encourage children to use blocks to create settings for dramatic play.

The outdoor play area also serves as a site for dramatic play. Children might hold picnics in the sandbox, or turn the climber into a space ship, or pretend to drive cars.

The house corner is the most popular site for dramatic play.

The house corner, where the scene is set and ready to go, is usually the most popular site for dramatic play. This area should feature props that encourage play revolving around the family—cooking, cleaning, caring for babies, going to the grocery store. A child-sized table and chairs can set the stage for a variety of dramatic play scenes—from family scenes to a restaurant or doctor's office.

As children gain experience in dramatic play, teachers can offer a variety of new props to build on their interests. Props might relate to a class experience. For example, you could offer new baking and cooking props after a field trip to a bakery. To build on the children's behind-the-scenes tour of a grocery store, offer a cash register, play money, empty food cans and boxes, and shopping bags. Help children recall what they saw and did so they can use the props to recreate and expand their experiences. Props may also relate to something important that has happened in children's lives—a child going to the hospital, or a neighborhood fire that the children witnessed.

Encouraging Dramatic Play through the Use of Prop Boxes

One way to extend children's dramatic play is to create prop boxes—collections of materials focused on a specific theme, such as a health clinic or a shoe store. To create a prop box, think of a theme that builds on children's interests or a recent experience. Then think of items children could use to engage in dramatic play around the theme. Collect the materials and put them in the prop box—any sturdy container will do for storage—until you are ready to introduce them to the children. On the following page are some suggested themes and materials to include in prop boxes.[2]

---

[2] Adapted with permission from Cheryl Foster, "Dramatic Play Kits or Prop Boxes," in *Competency-Based Training Module No. 24: Dramatic Play* (Suppl. No. 5) (Coolidge, AZ: CDA Training Program, Institute of Human Development, Central Arizona College, 1982), pp. 41-46.

Prop Boxes for Preschool Children

Health Clinic

Gauze
Cotton balls
Height-weight chart
Prescription pads
Tongue depressors
   (disposable)

Real stethoscope
Plastic eye droppers
Dolls
Scale
Red finger paint for blood

Bandages
Play thermometer
Paper and pencils
Stretcher or cot
Cloth for making bandages

Beds
Stop watch
Telephone
Hospital gown
Uniforms

Unisex Hair Stylist

Large mirror
Rollers or curlers
Bobby pins
Manicure set
Paper
Hair dryer and curling
   iron without cords

Hand mirrors
Hair nets
Hair clips
Nail file
Pencil
Hair care products
   (empty containers)

Hairpins
Plastic basin
Barrettes and ribbons
Magazines
Shaving brushes
Hairbrushes and combs
   (wash after use)

Towels
Scarves
Headbands
Play money
Shaving cream
Razors (toys or real
   ones without blades)

Beach

Sunglasses
Umbrellas
Playing cards
Buckets and shovels
Blankets or beach
   towels

Sun hats
Picnic basket
Swim goggles
Sand molds
Suntan lotion (empty)

Beach bags
Fishing poles
Inflatable tubes
Frisbees®
Paper plates and cups
   and plastic utensils

Sea shells
Portable radio
Flippers
Plastic thongs
Food (pictures or empty
   cans or boxes)

Gas Station and Automobile Repair

Work shirts
Flashlights
Key ring and keys
Parts (used and washed
   spark plugs, filters, gears)

Caps
Wiring
Rags
Auto supply catalogs

Tire pump
Empty oil cans
Work gloves
Tools (pliers, hammers
   screwdrivers)

Oil funnel
Windshield wipers
Short lengths of hose
Small tool set

Post Office/Mail Carrier

Index card file
Stamps from "junk" mail
Gummed labels
Mailbox(es) (arch
   cardboard over a box,
   paint, cut slot)

Play money
Rubber stamps
   and ink pad
Writing pads

Crayons
Envelopes of different sizes
Rubber bands
Mailbags (shoulder-strap
   purses or paper bags
   with straps attached)

Pencils
Junk mail
Mail carrier hat

Guiding and Extending Children's Play

As a teacher, you can play an important role in helping children become fully involved in dramatic play. By observing, you can see which children do and do not get along with one another, what roles they play in the group, and what problems or anxieties individual children are experiencing. Observation also lets you know what is going on in the play situation and when your guidance is needed. Your interventions should be gentle and indirect, such as providing a suitable prop to help a child get involved in the play. "Kia, here is some money to give the storekeeper. I think he has run out of change."

Participating in dramatic play is one of the best ways to teach play skills.

One effective way to guide children's play is to take a role and participate in the play. Sit at the table in the house corner for 20 to 30 minutes, while a colleague handles the rest of the room. Chat with the children as they come and go, or pretend to talk on the telephone. From this vantage point you can observe the children, comment on what they are doing, offer information, and give indirect suggestions of what to do next. Here are some examples.

- Sergio is holding the coffee pot. The teacher says: "I'd really like a cup of coffee. Could you please put the coffee on the stove to get hot."

  This involves Sergio in playing "house," tells him that stoves are used to heat food and coffee is served hot, and suggests an action—putting the pot on the stove.

- Mara starts to leave the house corner. The teacher says: "Where's Mara going?"

  This stops Mara from just wandering away and helps her feel included. Mara says, "I'm going to the store."

  Picking up on this, the teacher offers a few ideas: "Mara, have you got your money? Could you please buy me some milk?"

  Mara feels free to leave but also has a good reason for coming back.

- Nigel is standing at the stove. The teacher talks to Ana on the phone: "Yes, we're pretty busy here. Nigel is cooking. Hey, Nigel, Ana wants to know what you're cooking."

  Nigel may not have had a purpose for his actions at the stove. The teacher's description helps Nigel focus on what he is doing. Nigel thinks before answering, "I'm cooking beans."

- Gemma is holding a doll. The teacher says: "Oh, is your baby sick? Did you call the doctor? Here, let's get her on the phone."

The teacher's questions help Gemma focus on a prop, the doll, as she assumes the role of parent in the play episode.

- Delia and Shanelle are playing with dolls. The teacher says: "Take the baby off the table. He might fall and hurt himself." "Is the baby ready for bed? Be sure to put the blanket on so she won't catch cold."

  The teacher helps Delia and Shanelle learn how real babies are cared for.

Here are some other ways in which teachers can help children play.

Refer to children in their role names.	"Doctor, could you move your patient over here? Your examining table is in the way of the construction crew."
Remind children of something they did in the past.	"Do you remember last week when we went on a trip to the park? We had a lot of fun."
Model playful behaviors yourself.	"I could smell your bread baking from way over by the easels."
Help children get started, then step back so they can express their own ideas.	"I really enjoyed my dinner, but I have to run to get my bus."
Remind children of classroom rules within the context of the play.	"I think this grocery store can only hold four customers. Susan, can you and Tony take a walk around the block until these customers are finished with their shopping?"
Reinforce positive social behaviors when you observe them.	"I liked the way the two campers took turns wearing the backpack."

Applying Your Knowledge

In this learning activity you will create a prop box to encourage children's dramatic play. After introducing the prop box, conduct a 30-minute observation of a group of children using the props. Next, use your observation notes to describe the children's roles and play theme. Record examples of the social skills children were developing or using during their play. Then develop a plan for extending the children's play. The plan might include a way to involve a child who was excluded, props to add, or words you can use to comment on the play. Finally, implement your plan and record what happens.

Begin by reading the example that follows. It is a shortened version of a complete 30-minute observation. Then, complete your own observations using the forms provided.

Promoting Children's Play
(Example)

Setting: *House Corner*   **Children:** *Tanya, George, Danny, and Carrie*

Prop Box Theme: *Camping out*

Props:

two sheets (to make a tent), two flashlights, backpack, thermos, cooler, plastic plates and utensils, three sleeping bags, tablecloth, rope, mosquito netting, nature books, binoculars, empty food containers, compass

What happened:

Tanya and George were in the house corner opening the camping prop box when Danny joined them. George said he would be the daddy and Tanya could be the mommy and Tanya agreed. Danny said he wanted to be the daddy. George said Danny could be the daddy's best friend and use a flashlight. Danny agreed and helped George make a tent with the sheets. George put on the backpack. Danny picked up the thermos and some food. Tanya got a bag and filled it with the plates, utensils, and tablecloth. Carrie joined them and Tanya said she could be the other mother. George said there could only be one. Danny said she could be his wife. That was okay with George. Danny gave Carrie the thermos to carry. George lined everyone up and they walked around the room and back to the tent. Then George said they should go to sleep. He and Danny put the three sleeping bags in the tent. They all wanted to lie down right away. Tanya said she didn't want to sleep. She and Carrie spread out the table cloth to have a picnic.

Social skills used or being developed:

The children negotiated with each other as they worked out who would play each role and shared props.

Danny shared the thermos with Carrie so she would have something to carry.

Danny acted as a negotiator, suggesting a role for Carrie.

The girls found a way to play so they could do more than what George told them to do.

Ways to extend the play:

The children didn't use the nature books. I could say to them, "I saw a lot of interesting plants out in the woods. I wonder if there are pictures of those plants in these books?"

I could add some more props so the children could have a pretend fire to cook their food on. I will add some logs and some pots and pans.

I can read Three Days on a River in a Red Canoe *by Vera Williams or* Sleep Out *by Carol Currick.*

What happened?

They used all the cooking props I added and continued to take turns in the tent.

I read the stories. The next day I saw Tanya and Danny go canoeing in the wagon.

Promoting Children's Play

Setting: _____ **Children:** _____

Prop Box Theme: _____

Props:

What happened:

Social skills used or being developed:

Ways to extend the play:

What happened?

III. Creating an Environment That Supports Children's Social Development

---

In this activity you will learn to:

- Set up the environment so that children are comfortable being in a group all day
- Plan the environment so that children can develop and use social skills

---

Many of the children who come to your program will have to adjust to group living. No matter how homelike the environment, the classroom is not a home. You can respond to children's questions and concerns by how you organize the environment.

Do I belong here? "Here is a special place where you can keep your things. It's called a cubby. We'll hang this photograph of you and your family and write your name above it so everyone will know it's yours."

Will the things I make and the things I bring here be safe? "I'll help you hang up your paintings until they're dry. Then you can store them in your cubby until you take them home, or I'll help you hang them on the class room wall."

Do I have to share the things I want to play with? "We know it's hard to share, so we make sure we have several of the most popular toys. After you've been here for awhile, you'll find it easier to share."

How will I know when it's my turn? "When Joe is finished using the wagon he'll ring the bell. Then you'll know it's your turn. He'll wait with the wagon until you get there."

How will I know what to do? "We'll help you get used to being at the center. Every day we do the same things, in the same order, just as you see in these pictures. Soon you'll be able to tell me what we do next."

Will I have friends? "First, I'll help you find out what things you like to do here. Then, I'll help you get to know other children who like to do the same things."

To create supportive environments, teachers make sure children have many opportunities to cooperate, share, and help. In addition, teachers minimize or eliminate the conditions that lead to disagreements and aggressive behaviors. One of the most effective ways to help children feel comfortable in a group setting is to create supportive physical and programmatic environments. The physical environment includes the arrangement of furniture and equipment in the indoor and outdoor spaces used by children, interest areas, and the way materials are displayed. The program environment refers to the daily schedule, routines, transitions, and adult-led and child-choice activities.

Planning the Physical Environment

Like adults, children respond to the characteristics of the physical environment. An attractive room with homelike features—walls painted in warm colors, curtains hanging in the windows, soft lighting, and pictures hung at children's eye-level with plenty of space between them—provides an uncluttered, calm setting for children's play. Several interior decorating rules—"less is more," "provide a place for everything," "form follows function," and "rearrange to meet current needs"—are guidelines that apply to any environment for preschool children.

Less is more. Offer a variety of materials to stimulate children's interests, but not so many that children are overwhelmed by too many choices.

Provide a place for everything. Display toys on low, labeled shelves, store play materials with loose pieces (such as Legos®) in separate open containers, and put materials together that are used together (paper and crayons). A well-organized environment allows children to find what they need. Clean-up time goes more smoothly because it's easy to see where things go.

Form follows function. Set up interest areas near necessary resources. For example, have the art area near the sink and the computer area near an electrical outlet. Children won't drip paint on the way to the sink or trip over extension cords.

Rearrange to meet current needs. Create a flexible room layout so teachers can move furniture and equipment when children need space to spread out or to store unfinished projects.

Accidents are common in preschool rooms. Children get in each other's way, knock down buildings, and bump into each other. Some children interpret these accidents as intentional and may respond with aggression. Limiting the number of children allowed to use an interest area or piece of outdoor equipment can minimize crowding and prevent accidents, thus reducing a source of disagreements. Children can monitor the area themselves if you set up a concrete system that lets them know if there's room for them to play, e.g., five hooks to hang name tags limits the area to five children.

Some disagreements take place when children can't get in or out of an area easily. They may feel trapped or frustrated because movement is limited. To avoid this problem, make sure there is more than one way to get in or out of each area. "Gwen, use the steps to climb up to the loft. The rope ladder is for climbing down."

Limit the number of children who can use an area at one time.

Provide more than one way to enter or exit an area.

Locate related interest areas near each other in order to extend children's play.

The location of interest areas can support or work against social development. To extend children's imaginative play in the house corner, you might create another complementary area nearby using prop boxes or other materials. A store, restaurant, or doctor's office can provide new play opportunities. Children in the house corner will have somewhere to go and the children in the new area will have "customers" or "patients." The new areas can stay in place as long as they are capturing children's interests.

Locating the block area away from the line of traffic offers protection and allows children to work on their structures without worrying about accidents. On the other hand, if the block area is in an unprotected space, children passing by are likely to get in the way of the builders and may accidentally knock down their creations.

Provide places where children can take "time out."

Although preschoolers spend most of their time playing in groups, even the most outgoing children sometimes want to be alone for a while. They may take time out from group living because they are tired and need to "recharge their batteries." Some children need to spend time alone because they are overwhelmed by strong feelings. Time away from the group allows them to handle their feelings and prevents them from losing control and acting out in inappropriate ways. Examples of time-out places include:

- a listening area with tape recorders or CD players with earphones;

- small enclosed spaces—a platform or lookout loft, a large cardboard box, a small defined area with pillows;

- a small bean bag chair; or

- a small table and chair for one child.

Provide places where a few friends can play together.

When children want to play with just one or two others, they need spaces sized to accommodate a few friends. Indoors, you can use shelves as dividers to create small spaces, group a pile of pillows in a corner, or turn a large appliance carton into a cozy nook. Outdoors, a tire swing can hold two children. Large hollow blocks and planks are ideal for children who wish to build their own spaces. A tractor-tire sandbox is the perfect size for a small group.

Provide lookouts so children can observe play.

To help children who find it difficult to enter a group, you can create lookouts—places from which a child can observe others at play until he or she feels ready to join in. A loft can be a lookout or a quiet area can serve as a lookout for a noisier one. For example, as Hussein paints a picture in the art area, he watches several children playing house next door in the dramatic play area. The art area serves as a lookout point for Hussein. He can watch the noisier, more social play in the dramatic play area and learn what the children are doing—cooking dinner. This information gives him the confidence to join in the play. "I'm hungry. What's for dinner?"

Planning the Programmatic Environment

Your daily schedule, routines, transitions, activities, and group time can also support social development. These aspects of the environment are less concrete than interest areas, materials, and equipment. However, your careful planning of these parts of the program can help children learn social skills such as helping others, cooperating, and enjoying the company of others.

Follow a daily schedule that has long blocks of time when children can make choices—what to do, what to use, who to play with, when to move on to something new. Include opportunities for children to play alone, with one or two others, in a small group, and in a large group.

Use routines and other opportunities to encourage children's independence. Children can use their self-help skills during personal routines such as washing hands or brushing teeth. When you set up a system for rotating assigned chores, children can share the responsibility for keeping the classroom running smoothly. In addition, ask for children's help at other times—to find a classmate's lost mitten, to carry something heavy outdoors, or to teach another child a skill.

Announce transitions before they occur to give children time to finish what they are doing. Some children find it difficult to move from one activity to the next. They may need several reminders that the transition is coming, one-on-one attention from a teacher, or extra time to finish what they're doing.

Plan activities that respond to the interests of a child who seldom joins in group play. This lets the child know he or she has been noticed, gives the child an opportunity to interact with others, and lets the other children see the child in a new light. You can also plan activities that encourage cooperation—painting a mural, making a collage, planting a garden, building an obstacle course.

Use group time to play cooperative games and teach social skills. Try using puppets to act out a conflict resolution strategy, reading a story in which the characters face and resolve a social problem, or involving children in setting rules for a new area or piece of equipment.

Try these strategies in your classroom.

The programmatic environment should offer a balance between structure and choice time.

An effective programmatic environment is balanced—neither highly structured by adults nor completely devoted to children's free play. Ideally, there is enough structure for children to feel secure, but not so much that children can't make choices and interact with each other. In a balanced environment, children spend most of the day in activities of their own choosing and teachers observe and guide their play. Teachers stay alert to opportunities to reinforce social skills and address aggression. They remind children of rules and guidelines, model social behaviors, offer new props, provide indirect suggestions to extend play themes, and let children know they value their social skills. "Jade, that was a good idea to offer to be a passenger instead of the bus driver. Toya, maybe on the next trip you can be the passenger and Jade can be the driver."

Applying Your Knowledge

In this learning activity you will select one aspect of your center's physical environment and one aspect of its programmatic environment to assess and improve, if necessary. Describe what you do now, how it does or does not support social development, and how you would like to change your practices. Next, implement one of the changes and report on what happens as a result. Begin by reviewing the example that follows.

Using the Environment to Support Social Development

(Example)

Select one aspect of the <u>physical</u> environment, then complete the chart.

- offering enough materials to stimulate interest without overwhelming children

- providing a place for everything

- setting up interest areas near necessary resources

- limiting the number of children who can use an area at one time

- providing more than one way to enter or exit an area

- locating related interest areas near each other to extend children's play

- providing places where children can take time out or play with one friend

- providing lookouts so children can observe play

What We Do Now	How This Affects Social Development	How We Could Change Our Practices
Some interest areas have two ways in or out, others do not. *The play house we made from a refrigerator carton has a front door, but no back door.*	*Children bump into each other which causes disagreements that sometimes get out of control.* *Sometimes children refuse entry to others who want to use the play house, saying "You can't come in."*	*We can rearrange the interest areas to create two entry points.* *We can cut out a back door in the play house.*

What change will you make in the physical environment?

We can make a back door in the play house.

What happened as a result?

The conflicts in the play house have almost disappeared. Children using the house are getting more involved in imaginative play.

Using the Environment
to Support Social Development

Select one aspect of the <u>physical</u> environment, then complete the chart.

- offering enough materials to stimulate interest without overwhelming children

- providing a place for everything

- setting up interest areas near necessary resources

- limiting the number of children who can use an area at one time

- providing more than one way to enter or exit an area

- locating related interest areas near each other to extend children's play

- providing places where children can take time out or play with one friend

- providing lookouts so children can observe play

What We Do Now	How This Affects Social Development	How We Could Change Our Practices

What change will you make in the physical environment?

What happened as a result?

Select one aspect of the <u>programmatic</u> environment, then complete the chart.

- following a daily schedule with long blocks of choice time

- offering meaningful opportunities to participate in routines

- announcing transitions before they occur

- planning activities in response to individual interests

- playing cooperative games and teaching social skills at group time

What We Do Now	How This Affects Social Development	How We Could Change Our Practices

What change will you make in the programmatic environment?

What happened as a result?

Discuss this activity with your colleagues. Implement other changes in the environment, as needed, to encourage children's social development.

IV. Helping Children Learn Caring Behaviors

> **In this activity you will learn to:**
>
> - Recognize caring behaviors in children
> - Help children develop caring behaviors

Caring or prosocial behaviors are valued by society. They include social skills such as sharing and taking turns, as well as the following behaviors:[3]

Showing empathy:
- Feeling and acting concerned when someone is upset or hurt
- Sharing another person's happiness or excitement

Showing generosity:
- Giving a toy or possession to another person
- Sharing a snack or toy with another person

Helping:
- Assisting another person do a job
- Stepping in when someone needs assistance

Children develop caring behaviors over a long period of time. Some infants demonstrate caring behaviors very early in life. They get upset and cry when they hear another infant crying. Between the ages of one and two, children begin to show real concern for others. When this concern is recognized and reinforced by parents and caregivers, children continue to develop caring behaviors. Between the ages of two and six, children begin to develop skills in responding appropriately to the needs and feelings of others.

As they learn to get along with others, young children are learning caring behaviors. The most direct way in which children learn such behaviors is by watching the adults who care for them. During a typical day you might help a child find a lost mitten, applaud a child who finishes a difficult puzzle, and listen to a child's concerns. In so doing, you are modeling caring behaviors for children. Your dependable and responsive interactions help children feel secure. This security allows children to show concern for others and to be cooperative members of the group.

---

[3] Based on Janice J. Beaty, *Observing Development of the Young Child* (Columbus, OH: Charles E. Merrill Publishing Co., 1986), p. 111.

You can think of caring behaviors as examples of the Golden Rule. When people behave toward others as they would like others to behave toward them, they are using caring behaviors. Teachers demonstrate these behaviors in their relationships with children, parents, and colleagues. They also help children learn these behaviors by letting children know that caring behaviors are valued by society.

Plan group activities that involve thoughtfulness and emphasize a sense of community. For example, make get-well cards for a child who is sick to let him know he is missed and that the class hopes he feels better.

Use each child's name often. Refer to children by their given names when you talk to them. Practice saying each name as it is pronounced by the family. Hang pictures of children and families on the wall at children's eye level and talk about who is who. Label the children's art work and cubbies. Use techniques such as singing songs with children's names in them to encourage children to call each other by name.

Give small groups of children cooperative play ideas. Suggest activities that call for cooperation. Cooperative activities may include moving a large box, folding a large blanket, or creating a collage.

Read books with themes of helpfulness and friendship. "What are some ways to be a good friend?" (after reading *Best Friends for Francis* by Russell Hoban).

Talk about exciting things that have happened to the children and teachers. When a child has had a happy experience, share that pleasure by giving out hugs or handshakes. "Tim, you baked such a beautiful loaf of bread. Can I shake your hand?"

Help children learn how to talk about their feelings. "When you are worried about something, you can talk to me about it. Everyone has worries. I will listen carefully, and I won't make fun of you."

Take pictures of children to record special occasions and typical daily events. Ask a parent to help by putting the pictures in small albums that children can easily handle. Children will enjoy reliving events and talking about what they did together. Families will enjoy seeing what their children do in your program.

Acknowledge what children say even when they can't have or do what they want. "I heard you ask for more French toast. There isn't any more left. If you are hungry, you can have a banana or a bowl of cereal."

Try these strategies for encouraging caring behaviors in children.[4]

---

[4] Adapted from a workshop handout, *Teaching Techniques to Encourage Friendly (Prosocial) Behavior in Young Children* (Ames, IA: Iowa State University).

Caring behaviors are not learned quickly; teachers need to be patient as children slowly learn the skills of negotiation, sharing, and cooperation. It is very natural for young children to put their own needs first. When their needs are met, children gradually learn to think about the needs of others. Frequently, you may have to reassure children with little experience in group living that their own wants will be satisfied.

Applying Your Knowledge

This learning activity has three parts. 1) Over the next three days, observe the activities in the room for five-minute periods, several times each day. Then review your notes and list examples of children learning caring behaviors. 2) Reflect on your own behaviors and interactions. Note some examples of ways you demonstrate and promote children's caring behaviors. 3) Make a book about the children's caring behaviors and read it with a small group. Read the examples that follow. Then use the blank forms that follow to record your examples.

1. Observation Summary: Caring Behaviors

(Example)

Caring Behaviors[5]	Examples
Showing concern for someone in distress	*Bonita fell down in the play yard. Susan put her arm around her and helped her get up. Then Susan got a teacher to help.*
Showing delight when someone experiences pleasure	*Tamila was very excited when Ms. Frilles hung up her picture. Charisse came over to look at it.*
Sharing something with another	*David gave Shawn part of his muffin at lunch time.*
Giving a possession to another	*Dean found a shiny rock outside and gave it to Maddie.*
Taking turns with toys or activities	*Billy and Lamont took turns putting blocks on their tower until it fell over.*
Helping another to do a task	*Maddie helped Felipe wipe up a spill.*
Helping another in need	*Carlos saw David trying to get a wagon out of the shed and went over to help him.*

2. How You Demonstrate and Promote Caring Behaviors

(Example)

When Trina's mom came to pick her up, I asked her how her day was. Then I gave her a flyer about our center's new toy lending library and invited her to the opening celebration.

Dean saw Kalisha having a hard time reaching the crackers. He moved them closer to Kalisha so she could serve herself. Later on I said to Dean, "I think Kalisha really appreciated your help."

Moki's mother dropped off the parent newsletters this morning. I asked the children to help me fold them in half and put one in each mailbox.

---

[5] Based on Janice J. Beaty, *Observing Development of the Young Child* (Columbus, OH: Charles E. Merrill Publishing Co., 1986), p. 30.

4. A Book About Caring Behaviors

(Example)

Write a book about children using caring behaviors. Illustrate the book with photographs, pictures from magazines, or drawings. Some children may want to help write and illustrate the book.

Describe your book and how you made it.

We wrote a book about Lamont and Billy's block tower. The boys rebuilt their tower while I took photos. We pasted each photo on a piece of cardboard and punched holes in each page. Then we put the pages in order. I asked the children to tell me what to write under each one. Max drew a picture for the cover. We used clear Contact paper to protect the pages and the cover. We laced the cover and pages together.

Read the book to the children and describe their responses.

Billy and Lamont liked hearing their names. At the end of the story several children said, "Read it again." Then I put the book in the library corner. During the next week the children "read" the book out loud to themselves and each other.

1. Observation Summary: Caring Behaviors

Caring Behaviors[6]	Examples
Showing concern for someone in distress	
Showing delight when someone experiences pleasure	
Sharing something with another	
Giving a possession to another	
Taking turns with toys or activities	
Helping another to do a task	
Helping another in need	

[6] Adapted from Janice J. Beaty, *Observing Development of the Young Child* (Columbus, OH: Charles E. Merrill Publishing Co., 1986), p. 30.

2. How You Demonstrate and Promote Caring Behaviors

3. A Book About Caring Behaviors

Write a book about children using caring behaviors. Illustrate the book with photographs, pictures from magazines, or drawings. Some children may want to help write and illustrate the book.

Describe your book and how you made it.

Read the book to the children and describe their responses.

Discuss this activity with your trainer and with a colleague who also cares for these children.

V. Helping Children Relate Positively to Others

> **In this activity you will learn to:**
> - Tell when a child needs your help to make friends
> - Help individual children develop friendship-making skills

Every young child needs to have at least one friend to talk to, play with, disagree with, make up with, and care for. Some children seem to know instinctively how to make friends and find their place in their group. Other children may take longer, but once they feel comfortable, they are able to join a group and make friends.

Children who feel rejected by others and don't know how to make friends need adult assistance. Such children often have low self-esteem, feel unloved, and lack the social skills they need to develop friendships. Because they aren't accepted by their peers, they have fewer chances to develop social skills. They cannot break the cycle of rejection. These children need to learn how to make friends so they can avoid serious problems in school and in later life.

Children who have trouble making friends may be shy or withdrawn, overly aggressive, or rejected by their peers for other reasons. You can make a big difference in a child's life by helping him or her break the cycle of rejection and learn how to relate positively to others.

Helping Children Who Are Very Shy Make Friends

Almost every group of children includes one or two who are very shy. Teachers may feel empathy for these children, but before offering assistance they need to observe to see if such a child is just moving at a slower pace than others. A shy child may need to play alone successfully first, or to sit back and observe other children at play to learn how to become part of the group. The child may begin by playing with one or two children. Then, after becoming more skilled, he or she will probably move on to playing with a group of children.

There are some children, however, who are so shy or withdrawn they need you to step in. It's best to be subtle. Saying "Be nice to Billy" or "Can you let Mary play too?" are not helpful. Remarks such as these tend to make the shy child feel self-conscious or embarrassed. The other children may go along with your suggestions for a time, but the shy child will not develop the social skills to cope when you aren't there to intervene directly.

Try the following suggestions for helping shy children develop social skills and make friends.[7]

Observe, observe, observe.

Watch what the child does and says, who the child talks to, and who the child watches. When the child is playing alone with Legos®, is he or she building with concentrated attention or also watching the firefighters in the house corner? Observe to find out what the child likes to do, where his or her favorite places are, whether the child behaves differently outdoors, and what skills the child has.

Establish a connection with the child.

Use your observations to help you talk with the child. "I see you are watching John and Pam playing at the water table." If the child responds positively, you can ask a question to extend the conversation. "Do you think John's cup will hold more water than Pam's? Perhaps you can play at the water table tomorrow and figure out the answer." You might also comment on what the child is doing. "I see you are lining up the shells by size." Such comments help the child feel more secure because he or she knows that the teacher is paying attention.

Notice when a child is particularly engaged in an activity and try to build on this interest.

"Jason, you seemed to really enjoy that story. What do you like to do on snowy days?"

Use what you know about the child's interests to create special situations.

For example, if you know that Holly really likes to cook, plan a cooking activity that involves several children working together. Include Holly when you conduct the activity and ask several open-ended questions to get her involved.

Help children find good friends.

Just as there might be several shy children in your room, there also might be several children who are socially competent and sensitive. Try asking one of these children and the shy child to help you do a task. "Drew, could you please help Tommy and me carry the toys outside?" Or let both children know about an activity that you think both would be interested in. "Drew and Tommy, I know you both like the woodworking bench. Ms. Johnson is getting the tools out now. I think there's room for two more carpenters."

Help the shy child understand his or her feelings of shyness.

"It's okay to want to play alone when you don't know the other children too well. After a while you'll feel more comfortable and be ready to play with Carlos, Portia, and the others."

---

[7]Adapted from Dennie Palmer Wolf, ed., *Connecting: Friendship in the Lives of Young Children and Their Teachers* (Redmond, WA: Exchange Press, Inc., 1986), pp. 58-62.

Helping Overly Aggressive Children Make Friends

In any group of preschool children there may be one or two who are not able to control their behaviors. They use aggression as a means to express their unhappiness or to get their own way. These children do not know how to take turns, negotiate, or cooperate with others. Because they are overly aggressive, other children do not want to include them in their play.

Although teachers also may have trouble relating to overly aggressive children, they must learn to overcome their negative feelings. It may help to remember that children who hit or bully other children are emotionally troubled or in pain. They feel unhappy or insecure, and they need help to learn positive ways of relating to other children. These children must feel safe and cared for before they can develop the social skills needed to make friends and play with other children.

Try these suggestions for helping aggressive children make friends.

Help the child understand the consequences of his or her actions.

"I think you want to play with Crystal and Susan. But when you knock their tower down it makes them angry. It doesn't make them want to play with you."

Try to redirect a child's angry energy.

"Shawn, I know you are very angry, but you may not hit Bonita. Use your hands to throw this ball at the wall. When you are ready, we can talk about what happened."

Identify a challenging physical activity the child really enjoys and set it up so several children can participate.

"Denise, you are a great jumper. Use this chalk to mark how far you and Lloyd can jump. You can take turns jumping."

Spend time alone with the child after he or she is no longer exhibiting aggressive behavior.

"David, let's sit in the big chair and read a story together. Ms. Johnson brought in some new books I think you might like."

Sit with the child and watch a group at play. Interpret the children's actions so the child can begin to understand how others use social skills.

"Carlos just came to the sandbox where Tamila and Renee are baking cakes. I think he wants to play with them. Carlos is making a cake to share. He's pretending to be a neighbor."

Help the child develop ways to achieve his or her goals without using aggression.

"I know you want to be the doctor, but Emily is being the doctor now. Let's find out if this is a hospital where there are lots of doctors."

Use the child's positive characteristics to help him or her be accepted by the group.

"Chaundra collected some beautiful leaves on our walk. Let's put them on the table where everyone can see them."

Helping Children Who Are Rejected for Other Reasons to Make Friends

There are children in every group who are neither aggressive nor shy yet still are excluded from play. These children, who may be loud, clumsy, or bossy, do not know how to get involved with their peers. They may play in the block area for a while, get up and move to the easel, try to join in with the house corner family, and then go back to the blocks. They appear to be unaware of the effects of their behavior. They seem to want to play with others, but because they are not able to understand what the other children are playing, they don't know how to get involved. You may hear a lot of complaints about these children. "She's always butting in." "He talks too loud." "He knocked our buildings over."

Often these children have some social skills but may not know how to use them. After observing carefully, think of ways to include such a child in a project with another child. Try these other suggestions to help children who are often rejected develop social skills and make friends:[8]

Teach the child how to ask questions to find out what other children are playing.	"What are you doing?" "Who are you pretending to be?" "What are you building?"
Suggest that the child watch and listen to find out what the other children are playing before trying to play with them.	"Delores, if you sit here and watch Bonita and Tim play, I'll bet you can guess what they're doing. Which one do you think is the firefighter?"
Encourage the child to discuss his or her feelings about being rejected.	"You look sad, Cynthia. Can you tell me what happened?" Describing what happened may help the child understand why she was rejected by the others.
Coach the child on how to follow the group's accepted social practices.	"Felipe, when it's time to go outdoors, try to get your coat on more quickly. Then the other children won't have to wait and we can all go outside and have fun."
Help the child state rules or the accepted behaviors of the group as a way to justify attempts to be included.	"I'd like to play, too. There are only three people in the sandbox and four children can play there."

Applying Your Knowledge

In this learning activity you will assist a child who needs help learning to make friends. Observe this child for five minutes at several different times of the day. Review your notes and summarize your thoughts about the child. Use this new information and the suggestions in this learning activity to plan ways to help the child play with others. Implement your plan over the next two weeks and record what happens. Begin by reading the example that follows.

[8] Adapted from Dwight L. Rogers and Dorene Doerre Ross, "Encouraging Positive Social Interaction Among Young Children," *Young Children* (Washington, DC: National Association for the Education of Young Children, March 1986), pp. 15-16.

Helping Individual Children Relate to Others

(Example)

Child: *Alex*   **Age:** *4 years, 3 months*   **Date:** *January 15-16*

Observation Notes	Summary
Time: *5:35 p.m.* *Alex is with a small group listening to Ms. Williams read a story. He sits at the edge of the group. The door opens. He turns to see who comes in. Kim gets up to greet her mother. Alex follows her when she gets her coat. The other children say goodbye to Kim. Alex walks back to the group. He says, "This is a dumb story."*	*Alex seems to want his dad to come. He is easily distracted. Perhaps he wants to go home. He doesn't notice that the other children want to hear the rest of the story.*
Time: *7:20 a.m.* *Alex comes in with his father. He smiles. His father says, "Say hello, Alex." Alex says hello in a loud voice. The other children turn to look at him. Ms. Williams asks Alex what he wants to do. "Blocks," he says. Kara and Donny are building a big tower. Alex builds beside them. Kara says, "Hey, we need all the blocks." Alex knocks down her building. He gets up and goes to the puzzle table.*	*If Alex knew how to join in with the block building group, he might have enjoyed himself.*
Time: *10:45 a.m.* *Alex is helping to serve snack. He carries a bowl of fruit to the table. He puts the bowl down, then stands behind the table. He is smiling. When all the children have their fruit, Alex takes his. He sits down next to Julia. She says, "I don't like bananas. Do you want mine?" Alex smiles and takes a piece of banana. He says, "I like bananas, but I don't like grapes." Julia says, "Can I have them?" Alex agrees and lets her reach over and take them.*	*Alex seems to like Julia. He lets her have his grapes. He seemed to feel good about helping, too.*

Plan:

I will tell Alex that I know it's hard to wait for his parents at the end of the day. I will ask him if there is something he would like to do instead of listening to the story. I will explain that the other children do want to hear the story.

When I see Alex watching other children, I'll point out how the children are working and playing together—for example, "Tony just gave Crystal that block because she needed one that size for her part of the road."

I'll encourage Alex and Julia to play together or help me do something. They both like to paint outside. I'll ask them to help carry the double easel outside one day next week.

Results (after two weeks):

Alex stays busy helping me clean up at the end of the day. He doesn't watch the door as often.

Alex joined a small group over at the water play table. He held the funnel while Tony poured.

Alex and Julia painted outside. She is very talkative so she kept the conversation going. Later in the week I saw them riding tricycles together.

Helping Individual Children Relate to Others

Child: _____ **Age:** _____ **Date:** _____

Observation Notes	Summary
Time:	
Time:	
Time:	

Make additional copies of this form if you need them.

Review your observation notes and summaries as well as the suggestions you have read. Develop a plan for helping this child. Implement your plan over the next week, then record the results.

Plan:

Results (after one week):

Discuss this activity with your trainer. If your strategies have not helped this child progress, you may need to talk with his or her parents to learn more about what might be causing the behavior. The child's behavior may be affected by a physical condition such as illness, allergies, physical or learning disabilities, lack of sleep, or poor nutrition.

Summarizing Your Progress

You have now completed all of the learning activities for this module. Whether you are an experienced teacher or new to the profession, this module probably has helped you develop new skills for promoting social development.

Before you go on, take a few minutes to summarize what you've learned.

- Turn back to Learning Activity I, Using Your Knowledge of Child Development to Promote Social Development, and add to the chart specific examples of what you learned about promoting social development while you were working on this module. Compare your ideas to those in the completed chart at the end of the module.

- Next, review your responses to the pre-training assessment for this module. Write a summary of what you learned and list the skills you developed or improved.

If there are topics you would like to know more about, you will find recommended readings listed in the Orientation in Volume I.

Your final step in this module is to complete the knowledge and competency assessments. Let your trainer know when you are ready to schedule the assessments. After you have successfully completed these assessments, you will be ready to start a new module. Congratulations on your progress so far, and good luck with your next module.

Answer Sheets

Overview
(pp. 103-105)

Helping Children Learn to Get Along with Other Members of the Group

1. **How did Ms. Frilles help the girls find a way to continue their play?**
    a. *She provided an indirect suggestion when she told them about a restaurant that had two waitresses.*

    b. *She stepped back to let them make their own decision about how to play.*

2. **How did Ms. Frilles help the girls feel good about solving their problem?**
    a. *She told them they used good thinking.*

    b. *She left them alone so they could continue playing.*

Helping Children Understand and Express Their Feelings and Respect Those of Others

1. **How did Ms. Kim let the children know that she understood and respected their feelings?**
    a. *She told them what she thought they might be feeling.*

    b. *She explained that she couldn't let them push each other.*

2. **How did Ms. Kim help the children to respect each other's feelings?**
    a. *She involved them in solving their own problem.*

    b. *She stepped back so the children could work things out for themselves.*

Providing an Environment and Experiences That Help Children Develop Social Skills

1. **How did Mr. Lopez use a daily routine—getting ready to go outside—as an opportunity to help the children develop social skills?**
    a. *He asked Jerry and Sukie to help Becky find her missing shoe.*

    b. *He said the bag of balls was heavy and asked for help to carry it.*

    c. *He said he likes it when children work together.*

2. **What social skills did the children learn as they prepared to go outside?**
    a. *They learned to work together and help each other.*

    b. *They learned to feel good about themselves because Mr. Lopez thinks all the children are important and he will wait until everyone is ready before going outside.*

Using Your Knowledge of Child
Development to Promote Social Development

(p. 113)

What Preschool Children Are Like	How Teachers Can Use This Information to Promote Social Development
They can help to make and follow a few simple rules and limits.	*Involve children in making the rules for the classroom. Play simple games such as* Lotto *or* Go Fish *to help children learn to follow rules in play situations. Offer positive reminders: "Walk indoors, please" to help children follow rules.*
They are learning to share, cooperate, and take turns.	*Provide duplicates of popular play materials. Model these social skills, yourself. Set up a system for taking turns, such as providing four hooks next to an interest area for hanging up name tags because there's only room for four children to use the area at once.*
They like to imitate adult activities.	*Provide a variety of dress-up clothes and props for dramatic play. Add new items to build on children's interest. Replace items children are no longer using. Encourage children to do as much as they can for themselves.*
They carry on conversations with other children, in pairs and also in groups.	*Observe and listen to children's conversations to learn about group dynamics—who initiates play, who negotiates, who solves problems, who thinks of new ideas, and so on.*
They may exclude other children from their play.	*Observe to see how often and in what situations a child is excluded by the others. Help the child become a part of the group by offering an interesting prop or material to share, suggesting a role, or explaining why the children might be excluding the child—"It scares the others when you knocked the Legos® on the floor."*
They are moving from parallel to cooperative play.	*Observe often to see the kind of play in which a child is involved. Provide duplicates of items such as telephones or firefighter hats that encourage two or more children to use together.*
They continue to need opportunities for solitary play.	*Provide a variety of materials children can use alone—beads and strings, puzzles, books, paints, tricycles, and so on. Observe often to see when a child plays alone by choice, and when he or she might want to join others, but doesn't know how.*

Using Your Knowledge of Child Development to Promote Social Development
(p. 114)

What Preschool Children Are Like	How Teachers Can Use This Information to Promote Social Development
They ask many questions.	*Use questions to engage children in a discussion but answer those that require a direct response. Include others in the discussion.*
They begin to develop friendships and may have a best friend.	*Follow a schedule that allows lots of time for children to choose their own playmates. Acknowledge children's friendships. "You and Paul had a good time riding tricycles together. I can tell you really like playing with each other." Tell parents who their children typically play with so they can support the friendship outside the center.*
They gain greater awareness of the larger community.	*Take the children on trips to the firehouse, parents' work sites, the pet store, the library, and so on. Prepare for trips by discussing what will happen and how children will be expected to behave. Invite parents and other visitors to come to the center to talk about what they do on the job or in the community.*
They engage in make-believe play alone and with others.	*Participate in play episodes by taking a role and helping children relate to others in the area. Suggest actions and offer props to promote play.*
They show pride in their own work, and they seek and value adult approval.	*Help children display their work. Take photographs to preserve block buildings and other creations that can't be saved. Give children lots of affection and encouragement. Let them know they are liked and that their accomplishments are noticed and valued.*
They have strong emotions and feelings and are learning to use words to name them.	*Encourage children to talk about their feelings. Help them understand how feelings and actions are connected and that they can have feelings without acting on them.*

Glossary

Cooperative play

The type of play that typically begins during the preschool years. Children play together in a group that they organize and control. The group has a specific purpose, such as making something, playing a game, or acting out a real-life or fantasy situation.

Parallel play

Play that happens when two- to three-year-old children progress from solitary play to playing alone with other children nearby. Children may use the same or similar kinds of toys or materials.

Peer

A friend or companion who is the same age or at the same developmental level.

Prosocial skills

Accepted behaviors, such as sharing or taking turns, which children learn and use to get along in society.

Social development

The gradual process through which children learn to enjoy being with other people and gain skills such as sharing, cooperating, and experiencing empathy.

Solitary play

The first stage of play, when infants and toddlers play alone, independent of other children. They use toys or materials that are the same as or different from those of other children in the group.

Module 10: *Guidance*

Overview

Guiding children's behavior involves:

- Providing an environment that encourages self-discipline
- Using positive methods to guide individual children
- Helping children understand and express their feelings in acceptable ways

---

Children need adult guidance to help them learn what is acceptable and what is not, and to help them learn how to live cooperatively with others. How you offer this guidance depends on your goals for the children you teach. What kind of people do you want these children to become? Do you want them to behave a certain way out of fear, or because they have learned what is acceptable and what is not?

Children need adult guidance to learn how to behave.

Self-discipline is the ability to control one's own behavior. People who are self-disciplined make independent choices based on what they believe is right. They are able to balance their own needs with those of others. They can accept the results of their actions.

Children are not born with self-discipline. As John Dewey, a famous American educator noted, adults need to provide positive guidance that teaches children to learn to make their own decisions, distinguish between right and wrong, solve problems, and correct their own mistakes. This module is about guiding children's behavior in ways that help them develop self-discipline.

Children misbehave for a variety of reasons. Joanne might be at a developmental stage where she needs to test the limits of her own control. Ross may be forced into a schedule that conflicts with his natural rhythm. Dana may be confused because the rules and expectations at home differ from those at the center. Michelle may have difficulty coping with transitions resulting from her parents' separation. Sometimes, children behave inappropriately simply because they are bored, tired, curious, or frustrated. To help children learn self-discipline, teachers need to think about the reasons for children's behavior.

There can be many reasons for children's misbehavior.

Because adults are powerful, they can force children to behave. But children who are forced to behave in certain ways, and are punished when they don't, learn the following lessons:

- I am a bad person.
- I need to watch out for adults.
- I had better not get caught.

These children are likely to behave only when someone is watching. Their goal is to avoid punishment. They do not learn to value acceptable behavior for itself, and they do not learn self-discipline.

Teachers can help children gain self-discipline in many ways. Some actions, such as setting up safe places for running, can prevent certain behaviors. Other actions, such as redirecting children to climb on the climber rather than the table, are responses to children's behavior.

Use the environment and appropriate strategies to help children learn self-discipline.

If you set up an environment that supports self-discipline, it will be easier for children to achieve this goal. If you set limits that fit children's development and individual needs, children will quickly learn the limits. If you are consistent in applying rules, children will try to follow them. And if you learn some techniques and words to use to guide children, you will help them develop self-discipline. Your caring relationships with the children in your room help them understand their feelings and those of others. Children depend on you and want your approval. They look to you to help them learn acceptable ways to express themselves.

Listed on the following pages are three sets of examples showing how teachers demonstrate their competence in providing positive guidance to children. Following each set of examples is a short reading and two questions to answer. When you have finished this section, compare your answers with those on the answer sheet at the end of the module. If your answers are different, discuss them with your trainer. There can be more than one good answer.

Providing an Environment That Encourages Self-Discipline

Make sure there are no safety hazards.	"Mr. Lopez, that was a good idea to replace the indoor climber. It was just too large for the children in this group."
Store toys and equipment on low, open shelves.	"Sammy, it's time to clean up. You know where the blocks go on the shelf."
Involve children in making up rules for the group.	"Everyone has been crowding around our new guinea pig and he's getting scared. Let's think about what rules we need for taking care of him."
Prepare children in advance for changes.	"In five minutes, it will be time to clean up and get ready for lunch. I'll set the timer so you'll know when the five minutes are over."
Arrange the materials and furniture to encourage appropriate behavior.	"When Jacey needs to spend some time alone, she sits in the reading nook."
Follow a schedule that allows children to initiate their own activities for most of the day.	"Good morning, Rion. What would you like to do during choice time today?"

"I'm glad it's Friday," sighs Ms. Kim. "This has been a frustrating week. It seems as if the children are constantly fighting over the toys. And getting them to help with clean-up is like pulling teeth." Ms. Richards nods her head in agreement. "I know what you mean," she says. "We need to make some changes." Ms. Kim responds, "I've noticed that some of the children have a hard time sharing, which leads to disagreements. Maybe if we had more duplicates, sharing would be less of a problem." Ms. Richards says, "That's a good idea. I think the children would help with clean-up more if we make picture labels and tape them to the shelves and containers. Then the children will know where the toys and materials are stored. That way clean-up time will be more fun." Ms. Kim agrees. "Let's try both ideas. Maybe we can address the behavior problems by changing the environment."

1. **What behaviors did Ms. Kim and Ms. Richards find frustrating?**

2. **How will changing the environment encourage children's self-discipline?**

Using Positive Methods to Guide Individual Children

Allow children to experience the consequences of their actions.

"Andrew, I'm very sorry you got wet at the water table. You can get a dry shirt from your cubby. What could you do differently next time so you'll stay dry?"

Redirect children to acceptable activities.

"Sukie's reading that book, Brandon. Pick another book to look at."

Help children who are screaming or thrashing regain self control.

"Dana, I'm holding you so you won't hurt yourself or anyone else. When you are calm and ready, I will let go and we can talk about what happened."

Use simple, positive reminders to restate rules.

"Please use the crayons on the paper, Jerry, not on the table."

Know when ignoring inappropriate behavior is constructive.

"Ms. Williams, I found one of the best ways to get children to stop using bathroom words is to just ignore them. If you don't react to the words, children soon stop using them."

Assume a firm, authoritarian role only when necessary to keep children safe.

"Stay on the sidewalk, Chaundra. A car is coming."

Ms. Williams and the children are outside in the play yard. Travis, a very active child, has collected some pine cones and is throwing them at other children. Ms. Williams walks over to him. She bends down, looks at him, and says, "Travis, you are learning to be a good thrower. But if you hit someone with a pine cone, they might be hurt or angry. Where can you practice your throwing safely?" Travis looks around and answers, "On the grass." Ms. Williams nods and says, "Yes, that's a good place. There aren't any children over there." Travis picks up his pine cones and walks over to the grass. Ms. Williams watches for a few minutes and then goes over to the sandbox to play with other children.

1. What did Ms. Williams know about Travis?

2. How did Ms. Williams let Travis know that she respected him?

Helping Children Understand and Express Their Feelings in Acceptable Ways

Make it easier to share or wait for a turn.	"I know it's hard to wait. Here's your name on the list. Your turn is next."
Redirect an angry or frustrated child to a soothing activity.	"Jane, I can't let you hurt other people or things. I think you might have fun at the water table."
Tell children you accept their feelings, even when their actions are not acceptable.	"Trish, I know you are angry with Elicia but I can't let you hit her. Tell Elicia you don't like it when she calls you names."
Help children understand the effects of their actions on the environment, materials, and people.	"Vanessa screamed because it hurt when you accidentally pulled her hair. If you want to play with hair you can use the baby doll."
Model acceptable ways to express feelings.	"Brett and Lien Chau, please use your inside voices. Your loud voices hurt my ears."
Work with parents to help a child with a challenging behavior learn acceptable ways to express feelings.	"Mr. Harper, Sheila had a great day today. Our strategies for reminding her to use words to express herself are working well."

"No!" screams Billy. His arm extended, he leans over ready to hit Sam, who has just grabbed a piece of orange from Billy's plate. "Billy," says Mr. Lopez, extending his hand between Billy's hand and Sam's arm. Billy looks up at Mr. Lopez. "That was good stopping," Mr. Lopez says. "I know you don't like it when someone takes your things. It's okay to have those feelings. You can talk to people when you are angry, but I can't let you hit them. Tell Sam not to take your orange." Billy looks at Sam and says, "I don't want you to take my orange." Sam puts the piece of orange down and goes back to eating his lunch.

1. **How do you think Billy felt when Sam grabbed his piece of orange?**

2. **How did Mr. Lopez help Billy learn to express his feelings in acceptable ways?**

Your Own Self-Discipline

Much of our behavior is automatic. We don't stop to think about what we should do; we just do it. When you put money in a parking meter, come to work on time, or thank a store clerk, you are probably acting without thinking about what you are doing. You have learned and accepted certain rules of behavior, and because you have self-discipline, you don't need to be reminded of them.

Self-discipline guides your behavior at work.

- You let the center director know when you're sick so a substitute can be called.

- You let a colleague know you are angry with her by telling her what you feel.

- You volunteer to help a colleague who's having difficulty meeting a child's needs.

List a few examples of how self-discipline guides your behavior at work:

Self-discipline also guides your behavior at home.

- You remember to water the plants because you know they'll die if you don't.

- You clean the frying pan so it will be ready to use in the morning.

- You resist eating a piece of cake because you are watching your weight.

List some examples of how self-discipline guides your behavior at home:

Think of a time when you did not use self-discipline. What affected your loss of control?

What does your own experience tell you about what children need if they are to gain self-discipline?

Being in control of your own behavior frequently results in enhanced self-esteem. Having positive feelings about your abilities will make you a more effective and skilled teacher. Your self-discipline is a good model for the children. They will learn a lot from being cared for by a responsible and competent person.

When you have finished this overview section, you should complete the pre-training assessment. Refer to the glossary at the end of this module if you need definitions for the terms that are used.

Pre-Training Assessment

Listed below are the skills that teachers use to provide guidance to children. Think about whether you do these things regularly, sometimes, or not enough. Place a check in one of the boxes on the right for each skill listed. Then discuss your answers with your trainer.

Providing an Environment That Encourages Self-Discipline

I Do This:	Regularly	Sometimes	Not Enough
1. Make sure there are no safety hazards.	☐	☐	☐
2. Store toys and equipment on low, open shelves.	☐	☐	☐
3. Involve children in making up rules for the group.	☐	☐	☐
4. Prepare children in advance for changes.	☐	☐	☐
5. Arrange the materials and furniture to encourage appropriate behavior.	☐	☐	☐
6. Follow a schedule that allows children to initiate their own activities for most of the day.	☐	☐	☐

Using Positive Methods to Guide Individual Children

	Regularly	Sometimes	Not Enough
7. Allow children to experience the consequences of their actions.	☐	☐	☐
8. Redirect children to acceptable activities.	☐	☐	☐

Using Positive Methods to Guide Individual Children
(continued)

	I Do This:	Regularly	Sometimes	Not Enough
9.	Help children who are screaming or thrashing regain self-control.	☐	☐	☐
10.	Use simple, positive reminders to restate rules.	☐	☐	☐
11.	Know when ignoring inappropriate behavior is constructive.	☐	☐	☐
12.	Assume a firm, authoritarian role only when necessary to keep children safe.	☐	☐	☐

Helping Children Understand and Express Feelings in Acceptable Ways

13.	Make it easier to share or wait for a turn.	☐	☐	☐
14.	Redirect an angry or frustrated child to a soothing activity.	☐	☐	☐
15.	Tell children you accept their feelings, even when their actions are not acceptable.	☐	☐	☐
16.	Help children understand the effects of their actions on the environment, materials, and people.	☐	☐	☐

Helping Children Understand
and Express Feelings in Acceptable Ways
(continued)

	I Do This:	Regularly	Sometimes	Not Enough
17. Model acceptable ways to express feelings.		☐	☐	☐
18. Work with parents to help a child with a challenging behavior learn acceptable ways to express feelings.		☐	☐	☐

Review your responses, then list three to five skills you would like to improve or topics you would like to learn more about. When you finish this module you will list examples of your new or improved knowledge and skills.

Begin the learning activities for Module 10, Guidance.

Learning Activities

I. *Using Your Knowledge of Child Development to Guide Behavior*

> **In this activity you will learn to:**
>
> • Recognize some typical behaviors of preschool children
>
> • Use what you know about child development to help children develop self-discipline

Helping children learn self-discipline begins with knowing what children can and can't do at each stage of development. Knowing which behaviors are typical at different ages allows you to have appropriate expectations and plan a program that reflects developmental characteristics. For example:

There are identifiable milestones in emotional development.

- Most preschoolers cannot sit still for more than 10 to 15 minutes. Teachers can plan group time activities that match this time frame.

- Some preschoolers have toileting accidents. Teachers can ask parents to provide extra clothes and respond in a casual way when accidents do occur.

- Many preschoolers are still learning to share and take turns. Teachers can provide duplicates of popular toys and set up simple systems to help children see when it will be their turn to use a toy or join an activity.

Dr. Stanley Greenspan has defined several early childhood milestones that are the foundation for healthy emotional development.[1] Children who master these milestones are more likely to learn self-discipline than those who do not. Greenspan's five milestones are described below.

The first milestone allows children to get involved in their play and activities. Most children begin learning this skill during the first few months of life. They enjoy being with their parents and caregivers; develop a regular schedule for sleeping; look at and listen to their environment; and in general, feel comfortable with life. Children who have accomplished this milestone can sit and listen to a story or the instructions for a new fingerplay. Children who have not reached this milestone are easily distracted and may have difficulty choosing what they want to do because the options are overwhelming.

"Security and the ability to look, listen, and be calm."

[1] Based with permission on Dr. Stanley Greenspan, *Playground Politics, Understanding the Emotional Life of Your School-Age Child* (Reading, MA: Addison-Wesley Publishing, 1993).

"Relating: the ability to feel warm and close to others."

The second milestone allows children to enjoy being with others. It is based on the trust that typically develops during infancy as a child interacts with and depends on parents and other caregivers. Most of children's early learning comes from their relationships with others. For example, infants begin to understand cause and effect when they learn their cries will bring someone to their side or that their smiles will get smiles in return. Children who feel close to others can play alone and easily join a group at play. Children who haven't developed warm, trusting relationships are likely to have difficulty making friends and becoming part of the group. They may use aggression to get what they want, or play and work alone because they fear rejection.

"Intentional two-way communication without words."

The third milestone allows children to understand and respond appropriately to nonverbal cues. Children build on the two previous milestones—paying attention and feeling close to others—as they learn to communicate with others. This milestone begins when infants learn that facial expressions and body language are signs of thoughts and feelings. An infant responds to a parent's frown by crying or wiggles with delight upon seeing a parent's open arms. Infants soon learn to use nonverbal communication to express their wants and needs—for example, a baby might point at a toy on the table so an older brother will get it for her.

Children who have mastered this milestone can observe nonverbal cues and accurately "read" other people's expectations, desires, and feelings. Children who have not mastered this milestone may misinterpret the actions of others and have trouble being accepted by the group. An example follows.

> Kate and Drew stand side-by-side talking and painting pictures. Drew becomes interested in what is happening in the house corner. He leaves the art area to join the group playing house. Kate doesn't understand why her friend left. She had not observed Drew's interest in the house corner area. She thinks he doesn't like her, and because she feels rejected, she calls after Drew, "You can't leave. You didn't clean up." The other children want Drew to join them so they take his side, "He already cleaned up." Kate has no idea what happened, but she now feels rejected by Drew and by the other children. Kate's teacher observes this episode and steps in to help Kate understand what happened. "You feel bad because Drew went to play with the other children. Drew is still your friend. He didn't want to paint any more. He watched the children in the house corner and decided to join them. Do you want to finish your painting or do something else?"

"Emotional ideas."

This milestone allows children to use words to express their feelings. Children with this ability can create mental pictures of what they want, need, or feel. When something happens that makes them feel angry they can give this feeling a name, rather than responding with tears, a tantrum, or pouting. A child who feels angry can say to himself, "I am angry." Preschoolers use this skill to explore feelings through dramatic play by imagining how a character might feel in a situation.

Children who cannot use words to express their feelings and ideas often have trouble controlling their actions. As a result, they tend to act without thinking because they don't know they can have a feeling without an action—be sad without crying, angry without hitting, or frustrated without tearing up a picture. Instead of using words to express their feelings, they respond by hitting another child, throwing a toy, or crying. Here is an example:

> Neil is watering the garden with a hose. When Quentin walks by, Neil aims the hose and says playfully, "I'm going to water you, too." When water drips on Quentin's sneakers, he grabs the hose, pushes Neil, and says, "You are stupid." Quentin had not noticed the playful tone in Neil's voice and he didn't know how to express his feelings—anger at having wet sneakers—so he pushed Neil and called him "stupid." Quentin's teacher can help him learn to recognize and understand nonverbal cues such as tone of voice and to use words instead of aggression to express his feelings.

The fifth milestone enables children to understand the consequences of their actions. Children learn to link different kinds of ideas and feelings to understand how one relates to another. For example, a preschool child might think, "I am disappointed because it's raining and now I can't play outside." An important part of emotional thinking is understanding that there are consequences to actions. Being able to consider consequences allows children to think what might happen as a result of their actions. This helps children learn to handle frustration, set aside immediate gratification for future rewards, and work hard at difficult tasks. Children who can't use emotional thinking may have difficulty understanding how their actions affect future events. Here is an example.

> Fran spent the whole morning on the computer. Each time Yancey asked for a turn she said, "No." After naptime, Yancey was using the computer. When Fran asked for a turn, he said, "No! It's my turn." Fran told Ms. Dodd, "Yancey won't let me have a turn on the computer." Yancey explained to Ms. Dodd that he had been waiting for a turn since the morning. Ms. Dodd took Fran aside and tried to explain why Yancey wouldn't let her have a turn. Fran responded, "It's not fair. I want my turn."

Greenspan's milestones are the foundation for developing self-discipline and positive behavior. Some of the children in your group will have reached these milestones, others will be working towards them. Your observations of children will help you determine what each child can do so help you can provide support and encouragement tailored to encourage each child's development of self-discipline.

"Emotional thinking."

Applying Your Knowledge

The chart on the next page identifies some typical behaviors of preschool children, ages 3 to 5. Included are behaviors relevant to developing self-discipline. The right column asks you to identify ways teachers can use this information to guide children's behavior. Try to think of as many examples as you can. As you work through the module you will learn new strategies and you can add them to the chart. You are not expected to think of all the examples at one time. If you need help getting started, turn to the completed chart at the end of this module. By the time you complete this module, you will find that you have learned many ways to guide children's behavior so they can develop self-discipline.

Using Your Knowledge of Child Development to Guide Behavior

What Preschool Children Are Like	How Teachers Can Use This Information to Guide Children's Behavior
They seek adult approval and attention.	*Notice and comment on children's positive behaviors and accomplishments, such as participating in clean-up, helping a friend, or finishing a difficult puzzle. Try to spend some one-on-one time with each child every day.*
They try new things and take risks.	
They can take turns and share, but they don't always want to.	
They sometimes lose control; they may scream or strike out in anger at children or adults.	
They are gaining new physical skills and have a lot of energy.	
They may swear or use bathroom words to get attention or without knowing what the words mean.	

Using Your Knowledge of Child Development to Guide Behavior

What Preschool Children Are Like	How Teachers Can Use This Information to Guide Children's Behavior
They want to do things for themselves, but may get upset if things don't go as expected.	
They can follow a few simple rules.	
They like to feel powerful and important, and they can be bossy.	
They are learning to use words to express their feelings and to solve problems.	
They are most comfortable when the daily schedule is consistent and predictable.	
They are learning to recognize how their actions affect the environment, materials, and other people.	

When you have completed as much as you can do on the chart, discuss your answers with your trainer. As you proceed with the rest of the learning activities, you can refer back to the chart and add examples of ways that teachers can guide children's behavior.

II. Creating an Environment That Supports Self-Discipline

In this activity you will learn to:

- Observe children's behavior to identify possible problems in the environment
- Create an environment that encourages children to develop self-discipline

---

There are times when no matter how hard you try, everything seems to go wrong. The children seem restless. They run around the classroom, fight over toys, and wander about unable to choose things to do. Most of the children seem easily distracted and have trouble sticking with tasks. They use materials roughly and are uncooperative at clean-up time.

The physical environment can be a cause of behavior problems.

There are many possible reasons for these behaviors. Most preschool children act in these ways sometimes, but, if you see many of these behaviors day after day, it's a good idea to check your environment by asking questions such as these:

- Does the furniture arrangement create open spaces that encourage children to run?

- Are the materials too simple or too difficult for the children's current skill levels?

- Do I limit or cancel outdoor play when it's cold or wet outside?

- Do I prohibit physical activities indoors?

- Do children spend most of the day doing adult-led activities?

If you answer "yes" to most of these questions, your environment may be negatively affecting children's behavior.

The chart on the following page provides examples of children's behavior, possible problems in the environment, and suggested solutions.

Behavior	Possible Problems	Suggested Solutions
Children can't find their belongings—hats, mittens, items from home. (They spend time trying to locate belongings or tell teachers they can't find them.)	Children don't have individual cubbies. Cubbies aren't labeled with children's names, photographs, or symbols.	Provide individual, labeled cubbies within children's reach. Help children make a rule about only taking things from their own cubby.
Children run indoors.	There is no limit to the number of children who can use each area. There are limits, but they allow too many children to use the area at one time. The room is not divided into various interest areas—too much open space. There are no indoor physical activities. Children need to have more time for outdoor play.	Establish a system to limit the number of children who can use each area at a time. Eliminate large, open spaces by creating interest areas. Provide equipment for indoor physical activities—climber, tumbling mats, hula hoops—or use the halls or an empty classroom for active play. Go outdoors daily unless the weather is very cold or wet.
Children fight over toys and materials. (They try to grab toys away from others, or push or shove other children away from toys they are playing with.)	There is only one of each toy and there aren't enough of materials such as crayons, scissors, musical instruments. There aren't enough toys and materials that match children's current skills and interests.	Provide duplicates of popular items so children don't have to wait too long to use them. Order sufficient art materials for the size of the group. Set up a system for waiting—provide timers, install hooks for hanging up name tags, or have a waiting list.
Children lose control and hurt others. (They shove others or throw objects at children or adults.)	There are no private areas where children can go to regain control of their emotions and actions.	Create private areas—a large box, a pile of pillows in the corner, a small table with room for one child, a sheet draped over three sides of a table.
Children refuse to participate in activities. (They respond negatively to an invitation to participate or walk away from an activity.)	Most of the day is spent in adult-led activities. The activities do not reflect children's interests.	Follow a schedule that allows ample time for children to select activities. Observe children and plan activities that respond to their interests.

The environment can promote positive behavior.

An appropriate environment for preschoolers can support their development of self-discipline in a number of ways. Children feel independent when they can select and replace materials that are stored on low, open shelves. Children learn to care for their own belongings when each has a cubby in which to keep personal items. Children feel valued when their interests, ethnicity, and culture are reflected in the toys, books, materials, and displays. Children gain a sense of competence when the materials offer challenges without being overwhelming. In such an environment, children feel respected and become involved in purposeful activities.

Applying Your Knowledge

In this activity you will review some common behavior problems and note how the environment can be the cause—or the solution. Then you will describe problem behaviors that occur in your group and plan ways to change your environment so it addresses these behaviors and promotes self-discipline.

Arranging the Environment to Promote Self-Discipline

Behavior	Possible Problems	Suggested Solutions
Children wander around and have difficulty choosing something to do.		
Children are easily distracted and have trouble staying with and completing tasks.		
Children use materials roughly and resist clean-up.		
Children frequently ask teachers for assistance in getting out materials.		
Children run around outside without using toys or equipment or participating in activities.		

Check your answers with answer sheet at the end of the module. There can be more than one right answer.

Now, think about a typical day with the children in your group. Use the following chart to describe the problem behaviors that tend to occur again and again. For each behavior, identify possible problems in the environment, then suggest one or more solutions and try them out.

Behavior	Possible Problems	Suggested Solutions

Discuss your ideas with your trainer and colleagues before trying them out. If the problem behaviors continue after you make changes to the environment, be sure to consider other causes for the behaviors of individual children and for the group.

III. Guiding Children's Behavior

In this activity you will learn to:

- Use positive approaches to guide children's behavior
- Tailor positive guidance to match each child's skills and needs

---

Often the words *discipline* and *punishment* are used to mean the same thing, but they are actually very different. Punishment means controlling children's behavior through fear. Punishment makes children behave because they are afraid of what might happen to them if they don't. Punishment may stop children's negative behavior temporarily, but it doesn't help children develop self-discipline. Instead, it may reinforce their bad feelings about themselves.

Discipline and punishment are very different.

Discipline means guiding and directing children toward acceptable behavior. The most important goal of discipline is to help children learn how to control their own behavior. Children are not born with self-control. It is learned through daily interactions with other children and adults. It takes a long time to learn self-discipline, but it is time well spent. Children who are self-disciplined tend to be more successful in school and in life. They can set goals and take the steps needed to accomplish them. They find it easier to get along with their peers and with adults.

Many preschoolers do not understand their feelings or how to express them. Even children with strong verbal skills might not understand feelings and can find it hard to express them with words. When children destroy materials, don't follow the rules, or hurt others, it is important to think about what their behavior means. What is the child trying to express? What are the reasons behind the behavior? Children's behaviors may be "telling" you many different things.

Children express feelings through behavior.

"I feel lonely because my friend is playing with someone else. That's why I can't find anything to do."

"I am angry because this morning I spilled juice on my favorite shirt and I had to wear something else. That's why I lost my temper and hit Shawn."

"I am afraid. That's why I won't let go of your hand."

"I want to be good at something. That's why I keep ripping up my pictures."

"I need some limits. That's why I'm running around the room."

"I can't do what you asked me to do. That's why I threw my sneaker at the wall."

Accept children's negative feelings.

It's important for teachers to recognize and accept children's negative feelings. We all have days when we feel bad or don't want to do certain tasks. Through observation, you can learn to recognize the signs that a child is feeling upset. Then you can respond by suggesting ways to express feelings without hurting oneself, other people, or the toys and materials. For example, when you see children who seem frustrated, redirect them to soothing activities that might help them feel better. Many children are comforted by pounding playdough, playing with sand or rice in a basin, or listening to music. There are no right or wrong ways to do activities such as these. Children can enjoy them without worrying about being successful. When children feel very angry, tossing beanbags or hammering may allow them to release their strong feelings.

Teachers can use a variety of approaches to guide children's behavior. No single approach works for every child or every situation. Effective discipline makes use of positive guidance techniques that are:

- based on realistic expectations for children's behavior and reflect an understanding of child development and each child's unique characteristics.

- individualized to match the situation and the child's skills and needs.

On the following page you will find suggestions of positive guidance approaches that might work for the children in your care.

Positive Guidance Approach	Examples
Reinforce children's positive behaviors during private moments.	"Peter, it was nice of you to give André the helicopter to play with."
Help children solve their own problems.	"I can see it is hard for you to share your bear, Carlos. Where can you put it until you go home?"
Anticipate problem behaviors and plan ways to avoid them.	"Let's talk about what will happen on our trip tomorrow. First, how are we going to get to the fire house?"
Discuss the possible reasons for a child's behavior with a colleague or your supervisor.	"Bonita's mother is going out of town next week. Maybe Bonita is afraid she won't come back."
See your environment and hear yourself through a child's eyes and ears.	"Was my voice too loud just then? I'll move closer and speak more softly to Joey."
Respond to the child's behavior, without labeling the child.	"I like the way you cleared your dishes." (Rather than, "You're a good girl for clearing your dishes.")
Help children understand the consequences of their actions, and, if appropriate, help them make amends.	"Felipe and Kim, the doll broke when you were both pulling its arms. Put it in the fix-it box. You can play with it again after it has been repaired."
Tell children what they can do, rather than what they cannot do.	"If you want to use the truck, you can roll it on the carpet. If you want to play in the house corner, you will have to put the truck away."
Be polite to children at all times.	"Could you please help me by holding my bag for a minute? Thank you."
Help children get over minor mistakes and accidents—their own or other children's.	"Whoops! Did your paint cup tip over? Did your silly elbow do it? Let's find a sponge to clean up the spill!"
Encourage children to move their bodies when they seem restless.	"Susan, you seem fidgety. Would you like to use the tumbling mats or join Tammy on the climber?"
Individualize rules and limits when needed to meet a child's needs.	"Eyonna, I see you need a few more minutes to finish your picture. We'll start cleaning up and you can join us when you're done."
Gain control of your own angry feelings before disciplining a child. Ask a colleague for help if needed.	"Mr. Lopez, could you please help Wendy pick up the Legos® she threw on the floor? I need to calm down before I talk to her about her behavior."

The chart that follows shows some typical behaviors of preschool children and some positive guidance approaches teachers can use to encourage self-discipline.

Typical Behavior	Positive Guidance Approach
Dana and Lorrie fight over a funnel at the water table. Lorrie is using the funnel.	Help the children find a way to take turns. Provide a prop for Dana to use while waiting for a turn. Write yourself a note to buy or make another funnel.
Mia writes on the table.	Calmly remind Mia of the classroom rule: "Draw and write on paper, not on furniture." Have her make amends by getting a wet sponge to clean the table.
Carla is very restless during group time.	One teacher can sit near Carla to help her focus on the activity. If Carla needs to get up, one of the teachers can help her select a quiet activity such as drawing a picture or reading a book.
The whole group is restless at group time.	Shorten the group activity and move on to choice time.
Jay and Raffi bump into each other by accident.	Make sure nobody is hurt. Encourage the children to laugh about the collision: "You guys made such a loud noise, I thought the building was falling down."
Janna, who used to forget, hangs up her coat three days in a row.	Use genuine praise to reinforce the behavior: "You remembered to hang up your coat three days in a row. You're doing a good job taking care of your belongings."

Applying Your Knowledge

In this learning activity, you will keep track of how you guide the behavior of an individual child over a three-day period. Take notes on the child's behavior, the possible reason for the behavior, and the positive guidance you use in response. After reading your notes, think about what you learned from the experience that you can use to promote self-discipline. Begin by reviewing the example that follows.

Guiding Children's Behavior
(Example)

Child: *Shawn*

Age: *4 years 3 months*

Setting: *Table Toys Area*

Date: *February 6*

Time: *10:45 a.m.*

Child's Behavior	Possible Reason for the Behavior	Positive Guidance Used in Response
Shawn was doing a puzzle. He couldn't get the pieces to fit. He knocked the puzzle pieces on the floor and left the area.	*Shawn was frustrated possibly because the puzzle was too hard for him. He might have been hungry because snack was late today. In the past, being hungry has affected his behavior.*	*I found Shawn in the book area and said, "Would you like some help picking up the puzzle pieces?" He came back to the table toys area. While picking up the puzzle we talked about how to take care of materials. I asked him if he was hungry. He said, "Yeah. My tummy is grumbling." I said, "Snack is late today. Would you like a graham cracker to take the grumbles away?" He nodded.*

What did you learn that you can use to promote self-discipline?

We should have some food available so children who are hungry don't have to wait.

Shawn needs help selecting puzzles that are neither too easy nor too difficult so he can experience success.

Shawn quickly recovered from his loss of control and was willing to make amends.

Guiding Children's Behavior

Child: _____ **Age:** _____

Day One

Setting: _____ **Date:** _____ **Time:** _____

Child's Behavior	Possible Reason for the Behavior	Positive Guidance Used in Response

Day Two

Setting: _____ **Date:** _____ **Time:** _____

Child's Behavior	Possible Reason for the Behavior	Positive Guidance Used in Response

Day Three

Setting: _____ Date: _____ Time: _____

Child's Behavior	Possible Reason for the Behavior	Positive Guidance Used in Response

How can you use what you learned about this child to promote self-discipline?

Discuss your observations and responses to this child with your trainer.

IV. Using Words to Provide Positive Guidance

> **In this activity you will learn to:**
>
> - Use words to guide children's behavior
> - Use words to remind children of rules and limits

Your words and tone of voice are powerful guidance tools.

Children listen to and understand what you say to them. Your words and tone of voice can be powerful positive guidance tools. Angry, insensitive words can make children feel sad, ashamed, or angry. Using words in a positive way, however, can promote children's self-discipline. Your caring words help children understand their own feelings and those of others.

Adults often use a loud "discipline voice" when talking to children. When adults shout, children sometimes get so startled that they don't really hear the words. It is better to talk to children in a natural though firm tone of voice. When children hear a quiet, firm tone, they are more likely to feel safe and cared for. When conversing with a child, try to get close enough to speak at a normal level. If you are having a private discussion, crouch or kneel at the child's level. Look into the child's eyes and gently touch an arm or shoulder. Give the child your full attention, and make sure you have the child's attention. (Note: In some families and cultures, children are taught that it is disrespectful to look an adult in the eye. Be sensitive to cultural differences.)

If you're not sure how your voice sounds when you're talking to children, try videotaping or audiotaping a part of the day. Play the tape and ask yourself, "Would I like to listen to this person all day?"

Choose your words carefully so children can focus on the real issues.

The words you use are very important. Sometimes, an adult who is angry with a child lets out an emotional flood of words. This may make the adult feel better, but the child probably does not hear the message. To help the child understand your message, use simple, clear statements, spoken once:

Describe what happened:

"Theresa, you tore Joey's pictures two times this morning."

Tell the child what behavior is not acceptable:

"I can't let you tear other children's work."

Tell the child what behavior is acceptable:

"Leave Joey's paper alone. It's his work."

Suggest a consequence and, if appropriate, a way to make amends:

"Joey feels bad because you tore his picture. Let's get some tape and fix it. Then you can tear some magazines for a collage, or you can read a story with me."

In this example, the child was offered two choices, both of which were acceptable to the teacher. Be careful to offer choices only when you mean them. When you ask a child "would you like to clean up now?" it sounds as if the child has a choice. The child could easily say "no." Probably you really mean, "it's time to pick up now."

Teachers can use words to give directions in a positive way. Instead of saying "no running" or "don't leave your coat on the floor," you can say "walk" or "hang your coat on the hook." Children respond well to positive directions because they tell them what to do, rather than what not to do.

Your words can show respect for children's feelings and help them feel good about themselves. Avoid comparing one child to another. Instead of saying "Susan is nice and quiet at story time—can you be quiet like Susan?" you could say, "Please be quiet now so we can begin the story." Avoid using phrases such as "four-year-olds don't suck their thumbs." They make children feel bad, and they do not change behaviors.

The chart on the following page provides some examples of words teachers can use to provide positive guidance.

Teachers should be positive and respectful in guiding children's behavior.

Situation	What a Teacher Might Say
Both Emilio and Tim want to sit next to Ms. Kim as she reads aloud to them in the book corner.	"There's enough space for each of you to sit right next to me. Emilio, you can sit on the right. Tim, you can sit on the left. Then we can share this big pillow and the book."
Maddie and Vanessa each want to use all of the cylinder blocks.	"There are many shapes of blocks for you to use on the shelves. There are only six cylinder-shaped blocks. Can you figure out a way to divide the cylinder blocks so you can each use some of them?"
Dean wants to play in the house corner with two children who don't want him to join them.	"Dean, it feels bad when your friends say they don't want to play with you. It's hard to understand why they want to just play with each other. Can I help you find something else to do? There's room at the work bench, or you could invite some friends to join you in starting a new game."
Lloyd and Chaundra each want to play in the same area but they think there isn't enough room.	"There is room for both of you to play with your trucks. You can share the space. I'll get some masking tape while you two decide how you want to divide the space."

Using words to guide children's behavior takes some practice. It may take some time before you feel comfortable talking to preschool children in new ways. You will be rewarded when the children you care for let you know how much better they feel because of your understanding and caring.

Applying Your Knowledge

In this learning activity you will practice using words to guide children's behavior and help them learn self-discipline. First read the examples that follow. Then write down words that you can use in typical classroom situations.

Words You Use to Provide Positive Guidance

(Example)

When a child pushes another child:

"Jorgé, you want to use the doll carriage but you may not push Debby out of the way. She was already wheeling the carriage. Ask Debby if you can have a turn. If she says yes, you can use the carriage. If she says no, you must wait for your turn."

When a child takes playdough from another child:

"You may have some of your own playdough. You may not take Tamila's playdough from her. Ask Tamila to share her playdough, or ask me for some."

When a child paints on another child's picture:

"You may paint a picture of your own. I can't let you paint on Lamont's paper. You can have your own piece of paper, and Lamont can have another piece too. Or, you can ask Lamont if he wants to paint a picture with you."

When a child is having a hard time waiting for a turn:

"Marguerite, you've waited a long time for the trike. You're getting tired of waiting so you called Ana stupid. You may not call her stupid. She is not stupid and neither are you. You can tell Ana that you have waited a long time and want your turn now."

When a child screams because there aren't enough of one kind of toy:

It's okay to want to have your own shovel like the other children. But screaming doesn't help you get a shovel. You need to use your words. Ask if anyone is finished using their shovel. Or, I can help you find something else to dig with."

When a child is upset because a friend won't play:

"You want to play with Kenny, so you feel sad when he says no. He feels like playing alone now. You can play by yourself on the jungle gym, or ask someone else to play with you."

Words You Use to Provide Positive Guidance

When a child calls another child "stupid":

When a child refuses to clean up:

When a child watches other children playing but doesn't know how to join in:

When a child talks very loudly:

When a child is upset because it's too rainy to go outside:

When (add your own example here):

Now share your words with your trainer. To help you get to used to using these words, you could write them on a piece of poster board and hang it in your room.

V. *Setting Rules and Limits*

In this activity you will learn to:

- Set clear, simple rules and limits
- Remind children of rules by using positive statements that tell children what to do
- Apply rules consistently, while also considering individual needs

---

Rules and limits help both children and teachers agree on what behaviors are acceptable. Young children need simple rules that are stated clearly and positively. For example, "Walk when you're indoors so you don't hurt yourself," rather than "Don't run indoors," tells children what they can do and why. Children feel safer when they know that adults have set limits. These feelings of security tend to make children feel freer to explore and experiment.

It's important to have just enough rules to keep your classroom functioning smoothly. If there are too few rules, the children might be unsafe and the environment disorderly. When there are too many rules, however, children can't remember what to do and might feel inadequate. Children feel a sense of mastery when they can remember and follow a few, simple, important rules.

Children respect rules when they understand the reasons behind them. They are more likely to follow rules if they help create them. Talk to children about the consequences of actions. "What might happen if we squirt water on the floor?" Children can answer the question and suggest a needed rule: "When the water spills, the floor gets slippery. Someone might fall and get hurt. Keep the water in the water table." (See Learning Activity V, Helping Children Learn to Keep Themselves Safe, in Module 1, Safe, for an example of children creating safety rules.)

Some rules and limits are set by the way the room is arranged. You can label the interest areas to show how many children can play there at a time. (How the environment affects children's behavior is discussed in Learning Activity II, Creating an Environment That Supports Self-Discipline.)

All adults in the room need to apply the rules and limits consistently so the children will learn what they are expected to do. "Ms. Williams, we should remind the children not to run near the water table—Kim slipped today." However, in some situations it is appropriate to "bend" the rules to meet a child's needs. Consider the following example:

Rhonda joined the class a few weeks ago. Her parents recently separated and this is Rhonda's first time attending child care. She has had a difficult time adjusting to the changes in her life and shows little interest in classroom

Children need a few simple rules.

Children can help create rules.

Sometimes it is appropriate to individualize the rules.

activities. Recently, Rhonda discovered painting. Painting seems to allow Rhonda to express her feelings and to release tension. One of the classroom rules states that if someone is waiting for a turn at the easel, children should limit their paintings to no more than two at a time. Because painting is helping Rhonda meet her needs, the teachers decide to bend the rules so Rhonda can paint for as long as she needs to. One teacher tells Rhonda, "I think you like to paint. It helps you feel more comfortable here. When you feel ready, you can try some of our other activities. For now, you can paint as many pictures as you like." The teachers also explain the situation to the other children, "Rhonda is still getting used to our classroom. Until she feels ready to try other activities, we will let her paint as many pictures as she likes."

Positive reminders help children learn what to do.

Many times during the day teachers need to remind children of the rules and limits. Children are more likely to internalize the rules when the reminders are positive and delivered in a brief, firm manner. Some examples of negative and positive reminders follow.

To Respond to This Behavior	Say or Do This
Several children are talking too loudly.	"Use quiet voices inside; you can talk loudly outside."
A child hits another child.	"I can't let you hurt other children. Tell me what happened. Maybe I can help you solve the problem."
A child throws a shovel.	"Use the shovel to dig with; if you want to throw something, you can throw the ball."
A child is climbing on the table.	"Keep your feet on the floor. Climb only on the climber."
A child pushes another child on the slide.	"Keep your hands off other children. It's dangerous to push someone on the slide."
A child stands up and gets in the way of the others at story time.	"Please sit down on the rug. I'll hold the book up high so everyone can see."
A child swears at another child.	"Please don't use those words here. I don't want to hear them, and I don't want the other children to learn them."
A child absent-mindedly drips paint on the floor.	"Wipe your brush on the jar, so the paint won't drip."

Rules should reflect what children are like at each stage of development. As children grow and mature, they can handle more freedom, activities, and responsibilities. Teachers need to be careful observers to see when individual children or the whole group can handle greater freedom. There is a fine line between keeping children safe and keeping them from growth and independence. The limits set for four-year-olds in September may need to be adjusted in a few months' time.

As children develop new skills, review and revise the rules.

Applying Your Knowledge

In this activity you will use positive phrases to list the rules you have in your room. Then you will answer some questions about one of the rules. First read the example, then complete the blank forms that follow.

Rules for the Preschool Room

(Example)

Staying healthy and safe:

Serve yourself as much food as you think you can eat.

Stay in the playground during outdoor play.

Respecting the rights of others:

Stay out of other people's cubbies.

When you want to be alone, you can sit on the pillows.

Not hurting yourself or others:

Blocks are for building, not for throwing.

Go down the slide one at a time.

Caring for our equipment and materials:

Everyone helps at clean-up time.

Turn the pages in books carefully so they don't tear.

Select a rule from your list and answer the questions below.

Rule: *Everyone helps at clean-up time*

Why do you have this rule?

Our room is set up so that children can get toys themselves and put them back when they are finished. They can be independent and learn self-discipline.

How do you fit this rule to each child's development, strengths, and needs?

Most of the children can clean up by themselves. For the children who need help, we break down the tasks into smaller ones—first, hang up the clothes, then put the pots and pans on the shelf.

How do you make sure that all adults apply the rule in the same way?

We both work with the children at clean-up time. If there are problems with consistency, we discuss them at nap time.

How do you follow through and support your words with actions?

If a child doesn't respond, I walk over to the child. Then I kneel or crouch and repeat the reminder: "Peter, it's pick-up time." If reminders don't work, I might lift a child off the climber, take a brush out of a hand, help put the puzzle pieces back, and so on.

Give an example of a simple clear statement that states the rule positively.

"It's clean-up time. After we put the toys away we can go outside."

What might you say to respect and acknowledge a child's feelings?

"Juana, I know it's hard to stop playing when you're having fun. You can play some more after nap time."

How do you act with authority and show confidence?

I always give children a ten-minute warning, then a five-minute warning. I never apologize when I announce that it's clean-up time. When a child is slow to stop playing, I walk over and restate that it is clean-up time. I don't ask the child to clean up. I just say, "It's clean-up time."

Rules for the Preschool Room

Staying healthy and safe:

Respecting the rights of others:

Not hurting yourself or others:

Caring for our equipment and materials:

Discuss these rules with a colleague who also works in your room.

Select a rule from your list. Answer the questions that follow.

Rule: _____

Why do you have this rule?

How do you fit this rule to each child's development, strengths, and needs?

How do you make sure that all adults apply the rule in the same way?

How do you follow through and support your words with actions?

Give an example of a clear, simple statement that states the rule positively.

What might you say to respect and acknowledge a child's feelings?

How do you act with authority and show confidence?

Discuss this activity with your trainer.

VI. *Responding to Challenging Behaviors*

> **In this activity you will learn to:**
>
> • Look for the reasons behind a child's challenging behavior
> • Work with parents to develop a plan for responding to challenging behavior

Some annoying behaviors are signs of normal development.

Some children's behaviors that drive teachers and parents crazy are actually signs of normal development. These behaviors give way to new ones when children move to the next stage of development. For example:[2]

Gerry (3 years) spills his milk at lunch almost every day. He wants to do things for himself and doesn't notice when he elbows his cup.

Kim (3 1/2 years) shouts, "I'm coming to get you monsters!" and chases the other children around the playground. This beginning stage of dramatic play helps her feel powerful and in control of her fears.

Chuck (4 years) is very interested in watching Sarah (4-1/2 years) get undressed. He is very curious about the differences between boys and girls.

Trevor (4-1/2 years) always wants to win and be the "biggest" and the "best." He is developing a sense of self and needs activities that don't involve winners and losers.

Katherine (5 years) bosses the younger children around. "No, not like that. Do it this way." She feels good about her growing skills and has a sense of competence.

There are many possible reasons for challenging behaviors.

Challenging behaviors, such as biting or having temper tantrums, are likely to occur again and again. Often these behaviors are an indication that something in the child's life is disturbing. The child doesn't know how to express his or her feelings with words, so he or she acts out. It is important to remember that, in most cases, there is a reason for a child's behavior. Some reasons children use challenging behaviors are described below:[3]

---

[2] Based on California Child Care Resource and Referral Network, *Making a Difference* (San Francisco, CA: California Child Care Resource and Referral Network, 1986), pp. 14-15.

[3] Based on Project ETC, Greater Minneapolis Day Care Association and Portage Project, *Special Training for Special Needs: Module 5, Program Implementation* (Minneapolis: Portage Project, 1989).

Children are affected by a physical condition. Health problems and conditions such as illness, allergies, disabilities, lack of sleep, poor nutrition, or hunger can contribute to children's misbehavior. Learning disabilities and conditions such as attention deficit disorder (ADD) can cause a child to have difficulty following rules or getting along with others. When a child frequently or consistently has difficulty behaving appropriately, consider the possibility of physical causes. You and your colleagues can discuss examples of the child's behavior with the parents and request that the child be evaluated by a physician.

Children don't know what they are supposed to do. Sometimes teachers give children brief instructions delivered in an authoritative voice. "Pick up." "Get ready." "Use the brush properly." They assume that children already know how to respond to these requests. However, some children don't understand vague words such as "properly" and aren't likely to ask what the strange word means. Other children need a teacher to show them what to do and how to do it. For example, a teacher could show a child how to hold a brush so the paint doesn't drip onto his or her hand.

Children need more attention than they are getting. Children need to feel important and valued. When children don't receive enough positive attention, they may act out to get negative attention. Their need for attention is so great they "misbehave" because it will get adults to notice them and spend time with them. Unfortunately, once children are successful in getting attention by misbehaving, they are likely to continue the unacceptable behavior until the cycle is broken.

Children feel bored or confined. Most children need new materials and activities that respond to their growing skills and changing interests. Even in the most interesting and varied environment, some children will be bored because they can't find something to do. It helps to make an extra effort to consider these children's unique characteristics when planning activities and selecting new materials.

Children are seeking more control of the situation. Some children have very few opportunities to make decisions or to have control over their lives. Perhaps between home and the center there are too many rules and too few opportunities to make choices. When children can choose what to do, which materials to use, and who to play with, they feel a sense of control over their lives and they begin to develop self-discipline.

Children feel frustrated or discouraged. Children feel a sense of accomplishment and success when they use materials and engage in activities that are interesting and challenging, but do not require skills that they have not yet mastered. When a child misbehaves often, perhaps the classroom materials and activities do not match his or her developmental skills. For example, a child may not have the fine motor skills needed to thread beads on a string. The teacher can encourage such a child to use toys with large pieces that are easier to hold and manipulate.

Teachers and parents need to work together to respond to challenging behaviors.

When a child repeatedly exhibits a challenging behavior over a long period of time, all the adults who care for the child need to discuss the possible causes of the problem. Perhaps a situation at home is causing the child to be upset or frustrated. Perhaps the environment at the center is causing the child's behavior—the schedule, activities, or room arrangement may not meet his or her needs. You can reassure the child's parents that there are times when some preschool children behave this way, but the behavior cannot be allowed at the center. Together, you can then agree on a plan for consistent responses to the behavior. It is very important to let the child know that he or she is still loved and cared for, even if he or she has a problem behavior. Several of the more common challenging behaviors are discussed below.

Physical aggression—hitting, scratching, kicking—must be responded to immediately. Get down to the child's level and clearly state the rule forbidding this behavior: "Alexa, I cannot let you hurt people. Use your words to say what you want." Involve the child in comforting the child who was hurt (if the hurt child permits this) so she can understand the connection between her actions and the other child's pain. "Alexa, please get the ice pack from the freezer so Neil can put it on his shin." Then help both children find something else to do. "Alexa, if you still feel upset you can do some hammering or tear paper." "Neil, are you ready to find something to do?"

When a child uses physical aggression and is out of control, you may need to hold her until she calms down. Ask a colleague to respond to the hurt child. Children feel scared when they lose control, and your firm arms can help a child feel safe because you have taken charge of the situation. It may take a few minutes, but the child will quiet down. Then you can discuss what happened: "Do you want to talk about what made you feel so angry? I could see that you were upset." Reassure the child that you want to listen to her feelings. It is best to let the child recover before discussing alternative ways to handle anger and frustration. You can do this during a quiet, one-to-one moment later in the day, or even the following day: "Yesterday, when you felt upset, you hit Neil. Next time you feel upset, what could you do instead?" This discussion can be a rehearsal so that the next time the child begins to lose control, she will have an alternative to lashing out at someone else. "That sounds like a good plan. You could do some hammering to help you feel better." Later, when the child has finished hammering, be sure to offer support: "I noticed that when you felt upset you tried some hammering to help you feel better. Do you want to talk about it?"

Biting is one of the most emotionally-charged challenging behaviors. Parents and teachers have very strong reactions to biting and may overreact, rather than trying to solve the problem. The parents of a child who has been bitten are likely to be horrified, and afraid that their child is not safe at the center. The parents of the child who did the biting may be embarrassed, ashamed, defensive, and unsure of how to respond. Teachers need to understand what may cause a child to bite and work with parents to stop this unacceptable behavior.

As with other forms of aggression, teachers should respond immediately when one child bites another. State the rule clearly, involve the child who did the biting in comforting the child who was bitten, and help both children find something else to do. In addition, you will need to talk with the child and the parents to find out what might be causing this challenging behavior. Some children have great difficult controlling their urge to bite. It may help to give the child something they are allowed to bite (for example, a clean washcloth) until they learn to control their behavior.

Temper tantrums are a child's way of expressing total frustration. The child typically loses control and screams, kicks, and cries. Temper tantrums often occur when children have many strong feelings that they can't express through words. During a tantrum, a teacher may need to protect the child, as well as other people and things in the environment, by firmly holding the child's arms and legs until the child calms down. The child will recover more quickly from the tantrum if no harm came to people or objects. Once calm is restored, you can talk about what happened and what the child could do differently in the future. It is important to let children know that you will listen to and accept their feelings.

Many tantrums can be minimized by providing an appropriate program. Children who are tired and frustrated are more likely to have tantrums than those who are well-rested, fed nutritious meals and snacks before they get too hungry, and provided with age-appropriate materials and activities. Teachers can also learn to recognize the signs that a child is getting tired and frustrated and direct the child to a soothing activity such as water or sand play or listening to soft music.

Applying Your Knowledge

In this learning activity you will think of a child in your room who exhibits a challenging behavior. Describe the behavior and how you and your colleagues respond. Then discuss the situation with the child's parents and jointly develop a plan for responding to the behavior at home and at the center. Review the example below, then complete the blank form that follows.

Responding to Challenging Behaviors

(Example)

Child: *Renée*   **Age:** *3 years, 3 months*   **Date:** *April 16*

What behavior is challenging?

Renée hits other children.

How long has it been going on? How often does it occur?

Two or three times a week.   *Two weeks.*

In what situations does it happen?

It happens when Renée wants a turn with a toy. Sometimes it happens when she's outside on the playground and wants to swing or slide but other children get in line first.

How do you respond now?

One teacher comforts the child who was hit and gets the child ice, if necessary. The other takes Renée aside and tells her she cannot hit people. Then she has to sit on the grass until we all go inside.

How does the child respond?

She cries and screams. Sometimes she pulls up the grass or sucks her thumb.

Complete the following after your discussion with the parents.

Did something happen at the center that might have upset the child?

We can't think of anything that has changed.

Did something happen at home that might have upset the child?

Renée has a new baby brother, who shares her room. She does not seem very interested in him. Renée doesn't hit at home.

What do you think might be causing the challenging behavior?

Renée may feel jealous of her new brother. We need to look at the ways we are responding now to see how we could improve. We think separating Renée from the other children is making her feel very bad about herself. We need to help her use her words to express her feelings about the new baby.

What are your plans for responding to this behavior at home and at the center?

Renée's parents will help her express her feelings about her baby brother. They will set up a special place at home that is just for Renée and will take turns spending time alone with her. They'll try to do activities that help her feel special.

At the center, we will also provide ways for Renée to talk about her brother. We will read A Baby Sister for Francis, *by Russell Hoban, at group time, then place it in the library area. We can ask the other children who have baby brothers or sisters at home to tell us what it's like.*

When Renée hits, one teacher will still comfort the hurt child. The other teacher will respond to Renée. This teacher will bend down, hold her firmly, look in her eyes and say, "It hurts people when you hit them. I won't let anyone hit you. I won't let you hit anyone." Then the teacher will try to get her involved in a calming activity, such as playing with playdough, water, or sand. We know Renée hits when she wants a turn on the swing or wants something another child has. We agreed that we will not let her have the turn or the toy if she hits.

What happened at home and at the center when you tried out your plans? Has the challenging behavior changed or gone away?

Renée's parents say that she is doing much better at home. They rearranged the kitchen to create a corner for Renée. She draws and tells them about her day while they cook dinner. Every Saturday morning, Renée goes to the park with one of her parents.

We've noticed a difference at the center, too. Renée liked the book and reads it to herself. She has started using her words more—to tell others what she wants and to tell us that her brother is a baby and she's a big girl.

Responding to Challenging Behaviors

Child: _____ **Age:** _____ **Date:** _____

What behavior is challenging?

How long has it been going on? How often does it occur?

In what situations does it happen?

How do you respond now?

How does the child respond?

Complete the following after your discussion with the parents.

Did something happen at the center that might have upset the child?

Did something happen at home that might have upset the child?

What do you think might be causing the challenging behavior?

What are your plans for responding to this behavior at home and at the center?

What happened at home and at the center when you tried out your plans? Has the challenging behavior changed or gone away?

Discuss this activity with your trainer and your colleagues. Continue using this problem-solving approach as you work with parents to respond to children's challenging behaviors.

Summarizing Your Progress

You have now completed all of the learning activities for this module. Whether you are an experienced teacher or new to the profession, this module has probably helped you develop new skills for guiding children's behavior.

Before you go on, take a few minutes to summarize what you've learned.

- Turn back to Learning Activity I, Using Your Knowledge of Child Development to Guide Children's Behavior, and add to the chart specific examples of what you learned about helping children develop self-discipline while you were working on this module. Compare your ideas to those in the completed chart at the end of the module.

- Next, review your responses to the pre-training assessment for this module. Write a summary of what you learned and list the skills you developed or improved.

If there are topics you would like to know more about, you will find recommended readings listed in the Orientation in Volume I.

Your final step in this module is to complete the knowledge and competency assessments. Let your trainer know when you are ready to schedule the assessments. After you have successfully completed these assessments, you will be ready to start a new module. Congratulations on your progress so far, and good luck with your next module.

Answer Sheets

Providing an Environment That Encourages Self-Discipline

1. **What behaviors did Ms. Kim and Ms. Richards find frustrating?**
   a. The children are constantly fighting over toys.

   b. The children resist cleaning up.

2. **How will changing the environment encourage children's self-discipline?**
   a. If there are duplicates of popular toys, children are less likely to get frustrated because they won't have to wait so long for a turn.

   b. If there are picture labels on the shelves and containers, children can see where things belong. They can choose what they want to use and return items after they have finished using them.

Using Positive Methods to Guide Individual Children

1. **What did Ms. Williams know about Travis?**
   a. Travis likes to throw things.

   b. Travis can help solve problems.

   c. Travis responds well when his behavior is redirected.

   d. Travis is a physically active child.

2. **How did Ms. Williams let Travis know that she respected him?**
   a. She walked over to him and bent down to talk to him.

   b. She commented on his skills by saying that he is learning to be a good thrower.

   c. She asked him to think of a safe place where he could throw pine cones without hurting anyone.

Helping Children Understand and Express Their Feelings in Acceptable Ways

1. **How do you think Billy felt when Sam grabbed his piece of orange?**
   a. *Angry*

   b. *Frustrated*

2. **How did Mr. Lopez help Billy learn to express his feelings in acceptable ways?**
   a. *He told Billy that it's okay to not like it when someone takes his things.*

   b. *He stepped in immediately to prevent Billy from hitting Sam.*

   c. *He told Billy it's okay to talk to people when you're angry, but it's not okay to hit them.*

Using Your Knowledge of Child Development to Guide Children's Behavior

(p. 166)

What Preschool Children Are Like	How Teachers Can Use This Information To Guide Children's Behavior
They seek adult approval and attention.	*Notice and comment on children's positive behaviors and accomplishments, such as participating in clean-up, helping a friend, or finishing a difficult puzzle. Try to spend some one-on-one time with each child every day.*
They try new things and take risks.	*Conduct regular safety checks to make sure the indoor and outdoor areas are free of hazards. Talk with children about taking risks safely. Point out the safety features in your environment, such as using cones to create a safe area at the bottom of the slide.*
They can take turns and share, but don't always want to.	*Provide duplicates of the most popular play items. Set up a system for taking turns—a sign-up sheet, name or picture cards to hang on hooks, a timer.*
They sometimes lose control; they may scream or strike out in anger at children or adults.	*Step in immediately to stop the hitting or kicking. Calmly but firmly say, "Hitting hurts. It's not okay to hit. Use your words to tell him how you feel." Stay with a child until he or she has calmed down and can listen your words. Observe children to identify signs they are about to lose control. When you see these signs, redirect the child to a soothing activity such as using playdough, tearing paper, or listening to music.*
They are gaining new physical skills and have a lot of energy.	*Offer sufficient time, materials, and space—indoors and outdoors—for children to move their bodies and practice their rapidly expanding physical skills. Change the schedule and activities when needed to allow children to take a break and expend some energy.*
They may swear or use bathroom words to get attention or without knowing what the words mean.	*Your response to this behavior will vary, depending on the reasons why children are using these words. You might calmly say, "We don't use those words here," and go on to something else. If children seem to be seeking attention, try ignoring them when they use the words. Provide the needed attention at another time.*

Using Your Knowledge of Child Development to Guide Children's Behavior
(p. 167)

What Preschool Children Are Like	How Teachers Can Use This Information To Guide Children's Behavior
They want to do things for themselves, but may get upset if things don't go as expected.	*Set up the environment so children can select and replace materials without adult assistance. When problems arise, allow children time to express their feelings. When children are ready, encourage them to move on: to paint a new picture, to get a sponge to wipe up a spill, to figure out a different way to do something.*
They can follow a few simple rules.	*Involve children in setting rules and limits. Use positive reminders to help children remember what to do, rather than what not to do: "Walk indoors. You can run when we go outside." Apply the rules consistently.*
They like to feel powerful and important, and they can be bossy.	*Ask children to help you do real chores so they feel useful and competent. Create situations in which children can be leaders: choosing a book for story time, teaching another child how do something; ringing the bell to let the group know it is almost time to go outdoors. Remember, being bossy is a stage that passes when children feel sure of their abilities.*
They are learning to use words to express their feelings and to solve problems.	*Offer genuine praise when children use their words to express their feelings and solve problems. As needed, tell children the words that label their feelings: "You are sad because your Dad left." Read books in which the characters discuss and solve their disagreements.*
They are most comfortable when the daily schedule is both consistent and predictable.	*Follow the same schedule each day so children will learn the order of daily events and feel a sense of control over their own activities. When you have to alter the schedule, explain the change in advance and pay special attention to children who have difficulty coping with changes in routine.*
They are learning to recognize how their actions affect the environment, materials, and other people.	*Point out the immediate and natural consequences of actions: "You put your carpet square too close to Shane's, so he got up and moved to another spot. He likes to have more space." Respond calmly to accidents and involve children in repairs or clean-up: "Whoops! You tripped over your shoelace. Would you like some help tieing your shoes?"*

Arranging the Environment to Promote Self-Discipline
(p. 171)

Behavior	Possible Problems	Suggested Solutions
Children wander around and have difficulty choosing something to do.	*Perhaps the room is too cluttered, choices are not clear, or there aren't enough appropriate materials. The materials and activities don't interest the children, so they are bored.*	*Eliminate the clutter. Put away toys and materials children no longer use and put out some new ones. Observe what children like to do, then choose new items in response to observed interests.*
Children are easily distracted and have trouble staying with and completing tasks.	*Areas are too open, with the result that children can see everything that happens in the room.*	*Use shelves or make fabric dividers to define the areas so children are not distracted by other activities.*
Children use materials roughly and resist clean-up.	*There is no order to the display of materials. Shelves are messy. Containers are filled with pieces from different toys.*	*Organize the materials so there is a place for everything. Use picture and word labels to show where materials go.*
Children frequently ask teachers for assistance in getting out materials.	*Materials and toys are stored out of children's reach. Or, they are stored so haphazardly that children cannot find what they need.*	*Store materials on low, open shelves. Use open containers for items such as Legos® so children can easily find what they want. Label containers with pictures of the items.*
Children run around outside without using toys or equipment or participating in activities.	*The outdoor area doesn't offer a variety of activities. Children are bored because there are seldom new materials to explore.*	*Organize the outdoors into interest areas. Bring materials typically used indoors, outside. Observe children's play and provide new materials to build on their interests.*

Glossary

Challenging behavior

Behavior such as biting or temper tantrums that occurs again and again and is often difficult to handle.

Consequence

The natural or logical result of a behavior.

Discipline

The actions that adults take to guide and direct children toward acceptable behavior.

Limits and rules

Guidelines set by teachers and children to define acceptable behavior.

Positive guidance

Techniques that help children learn to behave in acceptable ways. These methods help children develop self-discipline.

Punishment

Control of children's behavior by use of force and fear.

Self-discipline

The ability to control one's own behavior

Overview

Working with families involves:

- Communicating frequently with parents to share information about their child's experiences and development
- Offering a variety of ways for parents to participate in their child's life at the program
- Providing support to families

Research has consistently shown that the most effective child development programs are those which actively promote and encourage parent participation. (In this module, we use the word *parent* to mean any nurturing adult who takes on the role of parent in a child's life—a mother or father, grandparent or other relative, or a close family friend.) When parents and teachers work as a team, they can share information and discuss ways to provide children with consistent care at home and in the program. Good working relationships with families enable teachers to recognize and be more responsive to children's individual characteristics and needs.

Parents are the most important people in children's lives. Children and parents are developing relationships that will continue long after the children leave your care. Enhancing the parent-child relationship is one of the key roles of an early childhood teacher. By building positive relationships with children's families, you acknowledge parents' roles as the first and primary educators of their children.

Parents can teach you a lot about their children—what they like to do, how they respond to new experiences, their strengths, and new skills they are developing. It is important for teachers to share similar information with parents on a regular basis. In this way parents can feel connected to their children's lives in the program. Parents who work in partnership with teachers become knowledgeable consumers who value the quality of care their children are receiving.

All families have a culture which defines and influences how they approach everyday experiences. A family's attitudes about play, discipline, food, and gender roles are often rooted in culture. The more teachers know about the cultural backgrounds of the children, the more effectively they can meet children's needs and communicate with parents. The communication and interaction practices accepted in your own culture may differ from those considered appropriate in another. To illustrate, in some cultures it is considered polite to answer a question as soon as it is asked. In others it is more respectful to pause and reflect on a question before giving a reply.

Teachers and parents work as a team to encourage children's development.

It is important to know about the cultural backgrounds of the children.

Teachers and parents develop partnerships in a variety of ways.

Because most parents are truly interested in their children's growth and development, sharing information is a good way to build strong lines of communication. Daily conversations with parents are opportunities to get to know each other and talk about a child's activities at home and in the program. You might describe a new skill that Donny has learned, and share a parent's excitement when she tells you how Kristi helped make breakfast or that Rigoberto talked about the trip to the clinic. It's important to let parents know that you are working to provide a quality program that meets their children's needs. This reassures them that you enjoy caring for their children.

You can encourage parents to become involved in the program by assuring them that they are always welcome to visit. When they do, offer a variety of specific ways to be involved, such as reading a story to children, helping with an activity, or simply observing for awhile. For parents who don't have time during the day, you can suggest other ways to participate. Don't be discouraged, however, if you have some parents who show no interest in becoming involved in the program. They may not yet feel comfortable with you and other staff, or they may be just barely coping with their responsibilities. It is the sense of partnership and mutual respect that is most important—not how often parents participate.

Teachers can offer support to families in need.

In addition to communicating and encouraging involvement in the program, a third aspect of working with families is providing support that enhances parent-child relationships. By sharing what you know about children, you can often help parents develop more realistic expectations and positive approaches to handling problems. Whether parents approach you or you approach them, part of your job is to relate to parents in ways that promote a sense of confidence in themselves and their children. Additionally, teachers are often among the first people to recognize when a family is under stress and having difficulty meeting basic physical and emotional needs of their children. You can help these families find the resources they need to cope with these challenges.

Listed on the following pages are three sets of examples showing how teachers demonstrate their competence in working with families. Following each set of examples is a short reading and two questions to answer. When you have finished this section, compare your answers with those on the answer sheet at the end of the module. If your answers are different, discuss them with your trainer. There can be more than one good answer.

Communicating Frequently with Parents to Share Information About Their Child's Experiences and Development

Share positive and relevant information about each child's routines and activities every day.

"Thank you for telling us that Max didn't eat breakfast. He was hungry before lunch so we gave him a snack."

Respond to parents' questions and concerns.

"If you think Nicki needs more physical activity, we can encourage her to ride trikes and stretch her muscles, indoors and outside."

Suggest ways to coordinate and build on a child's home and program experiences.

"Mark loves water play. At home he could practice pouring with plastic cups and bottles in the bathtub."

Learn parents' names and something about them as a way to build trust.

"I thought of you last night, Mr. Parker, when I watched the special on Mardi Gras celebrations in New Orleans. That's where your family lives, isn't it?"

Tailor communication strategies to meet parents' individual needs.

"Bianca, your grandma pinned a note to your bag. Let's see what she has to say."

Hold parent-teacher conferences regularly and as needed to share information about children's progress and to plan for the future.

"Ms. Khan, here's a planning form to help you think about what you want to discuss at next week's conference."

Yesterday, for the first time, Gina Carter climbed to the top of the ladder and went down the slide by herself. Ms. Kim gave Gina a big hug when she reached the bottom. For several weeks, Ms. Kim and Gina's parents have been sharing information about Gina's progress. First, Gina watched the other children use the slide, then she climbed up the ladder holding Ms. Kim's hand. Recently she climbed up and down the ladder by herself. Ms. Kim knew that the Carters were very pleased that Gina was learning to conquer her fears. She decided to say nothing about Gina's accomplishment so they could see it for themselves. Today Gina and her mother arrive a little early. "Guess what," Mrs. Carter says. "Gina went down the slide at the park by herself." Ms. Kim smiles and says, "That's a big accomplishment. Now that Gina has learned to take a risk she is going to explore the world in different ways. We'll have to help her explore safely."

1. Why did Ms. Kim decide not to share the news about Gina's accomplishment?

2. What kinds of information will Ms. Kim and the Carters need to share, now that Gina has learned to take a risk?

Offering a Variety of Ways for Parents to Participate in Their Child's Life at the Program

Encourage parents to visit the program at any time.

"Mr. Jackson, we're looking forward to your visit at lunch today.

Provide opportunities for parents to make decisions about their child's routines and activities in the program.

"Deena seems ready to use puzzles with more pieces. What do you think?"

Invite parents to share aspects of their culture.

"Could Young Lee bring in the photographs of your trip home? She told us about her new clothes and getting to know her grandparents."

Offer workshops and resources on topics about which parents have expressed interest.

"Many parents want to know more about helping young children cope when their parents have to travel for work, so we're planning a workshop."

Hold regularly scheduled meetings and informal family events at times that are convenient for most parents.

"Ms. Hanes, the children are having a great time jumping on the old tires you set up at last Saturday's fix-up day."

Offer a variety of parent involvement options to accommodate different schedules, interests, and skills.

"Thanks so much for typing this month's newsletter for us, Mr. Peterson."

At the mid-year orientation for new families, Mr. Bradley says to Ms. Williams, "I don't know much about young children, but I want to be a part of Jerry's life in the program." Ms. Williams asks Mr. Bradley about his work and interests, then says, "The children would enjoy learning about something you are interested in. It sounds like you enjoy cooking. That's something the children like to do, too. Your excitement would be contagious. We could plan a cooking activity together, and you could do it when you visit." Mr. Bradley thinks for a minute, then says, "If you can give me some tips on cooking with preschoolers, I'll try it. Let me check my schedule to see when I can take time off work." A few weeks later Mr. Bradley spends all morning in the program. He helps several small groups of children make "healthy bars" and talks about the nutritious ingredients they are using. All the children eat "healthy bars" for a snack. As he leaves, Mr. Bradley turns to Ms. Williams and says, "Thank you for showing me a way to be involved. This was fun, and it was great to see Jerry with his friends. I can't wait to come back again!"

1. How did Ms. Williams help Mr. Bradley find a way to be involved?

2. How did Ms. Williams help Mr. Bradley prepare for his visit?

Providing Support to Families

Maintain confidentiality about children and families.

"Thank you for sharing this information. With your permission I'll tell the director. It won't go any further."

Recognize when families are under stress and offer additional support.

"Most families find it hard to adjust when there's a new baby at home. We'll help Charisse here at the program."

Work with parents to develop strategies for dealing with a child's behavior.

"Many children go through a phase of using 'bathroom' words a lot. If we ignore them, it usually stops.

Help parents understand what their children learn through daily routines and activities.

"Jessica is building with blocks. She is learning math concepts she'll use to add and subtract."

Use familiar terms instead of jargon when talking to parents.

"When Mia plays with the pegboard and beads, she's strengthening her hand and finger muscles. She'll use those muscles when she begins to write."

Provide parents with information on child development and typical preschool behaviors.

"Like many 3-year-olds, Jody can be so involved in play that he wets his pants. As he gets older he'll learn to respond to his body's messages."

Notify a supervisor when it seems a parent needs professional help.

"Ms. Grimaldi, do you have a few minutes to talk? I've had several disturbing conversations with Mr. Lee and want to discuss them with you."

"I don't know what to do," says Ms. Thomas as she drops off three-year-old Marita. "Marita's been coming here for a month, and she still cries and clings to me when I leave. I have to work. Do you have any suggestions?" Mr. Lopez says, "Marita usually stops crying a few minutes after you leave. It takes some children a while to get used to being separated from their parents. We'll keep working with her to help her feel secure. Would you like to make an appointment to talk about how Marita spends her time here? Then you can talk to Marita about her activities. That may help her feel a stronger connection between home and the program." Ms. Thomas agrees, "You may be right. Can we talk tomorrow afternoon?" Mr. Lopez says, "Of course. Remember, we're a team, working together to support Marita." While Mr. Lopez and Marita read a book about what grown-ups do at work, Ms. Thomas leaves for work looking a lot less worried.

1. How did Mr. Lopez help Mrs. Thomas understand Marita's behavior?

2. How did Mr. Lopez help Marita and her mother cope with separation?

Your Own Family Experiences

What is a family?

Early childhood teachers bring many firsthand experiences to their work with families. Most of us grew up in a family. Some of us are raising families of our own or have grown children. Think for a moment about what the word *family* means to you. Do you think of a mother, father, and children living together? Or, do you think of different kinds of family relationships? Our experiences influence our views on families and how parents should raise their children.

The traditional view of a family as a mother and father with several children does not always apply today. Very few families in the United States look like the traditional one of a mother who works in the home, a father who works outside the home, and their two children. Children may be growing up with a single mother or father or with step-parents. They may live with several relatives—their mother, a grandmother, an aunt and her children—or they may live with a grandparent who has legal custody. A family might include children, a parent, and his or her partner of the same or different gender.

Parenting can be a difficult job.

In addition to "looking" different, many of today's families are affected by multiple sources of stress that can make parenting a very difficult job. In affluent, "family-friendly" communities, there are parks and recreation facilities, good public transportation, and public facilities for adult education and job training. Residents in these communities have adequate housing, nutritious foods, and health care. In less affluent communities, many families make do with far less—for example, substandard housing, limited transportation, and health care systems that do not meet their needs. These factors, accompanied by violence, drug and alcohol abuse, poverty, and other sources of stress, can challenge the innate resources of even the strongest families.

It is not uncommon for teachers to blame parents for their children's problems, especially when teachers see parents who don't behave toward their children as the teachers think they should. If you have difficulty accepting the values and life-styles of some children and families in your program, examine the source of your negative reactions. Do you expect children's families to conform to your own personal values? Are you willing to learn about different cultural practices and parenting styles? It may help to remember that most parents want the best for their children and try hard to be good parents. They too are guided by their own experiences growing up in a family.

Before you begin the learning activities in this module, spend a few minutes thinking of how your own views and experiences may affect the way you work with families. Answer the questions that follow.

Whom do you consider to be part of the family in which you grew up?

How are the families of the children in your care similar to and different from your own family?

What pressures do parents have today that your parents didn't experience?

Which pressures are the same?

How do you think your own views and experiences affect your work with families?

Discuss your responses with your trainer and a group of staff. When you have finished this overview section, you should complete the pre-training assessment. (Note: There is no glossary for this module.)

Pre-Training Assessment

Listed below are the skills that teachers use to promote partnerships with families of preschool children. Think about whether you do these things regularly, sometimes, or not enough. Place a check in one of the boxes on the right for each skill listed. Then discuss your answers with your trainer.

Communicating Frequently with Parents to Share Information About Their Child's Experiences and Development

	I Do This: Regularly	Sometimes	Not Enough
1. Share positive and relevant information about each child's routines and activities every day.	☐	☐	☐
2. Respond to parents' questions and concerns.	☐	☐	☐
3. Suggest ways to coordinate and build on a child's home and program experiences.	☐	☐	☐
4. Learn parents' names and something about them as a way to build trust.	☐	☐	☐
5. Tailor communication strategies to meet parents' individual needs.	☐	☐	☐
6. Hold parent-teacher conferences regularly and as needed to share information about children's progress and to plan for the future.	☐	☐	☐

Offering a Variety of Ways for Parents to Participate in Their Child's Life at the Program

	Regularly	Sometimes	Not Enough
7. Encourage parents to visit the program at any time.	☐	☐	☐
8. Provide opportunities for parents to make decisions about their child's routines and activities in the program.	☐	☐	☐

Offering a Variety of Ways for Parents to Participate in Their Child's Life at the Program

(continued)

	I Do This: Regularly	Sometimes	Not Enough
9. Invite parents to share aspects of their culture.	☐	☐	☐
10. Offer workshops and resources on topics about which parents have expressed interest.	☐	☐	☐
11. Hold regularly scheduled meetings and informal family events at times that are convenient for most parents.	☐	☐	☐
12. Offer a variety of parent involvement options to accommodate different schedules, interests, and skills.	☐	☐	☐

Providing Support to Families

	I Do This: Regularly	Sometimes	Not Enough
13. Maintain confidentiality about children and families.	☐	☐	☐
14. Recognize when families are under stress and offer additional support.	☐	☐	☐
15 Work with parents to develop strategies for dealing with a child's behavior.	☐	☐	☐
16. Help parents understand what their children learn through daily routines and activities.	☐	☐	☐
17. Use familiar terms instead of jargon when talking to parents.	☐	☐	☐

Providing Support to Families
(continued)

	I Do This: Regularly	Sometimes	Not Enough
18. Provide parents with information on child development and typical preschool behaviors.	☐	☐	☐
19. Notify a supervisor when it seems a parent needs professional help.	☐	☐	☐

Review your responses, then list three to five skills you would like to improve or topics you would like to learn more about. When you finish this module you will list examples of your new or improved knowledge and skills.

Begin the learning activities for Module 11, Families.

Learning Activities

I. Developing a Partnership with Parents

In this activity you will learn to:

- Work with parents to share information about each child
- Develop and maintain a partnership with parents

High-quality early childhood programs depend on strong partnerships between teachers and parents. Successful partnerships are based on mutual respect, trust, and the understanding that a child's development is enhanced when all the adults who care for the child work together.

Strong partnerships benefit everyone involved. Parents who learn more about their children strengthen their parenting skills. Teachers who also learn more about the children feel more competent; sharing information and strategies with families allows teachers to respond to children's individual needs, interests, and strengths. Children feel more secure knowing that their parents and their teachers can keep them safe and help them learn. They feel proud of their parents' involvement.

Strong partnerships benefit everyone.

Developing partnerships can be both challenging and time-consuming. Sometimes a child's teacher and parents have different views on child rearing. They may even have different ideas about the child's strengths, interests, and needs. Parents and teachers may not always understand each other's point of view and may disagree about how to solve a problem. What they almost always have in common, though, is genuine concern for the child's well being.

Although both the teacher and the parents know a great deal about a particular child, this knowledge and information must be combined to create a total picture. Here are some examples of the kinds of information each half of a partnership can provide.

Parents have information about the following areas of a child's life:

Parents have a lot of information to share.

Health and growth history. "The pediatrician said that Ben's allergies are under control. Thank you for working with us to coordinate his treatment."

Relationships with other family members. "Carla really enjoys being with her older cousin. They like to cook together and they can talk for hours."

Ways the child likes to be comforted. "When Yancey is tired he likes to have his back rubbed. It helps him settle down."

Food preferences and allergies. "Alfredo tried broccoli for the first time last night. He really liked it." "Donna is allergic to all kinds of berries."

How the child reacts to changes in routines. "Sonia gets very upset if I ask her to dress before breakfast. She likes to eat first, then put on her clothes."

The child's favorite activities at home. "Jake loves his bath. He wants to stay and play in the water."

The child's fears. "Lamont is afraid of clowns. We're not sure why, but he always cries when he sees one."

The family's lifestyle. "We like to get outdoors as much as possible. Peter likes to go hiking with us in the mountains."

How the child "used to be" as well as how the child is now. "When he was three, Nick liked trucks. Now that he's four, he's more interested in playing make-believe with other children."

What happened last night, over the weekend, or on vacation. "Kent woke up three times last night. I think he might be a little tired this morning." "Roxanne had a great time collecting shells at the beach."

Teachers know about a child's experiences in the program.

Teachers have information about the following areas in the child's life:

Favorite interest areas and materials. "Tanya loves the blocks. Her tall buildings are amazingly well balanced and detailed."

Which toys are too frustrating. "Tory isn't ready to do the farm puzzle yet. He chooses the ones that don't have as many pieces."

What challenges the child enjoys. "Shauna spent a lot of time today taking apart an old clock. She really wants to see what's inside."

How the child plays with others. "Jan likes to watch before she joins in with the other children."

How the child reacts to changes in the environment. "Whenever we put new props in the house corner, George is the first child to use them."

What the child talks about during the day. "Today Carlos talked a lot about going to see his grandparents. He's very excited."

What the child does when his or her parents leave. "Today I heard Jerry telling Sandy, 'Don't cry, your mom will come back soon!' I think that's his way of assuring himself that you will always come back."

What the child did today. "Marcus helped make snack today. He grated the cheese for our burritos."

Establishing the Partnership

Your relationship with a child's parents begins when their child first enters your room. Although the parents probably don't know you, you are the person who will care for their child for most of the day, five days a week. It is natural for them to want to learn as much as they can about you, the other children in the group, and how their child will spend each day. Provide a copy of the daily and weekly schedules and describe a typical day. Let the parents know something about yourself and why you enjoy working with children.

Begin to get to know the parents, too. Find out about their interests, the kind of work they do, how they feel about leaving their child in the program, and what kinds of stress they might be handling. Reassure parents that you recognize them as their child's first teacher. Describe some of the strategies you and the other parents use to share information and make decisions about children's routines and activities.

At first, you and the parents will get to know each other through brief conversations at drop-off and pick-up times. Be friendly and respectful; always greet each parent by name. Share interesting, positive information about their child's day. It's not necessary to report every time their child has a fight or loses his or her temper. Let them know by your attitude and tone of voice that their child is appreciated and well-cared for. "Susanna played with Carrie in the sand box, she painted, and she sat in my lap at story time." These ongoing communications build trust and acceptance, which will lead to a stronger partnership.

Let parents know you appreciate and will take care of their child.

If parents don't respond to your efforts to establish a partnership, try to understand their feelings about leaving their child in the program. Often parents are concerned about not spending as much time as they would like with their children. It is helpful to consider your feelings toward the parents and how you may be conveying these feelings through your tone of voice, facial expressions, or the kinds of information you share. Be careful not to make assumptions about parents or judge them because their lifestyle differs from yours.

Parents frequently raise concerns about their children. ("Why can't Sam zip his coat like the other children do?") or ask questions about the program ("What will you be doing on the field trip?"). If possible, respond immediately by providing the needed information. If it will take more time to discuss the issue, schedule a meeting at a time that is convenient for the parents. Sometimes parents offer their own suggestions about how to care for their child. Their ideas may differ from what you would do. Unless you think the suggested strategy will hurt the child, follow up on the parent's suggestions. "We'll be sure to let Jedi slice her sandwich in four pieces if you think she likes it better that way."

Respond to parents' concerns or questions.

Maintaining a Strong Relationship

Once a trusting relationship has been established, it is important to continue to communicate regularly with parents and involve them in their children's experiences in the program. A partnership is strengthened when parents and teachers can see how the child benefits from their teamwork. "Janine doesn't cry any more when you leave. When she feels sad, she looks at the family photo album you made for her that she keeps in her cubby."

Try these suggestions.

Some suggestions for maintaining strong partnerships follow.

Help parents focus on their child's special characteristics instead of comparing a child to others the same age. "Kwame always has a smile ready. He makes us all feel happier."

Help children and parents feel good about belonging to the same family. "Mr. Bent, Eli gets excited when he knows you're coming for lunch. He really likes it when the other kids talk about your visits."

Wait until asked before offering advice. When you are asked, make sure you are clear about what is fact and what is opinion. "Child development experts say that most preschoolers aren't really ready for formal academic lessons."

Acknowledge events and transitions in the families' lives. "Congratulations on your promotion. Your husband told me the whole family had a party to celebrate."

Help children and parents cope when one parent is away. Suggest sending art work, letters, tapes, or stories to the parent who is away. Remind children that their parents love them even when they are gone.

Keep in touch when a child is absent or ill. "Hello, Ms. Hon, I'm calling to see how Sooki is feeling today."

Maintain confidentiality when parents share something private with you. "I'm glad you told me about this. It will help me work with Luis, and I assure you I won't share it with anyone."

Although you do many things for children that parents also do (such as providing guidance or serving lunch), your role as a teacher is not the same as that of the parents. Always remember that parents need your support, but they don't need you to take over their role.

Applying Your Knowledge

In this learning activity, you focus on strengthening your partnership with the parents of one of the children in your care. Select a family you feel comfortable with but would like to know better. Explain the activity to the parents and ask for their permission to proceed. Then, for two weeks, record your daily communications—any information you each shared. At the same time, look for any changes in how you respond to this child. Begin by reading the two-day example that follows. Then make as many copies of the forms as you will need to complete this activity.

Parent-Teacher Daily Communication Record

(Example)

Child/age: *Donna, 3-1/2 years*   **Length of enrollment:** *4 months*

Parents: *Karen Parker and Frank Anderson*

Date: *June 6*

A.M. *Greeted Ms. Parker and reminded her I was starting this activity. She told me Donna is excited about playing dress-up.*

P.M. *Mr. Anderson came to pick up Donna. I told him that Donna played dress-up with Sheila. They put on lots of jewelry. He said she likes to wear her grandma's jewelry. His wife had told him about the activity.*

Date: *June 7*

A.M. *Mr. Anderson brought Donna. I told him about our plans to bring the water play table outside and that Donna likes using the turkey baster to fill up cups and bottles. He asked if she could do that at home. I told him she could do it at the sink, in a dishpan, or in the bathtub. He seemed pleased with my ideas.*

P.M. *Ms. Parker picked up Donna. I told her that Donna carried out the water play toys and made fruit smoothies. She was surprised because Donna doesn't eat much fruit at home. I said that some children eat more when they help make it. She told me Donna would be late on Friday because she has her first dentist appointment. I asked if Donna seemed worried about going to the dentist. She said, "Yes, a little. She doesn't know what to expect." I said she could borrow our book, Going to the Dentist. She and Donna can read and discuss the book so Donna will have some idea of what to expect. Ms. Parker thanked me.*

Weekly Summary

(Example)

Information you shared:

Donna played dress-up with Sheila and likes to use the baster during water play.

Suggested ways Donna could play with a turkey baster at home.

Donna carried the water play toys and likes to make and eat fruit smoothies,

Information parents shared:

Donna likes dressing up and wearing her grandma's jewelry. She doesn't eat much fruit at home. Donna is going to the dentist and she's a little scared.

How has the partnership helped you meet this child's needs?

I know more about what Donna likes to do. I can suggest things for her parents to do with her at home. I suggested a book to help Donna learn about going to the dentist.

*Parent-Teacher Daily Communication Record**

Child/age: _____   **Length of enrollment:** _____

Parents: _____

Date: _____

A.M.

P.M.

Date: _____

A.M.

P.M.

• Copy the first three pages of this form so you will have room to record your communications during the two-week period.

Date: _____
A.M.

P.M.

Date: _____
A.M.

P.M.

Date: _____
A.M.

P.M.

Weekly Summary
(Complete one at the end of each week.)

Information you shared:

Information parents shared:

After two weeks, review all your notes and answer the following question.

How has the partnership helped you meet this child's needs?

Discuss this activity with the parents who were the focus of this activity and your trainer.

II. Keeping Parents Informed About the Program

> **In this activity you will learn to:**
>
> • Keep parents informed about the program
>
> • Improve parent-program communication

Parents feel more involved when they know what's happening.

One of your most important responsibilities is to work with your supervisor and other staff to keep parents up to date on activities in the program. Parents feel more involved when they know what's happening. Most parents would appreciate knowing, for example, that there's a new climber on the playground, several staff are attending a training course, the children will be making pumpkin muffins for snack, one of the teachers will be on vacation next week, and this month's parent workshop is on encouraging creativity. Some of this information can be passed from teachers to parents during the times when children are picked up or dropped off. These times, however, are usually too brief to ensure that everyone is informed about everything that goes on in the program. Teachers need to use a variety of ongoing communication techniques to keep all parents informed about the program's current activities and future plans.

Program newsletters can keep families informed.

One of the most common ways to keep parents informed is through a newsletter. General information of interest to all families can be included, as well as specific news about each classroom. Generally, one staff member serves as editor; however, all staff contribute news. Parents might contribute to the newsletter by gathering information, writing articles, or producing an issue on a home or program computer. In addition to news and information about coming events, the newsletter might include the month's menus, suggested activities for parents and children to do at home, information on community events of interest to families, reviews of children's books, and books on parenting and related topics. The newsletter can include space for parents to make suggestions for future issues or provide news, information, or a favorite recipe.

Room newsletters can offer more detailed information about children's activities.

Another kind of newsletter covers the activities and news of one room. A parent may volunteer to help produce such a newsletter, or the teachers can take the lead. This type of newsletter can include the same kinds of information discussed in the previous paragraph, and it can be more personal, providing details about what takes place in the room: "When the children made muffin pizzas for snack they invented some unusual topping combinations." If you mention children by name, be sure to include something positive about each child.

Here are some other ways to keep parents informed about your program.

Establish a message program where each family has a box, folder, or pocket (shoe bags work well for this). Use the message program to provide parents with general news as well as specific information about their child.

Provide individual family journals that stay at the program and can be used by parents and teachers to share information about the child. Notices or flyers can be tucked in the journal so parents will see them.

Create a parent bulletin board in the lobby or some other area through which all parents pass. Post articles, a calendar of events, reminders of upcoming meetings, the week's menus, and other items of general interest.

Develop and maintain a parent handbook that presents the program's policies and procedures and lists opportunities for parent involvement. Organize the handbook by topic (calendar, holidays) or alphabetically. Give a copy to each family and provide updates whenever necessary.

Create a family photo board to help parents learn more about other children and families. Invite each family to provide a recent photograph and complete a brief questionnaire about their favorite foods, sports, recreation activities, hobbies, and places to visit. When new families enroll, add their photos and descriptions to the board.

Applying Your Knowledge

In this learning activity you answer some questions about one communication technique that your program uses to keep parents informed. First review the abbreviated example that follows. Then select a communication technique, suggest ways to improve it, implement your suggestions, and report on the results.

Communicating with Parents
(Example)

Communication technique: *Classroom newsletter*

What information is included?

Upcoming field trips, birthdays, something about each child, new toys or other materials, trips, and activities parents and children can do at home.

How often is the information shared or updated?

Bi-weekly.

What is the role of the program director?

She reads it and includes some of the information in the program newsletter before I make copies.

What is the role of teachers?

We take turns writing, proofing, and making copies.

What is the role of parents?

They read it.

How could this communication technique be improved?

We could ask parents to help produce the newsletter. They could provide information or articles to include. We could send home a questionnaire asking parents for suggestions and for help preparing the newsletter.

Implement your suggestions for improving the communication technique, then describe the results.

The parents provided lots of suggestions through their completed questionnaires. Two parents offered to help and worked on the latest issue. We used some parent-written articles, including one about a new park that one of the families visited last month. Several parents mentioned that they really liked this issue.

Communicating with Parents

Communication technique: _____

What information is included?

How often is the information shared or updated?

What is the role of the program director?

What is the role of teachers?

What is the role of parents?

How could this communication technique be improved?

Implement your suggestions for improving the communication technique, then describe the results.

Discuss this activity with your trainer and colleagues.

III. *Providing Ways for Parents to Be Involved*

> **In this activity you will learn to:**
>
> • Provide a variety of parent involvement opportunities, tailored to meet family needs
> • Plan and implement a parent involvement strategy

Create a variety of parent involvement options.

Most parents want to be involved in their child's life in the program but may not know how they can contribute. Some parents can arrange their work schedules so they can eat lunch with the children once a month, go on field trips, or volunteer in the classroom on a regular basis. However, many parents are not able to participate in this way. It's important to offer a variety of parent involvement options that match parents' interests, skills, and schedules. When parents first register their children, ask them to complete a brief questionnaire about how they would like to be involved in your program.

Make it a point to let parents know how much you value their participation and how it benefits the program. Parents who come along on field trips may enjoy themselves so much that they need little or no encouragement to offer to do it again. The parent who sews new curtains for the children's puppet theater, however, may never see the theater in action. In such a case, be sure to send a thank-you note home. Describe how the children are using the theater and enclose a photograph of the theater in action. Similarly, the parent who produces the newsletter should be credited in every issue.

Try these suggestions.

Here are some suggestions for helping parents become more involved in your program.

Hold a new parents' orientation several times a year. Because you are likely to have new families enrolling in your program during the year, you may need to provide more than one orientation.

Keep a job jar in your room. On index cards, list program-related jobs you never get around to doing that a parent could do at home. Parents can select a job from the jar, then see you for additional instructions. Jobs could include repairing broken toys, making name tags for future field trips, shopping at yard sales for dramatic play props such as cooking utensils, or making lotto boards or other materials for the room.

Organize a family dinner. Plan the event so that parents can come and have dinner on their way home. Dinner might be a meal planned and prepared by the children, or something simple such as pizza.

Involve parents in building or landscaping projects. Interested parents can work on these types of projects at their own convenience over time. When a project is completed, hold a celebration party.

Hold a family movie night. Parent volunteers can plan and host the event. They might, for example, sell popcorn and juice to raise funds for extra materials or field trips.

Schedule an evening or weekend "fix-it" session. At this session, families can work together to spruce up the program, paint walls, make a tire playground, or prepare a plot of ground for a garden.

Open the program for an evening or a weekend afternoon. Children can come to their room as though it were a regular day. Parents come too and play with the children, lead activities, serve snacks, or sit back and observe their child playing with others. Set this up so small groups of parents take turns being with the children while the rest of the parents are involved in another activity.

Set up a parent corner. Include books, magazines, brochures, and other resources of interest to parents. If possible, provide comfortable chairs and refreshments.

Ask a parent to organize a photo album about the class. You can provide the pictures and the book; the parent can put it together. Display the photo album prominently and include a cover page thanking the parent.

Invite parents to be book reviewers. Parents could read children's books or books on child development or parenting. Provide a book review form, listing the title, author, publisher, price, and comments. For children's books, leave space on the form for parents to record what ages the book is appropriate for, what the book is about, and why they and their child liked it. Use these recommendations to select books for your room.

Send home a wish list of materials for the classroom. A list of needed resources should be updated regularly. Parents might make contributions themselves, or they could put you in touch with businesses, community groups, or individuals who could make contributions.

Applying Your Knowledge

In this learning activity you try out a parent involvement strategy. Select from those mentioned earlier or make up one of your own. Discuss the strategy with your supervisor and other teachers in your room. If your supervisor or colleagues think this strategy is not appropriate for the parents at your program, then select another one. First read the example; then complete the chart that follows to describe the strategy you chose and how it encouraged parent involvement.

Parent Involvement Strategy
(Example)

Strategy:

Invite parents to help us make new story tapes of some favorite books.

Plans:

I will send a notice home with the children asking for volunteers. The program will supply blank tapes and zipper bags to hold each book and tape. We can provide the books or parents can read favorites from the library. I'll try to make sure we tape a variety of books. I'll explain that the tapes will be used in the quiet corner, where children like to go to be alone for a while.

Results:

Four parents volunteered to make tapes. Each parent made four tapes so now we have a good supply for the quiet corner. The children really enjoy hearing their parent's voices on tape. All four parents said they would be happy to make more tapes whenever we need them.

Follow-up:

I will make this an ongoing parent involvement project. I asked Ms. Porter, one of the four parents who made tapes, to help me keep track of which books we tape and which parents help. I think the children would like it if all the parents took a turn making story tapes. This could be a good project for parents who find it difficult to participate in the program.

Parent Involvement Strategy

Strategy:

Plans:

Results:

Follow-up:

Discuss this activity with your trainer and the other teachers in your room.

IV. Planning and Participating in Parent-Teacher Conferences

In this activity you will learn to:

- Prepare for a conference by reviewing information about the child's skills, needs, interests, and progress
- Participate in a parent conference

Parent-teacher conferences are opportunities for in-depth discussions.

At least twice a year, and whenever a need arises, parents and teachers need to meet to review how each child is progressing in all areas of development and to set goals for continued growth and learning. Parent-teacher conferences are opportunities to focus on one child and family without any distractions or interruptions. Although much information about the child is shared daily, conferences allow for in-depth discussions. They should be carefully planned and handled.

Planning for Conferences

At enrollment, explain to parents how often conferences take place, their purpose, and what is discussed. When it's time to schedule a conference, ask parents what time would be most convenient for them to attend. Offer several options and provide adequate advance notice so parents can make plans. Allow enough time for the conference so you and the parents won't feel rushed. Remind parents that the conference is an opportunity for you to learn more about the child's life at home so you can better support the child's development at the program.

Parents often have their own goals for the conference. Most importantly, they want to know you understand and like their child. In addition, they may have a specific concern they would like to discuss or a suggestion for how they would like you to work with their child. It's also possible that a parent might have a concern about the program's philosophy and curriculum or a complaint about something you did or didn't do. It's helpful to know about these issues ahead of time so you can be prepared.

Encourage parents to prepare for the conference.

To help parents prepare for the conference, you can provide a planning form asking what questions they want to address and inviting them to list the topics they want to cover. Ask parents to bring some photographs, observation notes, art work, and other items that demonstrate the child's experiences and accomplishments away from the program. These can be added to the child's portfolio—an organized collection of information about the child's interests, needs, development, and progress. (Work samples and portfolios are discussed in Module 12, Program Management.) Provide a copy of the goals and strategies agreed on at the previous conference (if there has been one).

To make best use of the time set aside for the conference, it's important to be well prepared. The teacher who will take the lead in the conference—usually the person with primary responsibility for the child—should examine the contents of the child's portfolio prior to the conference. This may include reviewing observation notes, anecdotal records, checklists, work samples, photographs, and any other written materials that provide objective information about the child's activities and progress. It is important to organize the portfolio items to make sure they address all areas of development: physical, cognitive, language, social, and emotional. If there are concerns about a child's health (such as evidence the child might need glasses) these concerns should be written down and supported with examples from observations. All adults who work with the child can provide information.

Many parents are interested in learning how their child gets along in a group setting with peers. They want to know as much as possible about their child's daily experiences in the program. For example: "What activities and interest areas does Nigel enjoy? Who does he play with? What makes him happy and sad?" Make sure your notes include examples that will help parents picture what their child does in the program and understand how these experiences support development.

Sometimes teachers feel a little uneasy before a conference. It may help to role play with your supervisor or a colleague. You can practice sharing your observations and answering the kinds of questions the parents are likely to ask.

Participating in the Conference

At the beginning of the conference, try to establish a relaxed and comfortable tone. Anticipate at least five minutes of social conversation before the more serious discussions begin. Start by explaining how the conference will proceed: "I'm so glad you could both come today. Let me tell you how we will proceed. We'll describe a typical day in the program for Karen. I'll use Karen's portfolio to give you information on her activities and progress in the program. Next, you can tell us what you've seen at home. . . ." This is a good time to stress that the conference is a time for sharing information and planning for the future. It is not in any way an evaluation of their child's performance.

During the conference, make sure there are many opportunities for parents to provide input and ask questions. Here are some other suggestions for conducting successful conferences.

Begin and end the conference with a positive statement. Focus on your relationship with the child. "We really enjoy watching A. J. take on challenges. He's always ready to try something new."

Respect cultural preferences related to communication practices. Maintain an appropriate physical distance, eye contact, and tone of voice; respect response times to questions; use or avoid physical contact, as appropriate.

Use portfolios to provide information about all areas of development.

Ask parents open-ended questions. This is especially helpful if they seem uncertain or reluctant to talk about their concerns. "What else about Rebecca or her activities in the program would you like to discuss?"

Invite parents to work with you by asking questions and seeking their advice. Stress the importance of consistency between home and the program. "It's helpful to know that sometimes you have to repeat directions to be sure Mai Le understands what to do. We'll remember to do that here as well."

Take notes during the conference. This is very important if you are discussing a complex or difficult situation. Explain to parents that the notes will help you follow up on their concerns.

Pay attention to body language. Note especially signs that a parent might feel tense, hurt, disappointed, or angry.

Listen carefully to parents' comments without interrupting or rushing them. Accept their feelings even if they are different from your own. Restate their comments and suggestions to make sure you heard them correctly. "You are concerned about Reneé being tired when she gets home so you would like us to make sure she naps every day."

Respond thoughtfully when parents ask you for advice about handling a specific situation. Always offer more than one suggestion; if you don't know the answer, say you will look into it and get back in touch. Most importantly, encourage parents to think about what would be best for their child. "Some parents find it helpful to allow their child to select what clothes to wear. Others offer a choice between two items, for example, the red sweater or the blue one."

Set new developmental goals and develop strategies for home and program.

After reviewing all areas of the child's development, the next step is to set some goals and develop strategies to encourage the child's development in the program as well as at home. These goals and strategies will serve as the framework for discussions at the next conference.

At the end of the conference, summarize your discussions and restate the actions you each have agreed to take and how you will follow up. "I will spend more time looking at books with Laura now that I know she likes to do that at home. And you'll bring in her special blanket, so she can have it during naps. That will make her feel more secure." Also, complete a conference evaluation form and record the new goals and strategies in the child's portfolio.

Applying Your Knowledge

In this learning activity you plan, conduct, and evaluate a conference with the parents of one of the children in your room. Begin by reviewing the information you and your colleagues collect about the child's activities, development, and progress. Complete the three planning forms: Conference Planning Summary, Developmental Summary, and Suggested Developmental Goals and Strategies. Hold the conference; then answer the questions on the Conference Evaluation form.

Conference Planning Summary

Child/age: _____ Parent(s): _____

Date of conference: _____ Date of last conference: _____

Which interest areas, materials, and activities does this child enjoy most?

What feelings does this child express (e.g., happy, sad, angry, frustrated)?

How does this child participate in routines?

With whom does this child play, and in what ways?

Anecdotes to share:

Concerns (if any):

Complete the developmental summary that follows.

Developmental Summary

Use this form to summarize the child's progress. For each area of development, list the goals set at the last conference (if there has been one) and describe the child's specific skills—for example, cuts with scissors, builds tall towers, usually plays with two or three others.

Goals	Skills
Physical (using large and small muscles)	
Cognitive (thinking and problem solving)	
Socio-Emotional (relating positively to others and developing self-confidence)	
Language (listening, speaking, understanding, and exploring reading and writing)	

List some suggested developmental goals and strategies on the chart that follows.

Suggested Developmental Goals and Strategies

List some suggested developmental goals for the next six months and strategies for encouraging the child at home and program.

Developmental Goals	Strategies
Physical (use of large and small muscles)	
Cognitive (thinking and problem solving)	
Socio-Emotional (relating positively to others and developing self-confidence)	
Language (listening, speaking, understanding, and exploring reading and writing)	

Hold the parent-teacher conference. Ask parents to suggest goals and strategies and add them to the list above if you all agree. You and the child's parents can use the completed chart to prepare for the next conference-six months from now.

Complete the conference evaluation on the next page.

Conference Evaluation

Think about what happened at the conference and answer these questions.

How did you establish a relaxed tone?

How did you start the discussion?

What information did you share to create a "picture" of the child's day?

How did you encourage parent input?

How did you show respect for the parents' communication style?

Were you asked for advice? If so, how did you respond?

How did you summarize the conference?

How did you end the conference?

What would you do differently next time?

Discuss this learning activity with your trainer and other teachers who work with the child and parents.

V. *Reaching Out to Families*

> **In this activity you will learn to:**
>
> • Recognize signs that families are under stress
>
> • Provide support to families to prevent or respond to stress

Teachers can lend a helping hand to families.

Many parents of preschoolers—especially first-time parents—are coping with stressful lives. Balancing the demands of a job and family, feeling unsure about sharing the care of their child, and not understanding changes in their child's behavior can leave parents feeling overwhelmed. Early childhood teachers are in an excellent position to lend a helping hand. Some parents will feel comfortable sharing their worries and seeking assistance; others will not. Regardless of whether parents approach you or you approach them, remember that helping them find their own solutions enhances their sense of competence.

Recognizing When Parents Are Under Stress[1]

Stress is a normal part of daily life for many families. Most parents can cope with typical frustrations and tension, so stress doesn't interfere with their work and home activities. Some families, however, are affected over a long period of time by significant sources of stress such as community violence, homelessness, substance abuse, or lack of basic necessities. The stresses are not caused by single events such as divorce or a car accident. Rather, they are routine, unrelenting, and woven into daily life. They are a result of societal conditions and pressures that are beyond the control of individual families.

The following are examples of sources of long-term significant stress that might be experienced by the children and families in your program. There may be other sources that are specific to your community.

- Unemployment.

- Lack of necessities such as food, clothing, shelter, medical care.

- Lack of transportation to work, job training, or a health provider.

- Exposure to violence in the home or in the community.

- Living in a shelter or other temporary housing.

- Living in overcrowded or inadequate housing.

- Chronic illness or disability of a child or other family member, along with lack of access to needed services and support.

- Substance abuse in the household or in the community at large.

[1] Adapted with permission from Derry G. Koralek, *Responding to Children Under Stress* (Washington, DC: Head Start Bureau, 1993), pp. 40-42.

- Abuse and neglect of a child, spouse, or other family member.

- Depression or other mental illness of a child or adult family member.

- Learning a new language and adapting to a new culture.

Regardless of the cause of high stress in their lives, families tend to have similar concerns, needs, and behaviors. Although some families have the skills and strength needed to cope with the stress, many are overwhelmed. They may experience effects such as the following:

Family life is unpredictable, unstable, and chaotic. If the family moves frequently, children must adapt to new child care programs, teachers, and classmates. Children may have difficulty focusing and lack a sense of order and discipline in their lives.

Adult family members are unable to give their children affection and attention. They may expect children to assume adult responsibilities such as caring for younger siblings.

Children and adult family members have unmet health and nutrition needs. The family may have no access to needed health care, including immunizations, dental checkups, and counseling.

Children receive inconsistent, overly punitive, or nonexistent parental discipline.

When a family is under stress, the parents may seem disorganized, frequently forgetting things such as mittens on a cold day or a child's special blanket. A parent might seem frustrated when a child is slow to get ready to go home. A parent might complain to a teacher about the difficulty of handling the child's growing independence. Parents under stress might be unwilling to accept help, or they might be more interested in talking about their own problems than their child's.

When you see signs of stress, it is important not to add to them. This is not the time to discuss the child's inappropriate behavior or changes in the program's vacation schedule. However, it would be appropriate to share information about their child that will help parents get through the evening. For example, you would let a parent know their child has been tired and cranky all afternoon so you can discuss whether the child might be coming down with the flu. When parents know the reasons for their child's behavior, they are less likely to be frustrated or angered by the crankiness and more likely to comfort the child. When parents feel less stress, they are more likely to interact positively with their children and less likely to lose control.

Always notify your supervisor when you think parents may need professional help. Do not counsel parents or refer them to social services or mental health professionals without first discussing the situation with your supervisor. Your job is to help parents get the support they need, not to provide it yourself.

When parents do confide in you, it's essential to maintain complete confidentiality. This means you should not discuss a child with anyone other than your colleagues or the child's parents. This holds true for information about families as well. In

High levels of stress can overwhelm families.

Recognize and respond to signs of stress.

addition, you should not share records with anyone who does not have a "need to know," nor should you hold discussions about children or families during times when other children are present. Ask your supervisor about your program's guidelines for maintaining confidentiality.

Helping Parents Locate Resources

Parents often need to know where they can get help for themselves, their child, or the family. Your director can provide you with information about parent education opportunities. Here are some things you can do to help.

- Encourage parents to connect with one another by introducing them to families that live in their neighborhood or have children of the same age. "Mr. Larsen, I'd like you to meet Mr. Wheeler. He and his wife have a son about the same age as your daughter."

- Develop an exchange list so parents can support one another through sharing responsibilities and errands such as carpooling, grocery shopping, and meal preparation. "Several families want to start a dinner club. Once a week each family would cook enough for all the other members."

- Call parents' attention to resources, articles, workshops, and television or radio shows on children and families. "Next Tuesday at 8 P.M., there's a show on Channel 8 about stepparenting and blended families."

- Display books on topics of interest to parents—playground safety, juggling home and work responsibilities, quick and healthy meals—and invite parents to borrow these resources.

- Tell parents about services and special programs provided by community groups. Provide as much information as possible—names, phone numbers, locations, and hours of operation.

Providing Information on Child Growth and Development

Parents sometimes do not know much about the typical development of young children. As a result, they may expect too much or too little of their children. Here are some things you can do to help.

- Invite a parent to join you in observing a child. Review and discuss the observation recordings and explain why the child's actions are typical of this stage of development.

- Provide information about parenting workshops on topics such as supporting emerging literacy, adjusting to a new baby, responding to children's growing independence, and other subjects that would be of interest to parents of preschoolers.

- Include information on child development in newsletters and on the parent bulletin board.

- Invite parents to attend staff workshops.

- Establish a parent lending library of books, magazines, and videotapes about child growth and development.

- Introduce parents who are dealing with, or have already successfully handled, similar developmental issues.

One of the most effective ways to provide information about child development is during drop-off and pick-up times and in longer visits during the day. Without any extra effort or planning, you can model for parents appropriate ways to interact with children. In the following example, parents witness the following exchanges between a teacher and the children in her care:

Model appropriate ways to interact with children.

> *Ms. Danforth encourages Ashleigh to help put away the blocks. She talks and laughs with Evan as she ties his shoes. And she asks Bart a question about his painting—"Tell me, how did you make these long, squiggly lines?"*

> *The children's parents comment: "I can't get Ashleigh to put any of her things away at home." "Evan squirms around so much at home that I just want to get his shoes tied as quickly as possible." "All of Bart's paintings look the same to me."*

> *Ms. Danforth uses these comments to begin conversations about:*
> - *promoting children's self-help skills,*
> - *using routines as times to talk with children, and*
> - *supporting creativity by asking children about their painting techniques.*

When you demonstrate positive ways to talk to and support children, you do a lot to help parents improve their interactions with their children.

Often parents turn to teachers for advice about ways to deal with frustrating or confusing behavior. When this happens, be sure to respond in a way that acknowledges parents' skills and helps them feel confident and capable. Remind parents that they are "experts" who know more about their children than anyone else. Asking what approaches they use at home helps parents discover or recognize what works for them and their child.

Remind parents of their expertise.

Applying Your Knowledge

In this activity, you will focus on times when you reach out to parents in response to their requests or because you noticed they need your support. Over the next two weeks, keep a journal describing the problem, what the parent asked for or what you saw was needed, how you responded, and what the outcome was. Begin by reading the example on the next page. Then, make as many copies of the blank form as needed to record your experiences reaching out to families.

Reaching Out to Families
(Example)

Child/age: *Larry, 4 years, 3 months*   **Parents:** *Betty and Dan Ingraham*   **Date:** *October 23*

Problem:

Last month a fire caused extensive damage to Larry's house. The family had to escape from the burning house in the middle of the night. Since the fire, Larry has been fearful and unable to fall asleep at night. The family is living in an apartment until their house is repaired.

What parents asked for or what I saw was needed:

Strategies for helping Larry cope with his fears and get to sleep.

My response:

We talked about the problem and I reassured them that Larry's behavior is typical of a young child who has had a scary experience. Mr. Ingraham said that before the fire Larry was more independent and almost fearless. Again, I tried to reassure them by stating that it can take a long time for young children to completely recover from a stressful event. I suggested taking Larry to visit the house to show him that the fire was out and to see how the repairs will make the house safe again. Another suggestion I made was to talk to Larry about his fears. This would confirm that his feelings about the fire are important and recognized. It can also reassure Larry that he is safe now. I mentioned some of the strategies we use to help children relax so they can fall asleep at nap time. I said that we would be sure to have plenty of firefighting props so Larry could use dramatic play to express and handle his feelings.

The outcome:

A week late Ms. Ingraham told me that the relaxation strategies were working—Larry is now finding it easier to fall asleep. He talks about the fire and how scary it was before he goes to sleep each night. Ms. Ingraham says either she or her husband stay with Larry until he falls asleep and he always seems to sleep better after they talk. She also said that visiting the house helped Larry understand that the house was no longer on fire. He was excited to see his room, repainted and almost ready to return. I told her Larry had been engaged in a lot of firefighter play. After putting out fires he says, "The fire is out. The family can come home now."

*Reaching Out to Families**

Child/age: _____ **Parents:** _____ **Date:** _____

Problem:

What parents asked for or what I saw was needed:

My response:

The outcome:

Discuss your experiences reaching out to families with your trainer.

*Make as many copies of this form as you need to record your experiences reaching out to families.

Summarizing Your Progress

You have now completed all of the learning activities for this module. Whether you are an experienced teacher or new to the profession, this module has probably helped you develop new skills in working with families. Before you go on, take a few minutes to summarize what you've learned.

Review your responses to the pre-training assessment for this module. Write a summary of what you learned and list the skills you developed or improved.

If there are topics you would like to know more about, you will find recommended readings listed in the Orientation in Volume I.

Your final step in this module is to complete the knowledge and competency assessments. Let your trainer know when you are ready to schedule the assessments. After you have successfully completed these assessments, you will be ready to start a new module. Congratulations on your progress so far, and good luck with your next module.

Answer Sheet

Communicating Frequently with Parents to Share Information About Their Child's Experiences and Development

1. **Why did Ms. Kim decide not to share the news about Gina's accomplishment?**
    a. *She wanted Gina's parents to be there when their daughter first went down the slide alone.*

    b. *Ms. Kim knew Gina would go to the park with her parents and they would enjoy the surprise.*

2. **What kinds of information will Ms. Kim and the Carters need to share now that Gina has learned to take a risk?**
    a. *Other challenges Gina is trying to master*

    b. *Ways to help Gina learn to take safe risks*

Offering a Variety of Ways for Parents to Participate in Their Child's Life at the Program

1. **How did Ms. Williams help Mr. Bradley find a way to be involved?**
    a. *She asked him about his work and interests.*

    b. *She told him she could tell that he enjoyed cooking.*

2. **How did Ms. Williams help Mr. Bradley prepare for his visit?**
    a. *She told him that the children liked cooking activities.*

    b. *She helped him plan a cooking activity for preschoolers.*

Providing Support to Families

1. **How did Mr. Lopez help Mrs. Thomas understand Marita's behavior?**
    a. *He told her that Marita usually stops crying a few minutes after she leaves.*

    b. *He explained that Marita was getting used to being separated from her parents.*

2. **How did Mr. Lopez help Marita and her mother cope with separation?**
    a. *He scheduled a meeting with Mrs. Thomas to tell her more about separation and what Marita does in the program.*

    b. *He read a book to Marita about what parents do at work.*

Module 12: *Program Management*

Overview

Program management involves:

- Learning about each child's culture, language, family, skills, needs, and interests
- Working as a team to offer an individualized program
- Following administrative policies and procedures

As an early childhood teacher, you play many roles. Your most important role is to provide for children's health and safety, and encourage their development. But as you know, working with young children involves much more. You help children feel competent and self-confident. You support families and help parents balance their work and home responsibilities. And, you and your colleagues use management skills to ensure the smooth operation of your program.

Teachers plan, conduct, and evaluate the program.

Many teachers do not see themselves as managers. Most likely your program has a director who performs a variety of management tasks. The director prepares budgets, makes hiring decisions, develops schedules, supervises staff, and provides training. Yet you and your colleagues are also managers. You work as a team to plan, conduct, and evaluate the program. Performing these managerial tasks allows you to create a supportive learning environment, guide children's learning, and handle other responsibilities.

Effective early childhood programs are both developmentally and individually appropriate. They are based on the child development theories, principles, and milestones that describe, in general, how most young children develop. In addition, they are tailored to respond to the characteristics of each child. Identifying each child's skills, needs, and interests and planning a program that responds to these characteristics is called individualizing.

Teachers use information about each child to plan an appropriate program.

Individualizing is an important part of program management. In some programs, teachers begin getting to know each child by conducting health and developmental screenings at enrollment. Teachers use information collected through these screenings to plan for each child. In addition, screening results may identify signs of possible developmental problems. In these instances, teachers meet with parents and specialists to discuss the screening results and determine whether the child needs a health or developmental assessment to pinpoint areas of strength and need. Information gained through these assessments helps parents, teachers, and specialists plan ways to address the child's needs in the classroom and through other interventions.

To keep track of and respond to each child's changing skills, interests, and needs, many teachers have a system for ongoing assessment. An assessment system might include strategies such as: observing and recording children's behavior, using standardized instruments and checklists, saving samples of children's work, and discussing children's progress with parents and team members. Teachers can use individual portfolios to organize and maintain the information collected through ongoing assessment.

Individualizing is most successful when programs use a team approach. Parents and teachers regularly share information about each child and work together to offer a program that builds on the child's interests, offers appropriate challenges, and reflects the child's family, language, and culture. For example, when Peter's father tells Ms. Thomas how much the family enjoyed a weekend kite festival, she decides to add books on kites to the library area and plan a kite-making activity.

The program's administrative policies and procedures ensure smooth operations.

Early childhood programs need policies and procedures that tell everyone—parents, children, staff, and volunteers—how the program normally operates. For example, program policies might describe the procedures for completing time sheets and required reports. Upholding policies, following procedures, and maintaining appropriate records help to keep the program running smoothly. These activities are part of your management role.

Listed on the following pages are three sets of examples showing how teachers demonstrate their competence in program management. Following each set of examples is a short reading and two questions to answer. When you have finished this section, compare your answers with those on the answer sheet at the end of the module. If your answers are different, discuss them with your trainer. There can be more than one good answer.

Learning About Each Child's Culture, Language, Family, Skills, Needs, and Interests

Communicate with parents often to learn about a child's family life, culture, home language, and unique characteristics.

"Could you please help us make some signs for the classroom? We want to use English and the children's home languages."

Observe each child regularly and use a recording system that is objective, accurate, and avoids labeling.

"Marita and Steven kicked a ball back and forth to each other."

Observe children in different settings and at different times of the day.

"Yesterday I observed Joey playing house with Stephanie. The next time I'll observe him playing by himself."

Collect examples and photographs of work that document children's skills, interests, and progress.

"This photograph shows Lydia cutting an apple with a knife during a cooking activity."

Play and talk with children to learn about their interests and abilities.

"Zach told us a long story at lunchtime about going to the lumber yard with his dad. He said he's going to help his dad build some shelves."

As Eric rips lettuce leaves in half, Mr. Lopez crouches near the table, note pad in hand. "You look ready to make a lettuce roll-up, Eric. What do you want to spread on the leaf—cream cheese or peanut butter?" "Peanut butter!" Eric answers. He places a leaf in his left hand. Then, he picks up a knife, holds it with his fist, and dips it straight down into a jar of peanut butter. He spreads peanut butter partly on the leaf and partly on his palm. "You could lay the leaf on the paper towel to do that," Mr. Lopez says. He demonstrates how to hold the leaf on the paper towel. Eric lays the leaf down. Mr. Lopez makes another suggestion, "You might find a more comfortable way to hold the knife." Eric experiments with several ways to grip the knife until he finds one that works. He rolls up the lettuce leaf and takes a bite. Mr. Lopez takes a photograph of Eric eating the snack, then makes some notes: "Eric chose peanut butter, responded positively to my suggestions, tried different ways to hold the knife, and kept trying until he succeeded."

1.   **How did Mr. Lopez take advantage of a routine to learn about Eric?**

2.   **What did Mr. Lopez learn about Eric?**

Working as a Team to Offer an Individualized Program

Meet regularly with colleagues to plan and evaluate the program.

"Let's discuss next week's trip to the farmer's market and also the props we can add to the house corner."

Use information gathered through observations to plan for individual children and the class.

"Sam and Travis have been quickly finishing all our puzzles lately. What else can we provide to support their eye-hand coordination skills?"

Include parents in planning for their children's growth and development.

"Let me tell you about the foods Pam especially likes in case you want to serve them at home, too."

Use creative thinking skills such as brainstorming in planning and in solving problems.

"We're seeing a lot of superhero play lately. Let's plan some strategies for dealing with this aggressive behavior."

Change the environment, materials, interest areas, routines, and activities to address children's individual characteristics.

"Alexis and Lily have taken quite an interest in bugs this spring. I'll add some Eric Carle books and posters on insects to the library area."

Appreciate and use the strengths of all team members, including teachers, parents, and volunteers.

"Ms. Red Cloud will be our guest next week. She's going to teach the children a special dance."

Ms. Richards and Ms. Kim agree to meet on Friday to talk about the children's outdoor activities and ways to offer new materials and challenges. For the rest of the week, they note the skills used by children outdoors. Ian collects some leaves, Justin makes a network of roads in the sandbox, and Katherine uses long strokes to paint the side of the building with water. Ms. Kim takes photographs of a village several children built from boxes. She notes that Martha is the leader of this project. Ms. Richards tapes voices of the children and a visiting librarian acting out *Ask Mr. Bear*. On Friday the teachers share the information collected during the week and make some plans. Ms. Kim says, "The children really enjoyed building a village. Let's get some more boxes and building props." "I was thinking the same thing," says Ms. Richards. "We could also read and act out other books." The teachers then consider ways to build on individual skills and interests. They think Ian might like to help plant a garden and Justin would enjoy using small cars in the sandbox. They decide to bring the easels outdoors to support Katherine's interest in painting.

1. How did Ms. Kim and Ms. Richards use a team approach to planning?

2. How did the teachers use observation recordings to plan for individual children?

Following Administrative Policies and Procedures

Review program policies and procedures before starting a new task.	"I need to find out how we arrange a trip to the Children's Museum."
Complete management tasks according to a schedule.	"I'd like to review the parent evaluations, Ms. Snyder, so we can respond to their concerns and suggestions."
Use the program's system for reports and recordkeeping.	"Can you keep an eye on the children while I fill out the accident report for Paul's skinned knee."
Keep informed about teachers' job responsibilities.	"I've heard that new regulations for reporting suspected child abuse are being developed. Will we have a staff meeting to discuss them?"
Share ideas about program policies and procedures with colleagues and the supervisor.	"All the classes schedule outdoor play at the same time, so the play yard is pretty crowded. Perhaps we can talk about staggering outdoor times so that we're not all in the play yard at 11:00 every morning."
Answer parents' questions about program operations and refer them to the supervisor, if appropriate.	"Mr. Kaplan, we have to follow the health department's rules for giving children medicine at the program. We need your written permission and a note from a doctor."

Ms. Williams is in the staff lounge reviewing the Staff Handbook. "Even though I've been working here for awhile," she tells Ms. Richards, "I need to review our policies now and then. Do you know where to find information on preparing for a field trip?" Ms. Richards replies, "It's in the section on program activities. The appendix has samples of completed field trip forms and a planning checklist. Before our class went to the fire station, we used the samples to fill out permission forms and to complete the form used to request use of the van." Ms. Williams finds the program activities section and locates the sample forms and checklist. She later submits a field trip request form, contacts the nature center to get information needed to complete the checklist, and sends permission slips home to parents.

1. How did Ms. Williams stay informed about administrative policies and procedures?

2. What tasks did Ms. Williams complete according to the program's policies?

Managing Your Own Life

Many of the things you do at home require use of management skills. Management skills such as observing, individualizing, and planning are used both in home and work settings. For example, when you plan a trip to the grocery store, you might begin by making a list. You consider how many people will be eating each meal, what foods each person likes, and what ingredients you need for each meal. You can do this because you observe each member of your household, include them in planning balanced meals, and follow recipes—the "policies and procedures" for food preparation.

The more orderly and efficient you are in managing your life outside of work, the more time you have to do things other than chores. The more planning you do as a team, the more likely you and your family and friends will enjoy spending time together. Think about times when careful management encourages efficient use of your time.

- You do all of your errands at the same time rather than making several separate trips.

- You make sure you have all the tools and materials you need before you start a project, such as painting a room or repairing a bicycle.

- You keep records of all bills and file receipts promptly.

- You keep emergency numbers posted beside the telephone.

- You plan trips or vacations that are of interest to everyone.

- You borrow a folding table and extra chairs from a neighbor when you are having a crowd over for a special meal or a neighborhood meeting.

- You make a list of what you <u>have</u> to do (have the car inspected), what you'd <u>like</u> to do (get a haircut), and what you <u>can</u> do later (shop for new running shoes).

- You remember the importance of relaxation and make time for exercise and spending time with friends and family.

Organizing your time and your environment to work <u>for</u> you rather than <u>against</u> you helps you manage more effectively.

Use the chart on the following page to record something you've already done to manage your life more effectively, and to plan a strategy you can use for solving a frustrating situation. The chart begins with an example.

Frustrating Situation	Solution
I used to spend time practically every day searching for my keys.	*I put a hook on the inside wall by the door. Now I hang my keys there every day when I get home*

When you have finished this overview section, complete the pre-training assessment. Refer to the glossary at the end of the module if you need definitions of the terms used.

Pre-Training Assessment

Listed below are the skills teachers use as program managers. Think about whether you do these things regularly, sometimes, or not enough. Place a check in one of the boxes on the right for each skill listed. Then discuss your answers with your trainer.

Learning About Each Child's Culture, Language, Family, Skills, Needs, and Interests

	I Do This:	Regularly	Sometimes	Not Enough
1.	Communicate with parents often to learn about a child's family life, culture, home language, and unique characteristics.	☐	☐	☐
2.	Observe each child regularly and use a recording system that is objective, accurate, and avoids labeling.	☐	☐	☐
3.	Observe children in different settings and at different times of the day.	☐	☐	☐
4.	Collect examples and photographs of work that document children's skills, interests, and progress.	☐	☐	☐
5.	Play and talk with children to learn about their interests and abilities.	☐	☐	☐

Working as a Team Member to Offer an Individualized Program

		Regularly	Sometimes	Not Enough
6.	Meet regularly with colleagues to plan and evaluate the program.	☐	☐	☐
7.	Use information gathered through observations to plan for individual children and the class.	☐	☐	☐

Working as a Team Member to Offer an Individualized Program
(continued)

	I Do This:	Regularly	Sometimes	Not Enough
8. Include parents in planning for their children's growth and development.		☐	☐	☐
9. Use creative thinking skills such as brainstorming in planning and in solving problems.		☐	☐	☐
10. Change the environment, materials, interest areas, routines, and activities to address children's individual characteristics.		☐	☐	☐
11. Appreciate and use the strengths of all team members, including teachers, parents, and volunteers.		☐	☐	☐

Following Administrative Policies and Procedures

	Regularly	Sometimes	Not Enough
12. Review program policies and procedures before starting a new task.	☐	☐	☐
13. Complete management tasks according to a schedule.	☐	☐	☐
14. Use the program's system for reports and recordkeeping.	☐	☐	☐
15. Keep informed about teachers' job responsibilities.	☐	☐	☐

Following Administrative Policies and Procedures

(continued)

	I Do This:	Regularly	Sometimes	Not Enough
16. Share ideas about program policies and procedures with colleagues and the supervisor.		☐	☐	☐
17. Answer parents' questions about program operations and refer them to the supervisor, if appropriate		☐	☐	☐

Review your responses, then list three to five skills you would like to improve or topics you would like to learn more about. When you finish this module, you can list examples of your new or improved knowledge and skills.

Begin the learning activities for Module 12, Program Management.

Learning Activities

I. Using a Systematic Approach to Observing and Recording

In this activity you will learn to:

- Complete observation recordings that are objective, accurate, and complete
- Work with colleagues to regularly observe and record each child's behavior

---

Observing children is an ongoing process for people with children in their lives. They watch infants play and thrill at seeing them respond to others with cooing, smiles, and laughter. They share stories with parents and grandparents about toddlers' first words and expanding physical skills. They watch preschoolers as they learn to play cooperatively with others.

Observations are a useful way to get to know individual children—what they like to do, what skills they are developing, who they like to be with. It helps to have a focus for the observation. For example, you might want to learn how different children respond to new materials or explore a new interest area.

Early childhood teachers observe children for a variety of reasons.

To determine each child's interests, strengths, and needs. "Bobby likes to organize new items on the science table. He sorts collections in egg cartons."

To plan an individualized program. "There's been a lot of interest in dinosaurs lately. Let's talk about using a dinosaur theme in several interest areas next week."

To document each child's progress. "I've recorded several examples showing Sarah's use of fine motor skills."

To address a challenging behavior. "I reviewed my notes, and it seems that Jim hits other children when he doesn't know how to enter a group."

To report children's progress to parents, colleagues, and specialists. "Ms. White, I'd like to share some of my observations of Jared's ability to solve problems. My notes show how his skills have developed since we last met."

To evaluate the effects of the environment and activities. "Please bring your observations of children's use of the reading area so we can discuss what's working well and what we might want to change."

Teachers use the information gained through observation to provide a quality program that meets individual and developmental needs. They share information with colleagues and parents and use it to plan activities, add or change materials, and guide their personal interactions with children.

Observation recordings must be complete, accurate, and objective.

The primary purpose of an observation is to collect accurate and useful information about a child. This requires a careful, systematic approach. You and your colleagues need to watch, listen to, and write down what children do and say as it happens, according to a particular method. The information you write down is called a *recording*.

To be complete, recordings must include several facts. These are:

- the child's name and age;

- the observer's name;

- the date of the observation;

- the setting (where the activity is taking place and who is involved—for example, "Debby and Ronisha sit on the floor in the library area looking at books"); and

- the behavior (what the child you are observing does and says).

Observation is an ongoing process.

A single observation cannot provide a complete picture of a child. Children, like adults, do not behave in the same ways all the time. Illness, reactions to events at home or the program, and other factors affect what children do and say. Several brief (five- to ten-minute) observations can provide the information needed to determine a child's interests, skills, and needs. You can observe during indoor and outdoor activities over a period of time, as children arrive and leave the program, and as they move from one activity to another, clean up, set the table for meals, and interact with other children and staff. Children change over time; therefore, observation is an ongoing process. Work with your colleagues to develop a schedule for conducting regular observations of all the children in the class.

A collection of observation recordings completed over a period of time should address all areas of a child's development. A single observation, however, can provide information about several areas at one time, particularly if the observation is focused on one or more aspects of the child's development. For example, you might observe a child's:

- fine motor skills

- self-discipline

- thinking and problem-solving skills

- self-help skills

- gross motor skills

- role during cooperative play

- emerging reading and writing skills

- self-confidence

- creativity

- social skills

When you have collected several recordings on a child, you can make comments such as the following:

- "Tara can retell a familiar story in her own words."

- "Sarah can build a tower with the unit and double-unit blocks, balance blocks of different sizes, and use a variety of blocks and unit cubes to add detail to her structures."

- "Leo can match primary and secondary colors, name 'red' and 'black,' and mix white paint with other colors to make lighter shades."

To draw conclusions such as these, you must be sure that your recordings are objective and accurate. Objective and accurate recordings include only the facts about what is seen and heard. They do not include labels or judgments. Compare the following excerpts from an observation of a child at the water play table.

Example 1: Objective and Accurate

Tony moved the water back and forth with the funnel. The water splashed inside and outside the basin. Some fell on other children's shoes. Tony began to giggle.

Example 1 is an objective recording. It includes only the facts of what Tony did ("moved the water back and forth"), what happened ("the water splashed inside and outside the basin"), and his reaction ("Tony began to giggle"). Accurate recordings include all the facts about what a child does and says in the order they happen. Information is not omitted or recorded out of order. Read the following two examples about the same observation.

Example 2: Not Objective

Tony was bad today. He angrily splashed the water on the floor and on other children at the water basin. Then he laughed at them.

Example 2 is not an objective recording. It uses a label ("bad") and makes judgments ("he angrily splashed the water," "he laughed at them"). Given what the teacher saw, he or she could not know what Tony was laughing at or whether he acted in anger. A recording that he was "bad" does not tell anything useful about his behavior, since "bad" is a word that means different things to different people.

Example 3: Not Accurate

Tony stood at the water basin looking to see if a teacher was watching him. He giggled and began to splash water on other children.

In Example 3 a fact is added that has not been observed ("looking to see if a teacher was watching him"). A fact is omitted ("Tony moved the water back and forth with the funnel"). And a fact is written out of order ("He giggled and began to splash water. . .").

Making an objective and accurate recording such as Example 1 requires practice. Opportunities for taking brief notes are present throughout the day. With practice, you will become skilled at completing recordings as you play with, care for, and eat with young children. Here are some examples.

Examples

Child: *Natalia* **Age:** *3 yrs, 3 mos.* **Date:** *February 4*

Setting:

Near the entrance, in cubby area, at morning arrival. Natalia with her Grandfather.

Behavior:

Natalia enters, holding her grandfather's hand. G-fthr pulls her parka off over her head. Natalia smiles at G-fthr as he pats her hair down. She sits on the floor and silently lifts her foot. G-fthr kneels down and takes her boots off. Then G-fthr leaves and Natalia stands by her cubby, looking around the room.

Child: *Anthony* **Age:** *4 yrs, 4 mos.* **Date:** *August 30*

Setting:

Outdoors, Anthony is kneeling by the 18" high slice of tree stump, with Ms. Ash (volunteer).

Behavior:

Anthony rubs the palm of his right hand on the tree stump. He traces a tree ring with his right index finger. He picks up the hammer in his right hand and a roofing nail in his left hand. Holding the nail between his left index finger and thumb, he begins to pound the nail into the tree stump. Looks up at Ms. Ash—says to her, "My Dad is building new steps on our house."

Child: *Julie* **Age:** *5 yrs.* **Date:** *February 14*

Setting:

Table toys area, Julie @ table with parquetry blocks & patterns.

Behavior:

Julie dumps blocks out of basket loudly. Takes pattern card. Looks at card, lays it down on table. Moves blocks, picks up rd, places it on matching shape on card. Picks up bl, places on matching shape. Continues, picking up blocks & matching each block to pattern..

Here are some suggestions for recording your observations of children:[1]

Use these tips for recording observations of children.

- Write what you see, not what you think is happening.

- Jot down notes frequently. Carry a pad or index cards and pencil with you.

- Use short phrases rather than complete sentences, to save time.

- Abbreviate what a child said—don't try to write all the words, but get the gist of what is said.

- Describe how a child is doing or saying something.

- Develop a system of abbreviations or initials; for instance, for areas of the room use *qu-quiet*, *dr-dramatic play*.

- Use arrows to indicate movement.

- Make diagrams of the environment showing the child in relation to the setting, other children in the room, and adults.

- Underline words to indicate a particular intensity (for instance, "said <u>loudly</u>").

In addition to recording in an objective and accurate way, teachers must be sure that they see and hear what others see and hear. Eyewitness accounts of accidents demonstrate how several people, seeing exactly the same event, have different stories to tell. This may happen to you as well.

To ensure accuracy, compare your observations with others.

For example, one teacher sees Linda feeding her baby doll dirt and Julie taking the doll from her and trying to drown it. Another, watching the same children, observes Linda smearing mud on a doll and Julie giving it a bath. Knowledge of what a child has done in the past, your feelings about certain behaviors, the child's tone of voice, and many other factors can influence what you observe and record.

It is useful to compare your recordings about a child to those made by a colleague. If they are similar, your are maintaining an accurate record. If they are different, the information collected may be not useful. Two teachers with different perceptions of a child's behavior should observe the child together over a short period of time. After each observation they can compare their recordings and discuss what they have seen. This method helps ensure accurate recordings. If the recordings still differ greatly, your director or trainer can assist in solving the problem.

Applying Your Knowledge

In this learning activity you practice observing and recording. You can use the form on the following page, or one of your own design. Select a child to observe over a one-week period. Observe the child for five to ten minutes each per day. On at least two occasions, ask your director, a colleague, or your trainer to observe the same child at the same time as you are observing. Compare your recordings after each joint observation and at the end of the week.

[1] Adapted from materials developed by the Head Start Resource and Training Center (College Park, MD: University of Maryland, 1975).

Make several copies of this form before recording your observations.

OBSERVATION FORM

Child: _____   **Age:** _____

Observer: _____   **Date:** _____

Setting: _____

Behavior:

Check to see if your recordings are objective, accurate, and similar to those of your co-observer. If your recordings differ and are not objective and accurate, select another child to observe and repeat this learning activity. Ask your trainer to observe with you again and record information about the same child. Then discuss your recordings with your trainer and begin the next learning activity.

II. Individualizing the Program

> **In this learning activity you will learn to:**
>
> • Observe children to learn about their culture, family, strengths, needs, and interests
>
> • Tailor the program to respond to children's individual characteristics

High-quality early childhood programs are based on two understandings: the typical developmental characteristics of three- to five-year olds and the characteristics of individual children. The environment, materials, activities, and interactions between adults and children in such programs reflect children's developmental levels and respond to each child's culture, family, strengths, needs, and interests. For example, while preparing for a neighborhood walk, Ms. Williams and Ms. Frilles use what they know about preschoolers and what they know about individual children.

High-quality early childhood programs reflect and respond to children's stages of development and individual needs.

Preschoolers can act without thinking, so the teachers make a group-walk rope to keep the children safe while walking on busy streets. Next, they fill a wagon with large balls, buckets, and shovels—items enjoyed by most preschoolers, including the children in their class. They add some items with individual needs, interests, and skills in mind. LaShon and Tony like quiet activities, so Ms. Williams puts large chalk for drawing on sidewalks and picture books in the wagon. Several children play games with rules, so Ms. Frilles brings a T-ball stand and plastic bats and balls. Knowing that even with the rope, Carlos and Andy have difficulty staying with the class, the teachers hold their hands on the walk to and from the park.

To offer an individualized program, you need to know what makes each child special. Each day, as you talk and play with children, you learn a lot about them: Alicia is a leader on the playground and during dramatic play; Reynaldo is learning to share; Teresa changes best friends several times a day; Berta's vocabulary is expanding rapidly in both Spanish and English. Through observations, discussions with colleagues, and one-on-one conversations with children, you keep up-to-date on how children are growing and changing. Getting to know children also includes learning about their cultures, languages, and families. Many of the strategies for establishing partnerships with families described in Module 11, Families, also help you recognize children's unique characteristics.

Teachers don't have to provide separate materials and activities for each child.

Individualizing the program does not mean you have to provide a separate set of materials or plan one-on-one activities for each child. Instead, you can respond to individual children during your regular planning process. To do this, you and your colleagues review observation notes, examine samples of children's work, and reflect on recent events and interactions. You think about what individual children enjoy doing, what materials they use, what skills they are developing, and what's happening in their lives. Here is an example of teachers planning an individualized program.

Ms. Thomas says she has observed three-year-old Brian trying to pedal a tricycle. He only just reaches the pedals, so he is having a hard time. Mr. Lopez agrees—he, too has noticed Brian's efforts. They discuss Brian's learning style. Rather than give up in frustration, Brian keeps trying to figure out a way to make the pedals work. Mr. Lopez reviews the checklist he used last month to assess Brian's physical skills and notes that last month Brian was not using the pedals at all. Ms. Thomas shares that Brian's house has a long paved driveway. His grandmother has mentioned that there is an old tricycle in their garage that needs to be repaired. The teachers develop a plan.

Background. Brian has a tricycle at home and a place to ride it. Ms. Thomas will tell Brian's grandmother about his efforts and ask if the tricycle has been repaired. If so, she will suggest encouraging Brian to ride at home.

Need. Brian needs to practice riding on a tricycle that is an appropriate size. Mr. Lopez will exchange the larger tricycle with a smaller tricycle from another classroom.

Skill. Brian is self-motivated and works hard to meet challenges. Everyone will let Brian know they realize he is working hard to master riding the tricycle.

Interest. Brian seems to really like trike riding.

Teachers will continue observing Brian to see if the above plans are effective. When Brian masters trike riding, they will build on his skills and interests by offering props such as a firefighter hat, street signs, or cones to ride around.

In the above example, the teachers responded to Brian by incorporating strategies within their existing approach and schedule. They didn't take Brian away from the class to teach him to ride. Instead, they planned to offer appropriate equipment, work with his family, offer encouragement, and build on his interests. These are all strategies that contribute to individualizing. The chart that follows provides some examples of how to individualize the different elements of your program. As you read this chart you will notice that many of the developmentally appropriate practices you already use contribute to an individualized program.

Individualizing Strategies

Program Element	How You Can Individualize
Daily Schedule (the sequence and timing of daily events)	Include long periods of choice time so children can decide what to do, what to use, and with whom to play. To help children pay attention and participate in group time, divide the class into several small groups. Include the same teacher and children in the groups each day.
Materials (toys, books, equipment, and other items available for the children's use)	Include materials that reflect children's cultures, languages, and families, including books, tapes, signs, and labels. Add new materials to the interest areas in response to the children's changing needs, interests, and skill levels.
Environment (indoor and outdoor interest areas and arrangement of furniture and equipment)	Create a new area or offer a prop box that responds to the children's changing interests. Set up a tent outdoors so the children who have been using the camping prop box can extend their play.
Routines (daily events such as clean-up, meals, and naptime)	Serve milk or juice in small pitchers so children can pour their own drinks or ask for help. Use techniques recommended by parents to help children fall asleep—rub a back, sing a song, sit near a child.
Transitions (the times between scheduled routines and events)	Play word games with children who have difficulty waiting. Allow child who is engrossed in an activity to continue playing while the rest of the class cleans up.
Small-group activities (times when children choose to join in an activity planned and led by an adult)	Plan activities that allow children to make choices, such as making collages, blowing bubbles, or moving to music. Plan activities such as cooking and singing songs that incorporate children's cultures, languages, and families.
Interactions (verbal and nonverbal communications between teachers and children)	Recognize when to help children resolve differences and when to allow them to solve their own problems. Tailor support offered a child to the ways he or she typically handles frustration and challenges.

Including children with disabilities can be a rewarding experience.

As required by federal legislation, many classrooms include children with disabilities. Disabilities might be developmental, such as mental retardation; physical, such as muscular dystrophy; a health impairment, such as human immunodeficiency virus disease (HIV) or asthma; a learning difference, such as attention deficit disorder (ADD); or a hearing, visual, or speech/language disorder. As they do for all children, teachers, parents, and administrators work together to identify and respond to the child's skills, needs, and interests.

When successfully implemented, including children with disabilities in a child development program can be a very rewarding experience for everyone involved. Inclusion provides an environment in which all children can succeed. It helps children with disabilities gain independence and enables all children to develop comfortable, fair relationships with others. It teaches children to resist stereotypes and name calling. Children with disabilities are children first. They thrive in an environment that accepts differences and where adults strive to meet each child's individual needs.

Consider your own feelings about persons with disabilities.

To offer an individualized program for a child with a disability, teachers may need to review their own attitudes and behaviors towards persons with disabilities. Some typical responses include:

- Avoiding or ignoring the child, "Can Carrie be in your group? I never know what to say to her."

- Feeling sad, "Every time I see her walker, my eyes start watering."

- Believing the disability can be fixed, "He'll outgrow his hearing problems."

- Denying there is a disability, "Lots of children can't pay attention."

Although these are commonly held attitudes and behaviors, they do a disservice to the child. To support the child's development, teachers must take time to identify, acknowledge, and address their own personal feelings.

It's important to get to know the child and learn about the disability.

When a child with a disability enrolls in your program, you need to learn about the child and his or her family as well as the characteristics, effects, and treatment related to the disability. Here are some sources of information:

The child. Make a home visit and/or invite the child to the classroom. This will help you get to know the child as a person, rather than focusing primarily on the disability.

The child's parents. Meet with the parents to learn about the child's favorite activities, overall level of development, strengths, and interests. Parents are the best source of information about the child's experiences and developmental history.

Doctors, specialists, and previous teachers. With the parents' written consent, your program can contact professionals who have provided treatment and supported the child's development. The information they provide will contribute to a total picture of the child's characteristics. If addressing the child's needs is beyond your expertise and experience, seek advice from these specialists. You cannot be expected to know about every type of disability.

Professional resources. Use books, journals, and other resources to research the range of abilities and needs that a child with a particular disability could have. Remember though, that the range of individual differences among children with the same disability is as great as the differences among children in general.

Contact regional and national support groups and clearinghouses. There are many excellent resources. Here are a few:

American Academy of Pediatrics
Department C
141 Northwest Point Boulevard
PO Box 927
Elks Grove Village, IL 60009

American Psychiatric Press
1400 K Street N.W.
Washington, DC 20005

Children and Adults with Attention Deficit Disorders (CH.A.D.D.)
499 N.W. 70th Avenue, Suite 309
Plantation, FL 33317

Council of Administrators of Special Education, Inc.
615 16th Street, N.W.
Albuquerque, NM 87104

ERIC Clearinghouse for Handicapped and Gifted Children
Council for Exceptional Children
1920 Association Drive
Reston, VA 22091

Learning Disabilities Association (LDA)
4156 Library Road
Pittsburgh, PA 15234

National Association of School Psychologists
8455 Colesville Road
Suite 1000
Silver Spring, MD 20910

National Information Center for Children and Youth
with Disabilities (NICHCY)
PO Box 1492
Washington, DC 20013

Woodbine House
5615 Fishers Lane
Rockville, MD 20852

Once you have an understanding of the child and the disability, you can meet with your colleagues, the child's parents, and specialists to plan an individualized program. In addition, you may need to make accommodations such as rearranging the environment to make the pathways wide enough for a wheelchair, creating books of textured fabrics to provide tactile experiences, or providing several large-print versions of books for a child with a visual impairment. Several additional examples of accommodations appear in Module 3, Learning Environment.

Applying Your Knowledge

In this learning activity you conduct observations of two children for a five- to ten-minute period at least once a day, for a week. Your recordings should include at least the information asked for on the form provided in Learning Activity I. You can use copies of that form, a notepad, or index cards.

Make two copies of the blank Individualizing Summary Form. Record what you already know about each child in the first section of the form. Then, conduct your observations. At the end of the week review your recordings, summarize what you learned about the children, and plan ways to individualize the program.

Read the example of a completed Individualizing Summary Form on the next page. Then, begin this activity.

Individualizing Summary Form

(Example)

Child: *Silvio*   **Age:** *3 years, 6 months*   **Date:** *March 15*

Describe what you know about the child's culture, home language, and family:

Silvio's parents are Italian-American, born in the United States. His grandparents, who live nearby, were born in Italy and came to this country as young adults. Silvio hears both Italian and English at home. His grandparents talk to him about life in Italy. His grandfather has promised to take Silvio out on his boat, but his parents want to wait until Silvio is a little older.

Provide some examples of this child's skills and strengths:

Silvio is cooperative and follows classroom rules with only a few reminders. He can balance blocks, fill and pour sand and water from a container, draw with markers and crayons, listen to a short story, set the table, settle himself for a nap, and roll and pound playdough.

List some skills this child is learning:

Silvio is learning to participate in group play and activities, use props such as the sifter, baster, and rolling pin, use eating utensils, and participate in a conversation.

Describe this child's favorite materials, activities, and special interests:

Silvio's favorite activities are sand and water play and block building. He's very interested in boats. He points to pictures of boats in books and says that his Grandpa has a boat.

Conduct your observations, then use the recordings to answer the following questions:

How did this child usually play (alone, with several friends, in a group)?

He frequently played alone. Sometimes he played with Roy or Clara. He also joined a group at the sand/water table and outdoors in the sandbox.

What materials, activities, and interest areas did this child select?

Indoors he chose the block area along with Roy or Clara and spent a lot of time at the sand/water table (prefers sand to water play). He rolled playdough with a thick, short dowel. Outdoors he used shovels, buckets, and pouring containers.

What skills did this child use?

He stayed involved with his play when alone or with one or two others. He balanced objects while building, poured without spilling, asked teachers for help when needed, and talked to Roy and Clara.

What did this child find challenging?

Joining and staying with a group at play. Large muscle activities, such as throwing and kicking a ball and balancing on one foot. Talking to children other than Roy and Clara.

Use what you already knew about this child, and what you learned through your observations to develop an individualized plan. You may not need to individualize all program elements.

Individualized Plan for: *Silvio*

Program Element	How You Can Individualize
Daily Schedule (the sequence and timing of daily events)	*No changes needed.*
Materials (toys, books, equipment, and other items available for the children's use)	*Provide large trucks in sand box for Silvio to lift and push.* *Provide more books about boats.*
Environment (indoor and outdoor interest areas and arrangement of furniture and equipment)	*Ask Silvio's family to suggest some props and dress-up clothes to include in the dramatic play area to encourage his participation.*
Routines (daily events such as clean-up, meals, and naptime)	*Sit with Silvio and model using utensils. Offer tips to help him master use of a spoon and fork.*
Transitions (the times between scheduled routines and events)	*No changes needed.*
Small-group activities (times when children choose to join in an activity planned and led by an adult)	*Invite Silvio to play balancing games outdoors as well as indoors.* *Ask Silvio's family for some simple recipes we could use in a cooking activity. Encourage Silvio to join in.*
Interactions (verbal and nonverbal communications between teachers and children)	*Join in sand and water play, start a conversation with the children there, and encourage Silvio to talk, too.* *Ask a child with more advanced play skills to join an activity with Silvio, Roy, and Clara.*

*Individualizing Summary Form**

Child: _____ **Age:** _____ **Date:** _____

Describe what you know about the child's culture, home language, and family:

Provide some examples of this child's skills and strengths:

List some skills this child is learning:

Describe this child's favorite materials, activities, and special interests:

*Make two copies of the form.

Conduct your observations, then use the recordings to answer the following questions:

How did this child usually play (alone, with several friends, in a group)?

What materials, activities, and interest areas did this child select?

What skills did this child use?

What did this child find challenging?

Use what you already knew about this child, and what you learned through your observations to develop an individualized plan. You may not need to individualize all program elements.

Individualized Plan for: _____

Program Element	How You Can Individualize
Daily Schedule (the sequence and timing of daily events)	
Materials (toys, books, equipment, and other items available for the children's use)	
Environment (indoor and outdoor interest areas and arrangement of furniture and equipment)	
Routines (daily events such as clean-up, meals, and naptime)	
Transitions (the times between scheduled routines and events)	
Small-group activities (times when children choose to join in an activity planned and led by an adult)	
Interactions (verbal and nonverbal communications between teachers and children)	

Discuss this activity with your colleagues and trainer.

III: Creating and Using Portfolios

> **In this learning activity you will learn to:**
>
> • Collect work samples and other items in a portfolio to document a child's progress and changing characteristics
>
> • Use portfolios to share information with parents, plan for individual children, and involve children in self-assessment

An important part of a teacher's management responsibilities is keeping track of children's growing skills, changing interests, and experiences that might affect their development. Individualizing relies on current information about each child. One way to ensure that your program responds to children as individuals is to create and use portfolios to plan ways to support children's development.

Portfolios include samples of children's work and information collected from a number of other sources to document a child's activities, progress, and interests. The items in a portfolio are concrete illustrations of a child's efforts, achievements, and learning style. Portfolios can include observation recordings, anecdotal records, notes from parents, developmental checklists, examples of a child's work, and other items that contribute to an up-to-date portrait of the child.

Work samples are records of children's progress.

Work samples are the major component of a portfolio. Teachers save these items, such as a child's paintings or photographs of the child participating in different activities, as records of a child's individual progress. Here are some examples of work samples that could be included in a portfolio:

Work completed at the program or at home:

- drawings, paintings, collages, weavings

- writing (scribbles, labels, letters, names and words, numbers)

- a book dictated to a teacher and/or illustrated by the child

- a book made by the child

- computer printouts

- graphs of a science experiment

Photographs of a child's work and play activities:

- block building or other block structure

- freshly-baked loaf of bread

- shells sorted by size and color

Photographs showing a child's accomplishments:

- standing on the top of the climber

- tying shoelaces

- completing a puzzle

Photographs showing a child involved in everyday routines and activities:

- using a serving spoon

- brushing teeth

- listening to a story

Written records of a child's interests:

- questions—asked or answered during a small group activity

- favorite books

- descriptions of drawings and other work

- comments after a field trip

Video and audio recordings of a child's use of language:

- singing, telling a story, or playing with others

- conversing during a family-style meal

- engaging in dramatic play

- identifying a solution to a problem

Teachers, parents, and children each play a role in selecting work samples and other items to include in the portfolio. Parents might contribute scribble writing done at home, descriptions of the child playing with a younger sibling, or examples of the child's use of self-discipline. Teachers can collect work samples and other items that illustrate the child's creativity, interests, and progress towards developing cognitive, physical, socio-emotional, and language skills. Children can help teachers and parents select items for the portfolio. To help children evaluate

A child's portfolio creates a balanced picture of development.

their own work and activities, ask questions such as: "Which of these books that we read this week was the one that made you feel that you were in the story?" "Which photograph of your block buildings would you like to put in your portfolio?" "Which of these paintings was most fun to do?" The items in the portfolio should present a balanced picture of the child's development through participation in all interest areas, indoors and outdoors, and all parts of the daily schedule—routines, transitions, choice time, and group time.

It's a good idea to try to add something to each child's portfolio every two weeks. Teachers usually share this responsibility, because each has a different perspective about a child. You may choose to set a staggered schedule for updating portfolios so you don't have to do them all at once.

Teachers use portfolios in several ways:

- To share information with parents: "It's easy to see Drew's progress when we compare the drawings he made six months ago to the ones he made last week."

- To review a child's progress, set new goals, and plan individualized strategies: "This videotape shows Aurora telling an imaginative but some-what confusing story. We'll help her expand her skills so her stories are easier to follow."

- To help children evaluate their work and recognize their own skills and progress: "Tell me about what you and Stacey are doing here in this photograph."

Portfolios should be organized collections.

Portfolios start with a few items but grow quickly! You will need containers large enough to hold the items and a system for organizing them. Containers should be of a size that fits in the locked storage file or closet where portfolios will be kept. Accordion files, magazine files, empty pizza boxes (unused, donated by a local business), or plastic containers with lids might meet your needs. File the portfolio items by date and group them by categories that make sense for your program. For example, you might group them by activity, type of development, or interest area.

Applying Your Knowledge

In this learning activity you create a portfolio for one of the children you observed in Learning Activity I or II. Review your records for the child and think about what else is needed to create a portfolio. During the next two weeks, collect items for the portfolio, with input from the child and his or her parents. If needed, refer to the examples of portfolio items in this learning activity. Develop a system for storing and organizing the portfolio items. List the portfolio items and explain why you collected them on the blank form that follows. Begin by reviewing the example that follows.

Creating a Portfolio
(Example)

Child: *Shanti*   **Age:** *4 years*   **Dates:** *February 12—23*

Describe the items you collected for this child's portfolio and explain why they represent the child's skills, interests, progress, or other relevant characteristics.

Portfolio Item	Why It Represents This Child
Easel painting of suns	*Shanti learned to mix a new color-orange. She has been painting a lot of pictures with suns and picked this painting as her favorite.*
Notes on conversation with Shanti's mother about trip to doctor	*Shanti used to be very fearful about going to the doctor because she hated getting shots. Her mother said she has overcome this fear.*
Photograph of Shanti and other children playing in the snow and written description of this experience and related activities she enjoyed	*When asked, Shanti said that playing in the snow was "the most fun I ever had." She had never seen snow before so this was a special experience. She listened to stories about snow and joined others in measuring snow before and after it melted.*

Describe your system for storing and organizing the portfolio items.

I used a legal size cardboard file box with a lid and handles as the portfolio container. I organized the items by area of development.

Creating a Portfolio

Child: _____ **Age:** _____ **Dates:** _____

Describe the items you collected for this child's portfolio and explain why they represent the child's skills, interests, progress, or other relevant characteristics.

Portfolio Item	Why It Represents This Child

Describe your system for storing and organizing the portfolio items.

Share the portfolio with the child's parents. Then, review the portfolio with your trainer and colleagues. Discuss how the items you included complement your observation recordings. You might also meet with your director to consider how to set up a system for creating, updating, and using portfolios for all of the children in the program.

IV. Working as a Team to Plan the Program

In this learning activity you will learn to:

- Develop daily, weekly, and long-range plans
- Evaluate the effectiveness of your plans

Planning involves thinking about what you want to do and how you will do it. It starts by considering children's recent activities and experiences and thinking of ways to build on their interests. When you plan you are better prepared. You have sufficient materials, and are more easily able to involve children in activities suited to their skills and interests. As a result, the program runs more smoothly.

Planning helps you be well-prepared for each day.

Everyone who cares for and interacts with children at the program—teachers, parents, and volunteers—should be part of the planning team. Many programs regularly include parents and volunteers in planning and implementing the program. The more involved in planning all team members are, the more likely they are to realize the important role they play in carrying out the plans.

Teaching teams often include individuals with particular strengths, interests, and talents. Ideally, each member's skills complement those of others on the team. One teacher might speak several languages; another might be a gifted storyteller. A regular volunteer might be an artist with a natural ability to share her talent with others. A parent could be a carpenter who can bring the program's old equipment back to life. Each member contributes something special to the team.

Two types of planning are useful for early childhood programs: long-range and weekly. Long-range planning involves thinking ahead—perhaps a month or more—to consider what materials, activities, and experiences you want to offer the children. For example, if you are going to set up a grocery store next to the house corner next month, you need to plan ahead. Your plan might list tasks such as the following:

Long-range planning covers a month or more ahead.

- Collect empty food containers and cans, and shopping bags for the store.

- Send a letter to parents asking them to save these items, too.

- Get the cash register and play money from the storage closet.

- Gather writing materials so children can make signs for the store.

- Call the local grocery store to schedule a behind-the-scenes tour.

- Ask the librarian to suggest and reserve some books about foods and shopping.

Long-range planning allows you to respond to changing seasons or to arrange a special event such as a trip, a family picnic, or a visit by a special guest. Thinking and planning ahead ensure that special events really happen.

Weekly plans are also needed.

Weekly plans are more detailed than long-range plans, but weekly planning does not need to be a lengthy process. However, finding time for planning can be difficult. In many programs, teachers who work together hold planning meetings before children arrive, after they leave, or during rest time.

In most programs, teachers use a format to guide their planning meeting and to record their weekly plans. However, what works well for one teaching team may not work for another. A good place to start is to ask yourself, "What do I need to plan that will help me be a better manager?"

Consider these planning categories.

The following categories may be useful for you and your colleagues.

Special focus—a theme or topic related to children's interests and experiences that guides planning of materials and activities for a week or more, depending on children's responses. The team plans a variety of activities and selects materials that are based on the theme. For example, after a trip to a neighborhood pet store, the children explore the theme, "fish." The teachers add plastic fish props to the block corner, plan a movement activity so children can swim like fish, and drape a net over a corner of the library area and stock the area with stories about fish.

Group time—a 10 to 15-minute meeting when children participate in an adult-led experience, such as reading a story or setting rules for using new playground equipment. Group time activities can build on the current theme or an ongoing project. Group time is also used to discuss the day's activities—near the beginning of the day or at the end. Teachers describe the plans for the day, note changes to the schedule, talk about upcoming events, and summarize what the children did. Children talk about what they did at home, their plans for the day, and activities they particularly enjoyed.

Small group activities—open-ended experiences for three to six children at a time, planned and led by teachers. Activities may support the special focus, respond to children's interests, coincide with the time of year—in the fall, a walk to collect seeds or dried grasses—or they may simply be activities the teachers think the children will enjoy, such as making applesauce or planting a garden. The teachers' special interests or talents are valuable here. An adult's enthusiasm for music or weaving is quickly communicated to children and can extend the children's interests.

Changes to the environment—adding or removing props or materials, or changing the arrangement of indoor or outdoor space. For example, teachers might add new transportation props to the block area, a collection of keys to sort and classify in the table toy area, or move the easels outdoors on warm days.

Outdoor activities—the choices offered to children in the program's outdoor space. Including the outdoors as a separate category helps teachers plan for outdoor experiences as thoughtfully as they do for indoor ones.

Teacher responsibilities—the specific tasks each teacher will complete to ensure that the plan can be implemented. For example, if the plan includes blowing bubbles outdoors, someone needs to collect a variety of frames (old eye glasses with lenses removed, berry containers, plastic 6-pack rings) and mix the soap solution. It is important to agree on who will do what and post a list reminding people of their assignments.

Target children—those children who have special skills, needs, or interests that teachers want to address during a given week. For example, a child whose mother is about to have a baby might need extra one-on-one time and books about new babies and older brothers or sisters. Target children also include individuals that teachers plan to observe during the week. To ensure confidentiality, do not include this category in the written plan posted on the bulletin board.

Teachers have many tools and strategies they can use to help them plan. First, they know typical characteristics of children at a given age and stage of development. Second, teachers have specific knowledge about each child. Information gathered through conversations with parents and daily interactions with children guide the planning process. Knowing, for example, that a child is going on a camping vacation, teachers can add backpacks to the house corner and books about camping to the library. In addition, daily observations provide important clues as to what changes are needed in the environment and other program practices.

> **Knowledge of children's individual and developmental characteristics guides the planning process.**

Anyone who has worked with young children knows that even the best plans don't always work out as intended. Relax and enjoy the experience when a walk to a neighborhood playground becomes a trip to a construction site where the dirt movers and cranes have captured children's interests. Join in the fun when the children find different ways to use materials than what you had planned. Extend the outdoor playtime when children are fully involved in a project or a dramatic play scenario. Teachers who work with this age group must be very flexible.

> **Early childhood teachers must be flexible.**

In many early childhood programs, teachers meet at the end of each day to discuss what happened. Questions such as the following can guide your discussions:

> **Evaluation is the last step in the planning process.**

- What did the children do in each interest area?

- Which materials did the children use?

- What worked well? What problems came up?

- Did the children have disagreements, conflicts, or other behavior problems? If so, how were they resolved?

- Which children had problems finding something to do? How did we respond?

- Did we welcome and provide meaningful roles for parents who visited the program?

- What changes are needed in:

    - the indoor or outdoor environment?

    - materials and equipment?

    - our interactions with children?

    - our interactions with families?

    - group time?

    - small group activities?

Plans are modified based on what you learn from evaluation.

Daily evaluation meetings tend to be short, but very effective, because the answers to the above questions are fresh in teachers' minds. As planning is an ongoing process, you and your colleagues can change the weekly plan, if necessary, to solve problems or to respond to children's interests. For example:

- *The storytelling activity went well, but there wasn't time for all interested children to participate. The teachers will offer storytelling again tomorrow instead of introducing a new fingerplay.*

- *Emma had a particularly stressful day. Ms. Kim will spend more one-on-one time with her tomorrow.*

- *Several children had trouble using the new climber. Ms. Kim and Ms. Richards will observe over the next few days to see if the climber continues to be a source of frustration.*

Teachers can use a similar evaluation process when meeting to develop weekly and long-range plans. These are times when observations carried out over time can be useful. For example, the same toys have sat in the same place on a low shelf for several weeks. Putting some toys away, adding new ones, or even changing the location of some items could spark children's interests. Observations also let teachers know when something planned is not working. For example, if children are unable to complete the puzzles and often leave them out unfinished, the puzzles may be too difficult. This observation suggests that teachers should try puzzles with fewer pieces and less complex shapes.

Applying Your Knowledge

In this learning activity you and a colleague develop, implement, and evaluate a weekly plan. Begin by reviewing the example. Agree on a time to hold a planning meeting with your colleague. You can use the blank form that appears after the example or one of your choosing. Implement the plan, then meet again to evaluate how it worked.

Weekly Plan[1]

Week of: *April 15*   **Special Focus:** *Bodies*

	Monday	Tuesday	Wednesday	Thursday	Friday
Group time	*Read Bodies*	*Introduce new fingerplay*	*Dance the hokey pokey*	*Imagine what it's like to be a giant*	*Weekly review*
Small group activities	*Face painting in front of long mirror*	*Body tracings-hands, feet, or whole bodies*	*Hang body tracings from tallest to smallest*	*Bake "people" and "animal" cookies*	*Taste fruits: kiwis, mangos, tangelos*
Outdoor activities	*Play body tag and crawl through hula hoops*	*Measure things with hands, feet, and tools*	*Wash dolls and clothes, hang to dry*	*Use colored chalk*	*Nature walk: look for animals and insects*

Changes to the Environment

Block Area
Wooden people

Sand and Water Play
Rubber dolls and clothes to wash
Clothespins to hang up wet clothes
Bubble blowing props

Computers
Install updated drawing program

Art Area
"People" color paint, crayons, and playdough
Butcher paper for body tracings

Library
Bodies, by Barbara Brenner, My Feet, My Hands, by Aliki, My Five Senses, by M. M. Mille, I Can Tell by Touching, by C. Otto

Discovery (Science and Nature)
Borrow guinea pig from Ms. Williams' class
Materials for making a maze

House Corner
Small suitcases
Remove dress-up clothes children don't use

Table Toys
People puzzle
Small blocks and people

Music and Movement
Hokey pokey tape; scarves; hula hoops

Outdoors
Colored chalk
Large boxes to crawl through

Cooking
People and animal cookie cutters

Miscellaneous
Measuring tools: shoes, tape, yard stick, scales
Unbreakable hand mirrors

Responsibilities: *Ms. Kim: bring hokey pokey tape and cardboard boxes, install drawing program, get small suitcases from storage; observe Roger, Tori, and Jamal. Ms. Richards: get books from library, borrow guinea pig and get instructions for care, stock interest areas, purchase fruit; observe Andrei, May, and Alison; lead cooking.*

[1] Adapted with permission from Diane Trister Dodge and Laura J. Colker, *The Creative Curriculum for Early Childhood, 3rd Ed.* (Washington, D.C: Teaching Strategies, Inc., 1992), p. 62.

Weekly Plan[1]

Week of: _____   Special Focus: _____

	Monday	Tuesday	Wednesday	Thursday	Friday
Group time					
Small group activities					
Outdoor activities					

Changes to the Environment

Block Area	Sand and Water Play	Computers
Art Area	Library	Discovery (Science and Nature)
House Corner	Table Toys	Music and Movement
Outdoors	Cooking	Miscellaneous

Responsibilities:

[1] Adapted with permission from Diane Trister Dodge and Laura J. Coker, *The Creative Curriculum for Early Childhood, 3rd Ed.* (Washington, D.C: Teaching Strategies, Inc., 1992), p. 62.

For one week, use the plan you developed as a guide. Meet daily to evaluate how well the plan is working and to determine whether changes are needed. Then answer the following questions.

How did you work as a team to develop and evaluate the plan?

What happened each day?

How did children respond to changes in the environment?

Which activities were successful, and which were not?

How did the plan respond to children as individuals?

What changes did you make in the plan during the week?

How could you build on the experiences children had this week?

Discuss your plan and your experiences using the planning form with your trainer and your colleagues.

V. Following Administrative Policies and Procedures

In this learning activity you will learn to:

- Identify your program's administrative policies and procedures
- Complete management tasks according to a schedule

You are part of a system.

As a teacher in an early childhood program, you are a part of a system. Your role in this system includes coordinating with other staff, with parents, and possibly with other offices or agencies in the community. If your program is located in a public school, you may also coordinate with the principal and other school staff.

A program runs smoothly when staff understand and follow administrative policies and procedures. These policies and procedures are outlined in staff and parent handbooks and usually address the following topics:

- hours of operation;

- acceptance/registration procedures;

- fees and service charges;

- safety requirements;

- medical and health requirements;

- fire prevention and evacuation procedures;

- policy on closing for bad weather;

- contingency plans for responding to emergencies;

- reporting accidents;

- using, ordering, and replacing consumable supplies;

- reporting suspected child abuse and neglect;

- reporting maintenance needs for furniture and equipment; and

- using positive guidance.

Policies and Procedures

All staff need to be aware of the program's policies and procedures so everyone follows the same regulations during day-to-day operations. In addition, parents may seek answers to questions about discipline, accidents, or other issues. When you know how such issues are handled, you can respond with accurate information or, if the issue is a sensitive one, direct parents to raise their questions with the director.

The program's policies and procedures also address your role in completing forms and maintaining files. Records for individual children might include:

Teachers collect and maintain children's records and other forms.

- results of child health examinations;

- observation recordings;

- developmental screening results;

- in-depth assessment reports;

- daily attendance records; and

- parent contact forms.

You might also complete forms such as:

- contagious disease exposure forms;

- medical emergency consent forms;

- weekly plans;

- field trip permission forms;

- food service reports;

- inventory records;

- supply request forms;

- staff time sheets; and

- staff leave request forms.

To follow the program's procedures for reporting and recordkeeping, you may find it helpful to keep a list of necessary reports and the date each is due. Some reports may be due daily or weekly. Others are completed when an incident, such as an accident, occurs. Still others, such as inventory reports, are used once or twice a year. Your role will vary according to the reporting task. Some information, such as observation recordings or portfolios, may be collected and reviewed periodically by teachers. Other reports, such as a parent-teacher conference summary, may be completed by one teacher but kept on file in case other people need to review the information.

Maintaining confidentiality is essential. This means you do not share personal information about a child with anyone other than the child's parents or other professionals who also work with the child. Maintaining confidentiality is a part of being a professional teacher.

Your input can help improve the program.

Because you and your colleagues have knowledge of individual children and awareness of developmentally appropriate practice in child development programs, you may be called upon to provide input on program issues. You can talk with colleagues and management staff about ways to improve the program as a whole. Administrators usually welcome suggestions on staffing patterns, class size and composition, enrollment policies, and other practices and procedures that aim to provide a high-quality program.

There are laws and regulations on including children with disabilities.

The past several decades have seen a succession of federal, state, and local laws and regulations which require that children with disabilities be included in regular education settings.[2] The landmark Education for All Handicapped Children Act of 1975 (P.L. 94-142), more recently amended and reauthorized as the Individuals with Disabilities Act (IDEA), calls for a "free and appropriate public education" in the "least restrictive environment" for children with disabilities. And the Americans with Disabilities Act (ADA) of 1990 extends the principles of non-discrimination with respect to people with disabilities to a wide variety of other settings, including child development programs.

These legal provisions reflect the importance of "supplementary aids and services" (e.g., classroom aides, consultations, or resource services) to achieve the inclusion of children with disabilities in regular programs. The law requires state and local regulations to ensure that staff receive "the technical assistance and training necessary to assist them in this effort" (IDEA, 1991). As noted in Learning Activity II, you should always seek the advice of specialists when addressing needs that are beyond your expertise or experience.

For more information on this Act, contact the Department of Justice Hotline at (202) 514-0301 (voice) or (202) 514-0381 (TDD) in Washington, DC, or the Child Care Law Center at (415) 495-5498 in San Francisco, California.

Applying Your Knowledge

In this learning activity you review your program's administrative policies and procedures for completing various kinds of reports. Then you complete a report schedule indicating when these reports are due and what teachers' responsibilities are with regard to completing them. Begin by reading the example of a report schedule.

---

[2] Adapted with permission from Diane Trister Dodge, Judy R. Jablon, and Toni S. Bickart, *Constructing Curriculum for the Primary Grades* (Washington, DC: Teaching Strategies, Inc., 1994), p. 27.

Report Schedule

(Example)

Report	Teacher's Responsibility	Date Due
Portfolios	Complete observation recordings, involve children in selecting work samples, collect other items documenting progress and changing interests, request and collect materials from parents, complete summary form	Update twice a month
Attendance	Record attendance for class	Daily
Time sheet	Fill in hours worked each day	Every Friday
Supply requisition	Request consumable supplies when inventory is low	15th of each month
Annual leave request	Complete leave request form	Two weeks prior to date for which leave is requested
Contagious disease exposure	Complete form when parent notifies teacher of child's illness	By 6:00 p.m. on the day parent notifies me of illness
Inventory	Record quantities of equipment, toys, and consumable supplies	January 15 and July 15

Report Schedule

Report	Teacher's Responsibility	Date Due

Discuss this schedule with your trainer. If you need additional space, duplicate this form. Review and follow your program's administrative policies and procedures throughout the year.

Summarizing Your Progress

You have now completed all of the learning activities for this module. Whether you are an experienced teacher or new to the profession, this module has probably helped you develop new management skills.

Before you go on, take a few minutes to summarize what you've learned.

- Turn back to Learning Activity I, Using a Systematic Approach to Observing and Recording and Learning Activity II, Individualizing the Program. Review the recordings completed for the children in your class. What makes them examples of objective and accurate recordings? How did you use this information to individualize the program for these children? How did you use this information in your weekly plans?

- Next, review your responses to the pre-training assessment for this module. Write a summary of what you learned and list the skills you developed or improved.

If there are topics you would like to learn more about, you will find recommended readings listed in the Orientation in Volume I.

Your final step in this module is to complete the knowledge and competency assessments. Let your trainer know when you are ready to schedule the assessments. After you have successfully completed these assessments, you will be ready to start a new module. Congratulations on your progress so far, and good luck with your next module.

Answer Sheet

Overview
(pp. 257-259)

Learning About Each Child's Culture, Language, Family, Skills, Needs, and Interests

1. **How did Mr. Lopez take advantage of a routine to learn about Eric?**
   a. *He recorded what Eric did and said while making snack.*

   b. *He took a photograph for Eric's portfolio of the child eating his lettuce roll-up.*

2. **What did Mr. Lopez learn about Eric?**
   a. *Eric can make a choice.*

   b. *He likes peanut butter.*

   c. *He can hold a knife and use it for spreading, with assistance.*

   d. *He can stick with a task until he's finished.*

   e. *He is open to suggestions.*

   f. *He uses trial-and-error methods to solve a problem.*

Working as a Team to Offer an Individualized Program

1. **How did Ms. Kim and Ms. Richards use a team approach to planning?**
   a. *They both agreed to focus on children's outdoor activities.*

   b. *They collected and shared information.*

   c. *They jointly made plans to build on group and individual interests and skills.*

2. **How did the teachers use observation recordings to plan for individual children?**
   a. *In response to Ian's interest in nature, they plan to plant a garden.*

   b. *In response to Justin's road building activities, they will add small cars to the sandbox.*

   c. *In response to Katherine's interest in painting, they will bring the easels outdoors.*

Following Administrative Policies, Practices, and Procedures

1. **How did Ms. Williams stay informed about administrative policies and procedures?**
   a. *She reviewed the Staff Handbook and discussed field trip procedures with a colleague.*

2. **What tasks did Ms. Williams complete according to the program's policies?**
   a. *She filled out the field trip request form, contacted the nature museum to get information needed to complete the checklist, and sent permission slips home to parents.*

Glossary

Administrative policies and procedures

The systems outlined in Staff and Parent Handbooks that ensure the smooth operation of an early childhood program.

Assessment

The process of observing, recording, and otherwise documenting the work children do and how they do it, and using this information as a basis for a variety of educational decisions that affect the child.

Individualizing

Offering a child development program in which the environment, materials, activities, routines, and interactions with children are tailored to respond to each child's culture, language, family, interests, skills, and needs.

Portfolio

A collection of items—including work samples, observation recordings, photographs, lists of favorite books, and audio and videotape recordings—that document a child's progress and interests.

Recording

A complete, accurate, and objective written record of an observation.

Systematic Observation

Watching and listening to a child's behavior and using accurate, objective language to write down what the child says and does.

Module 13: *Professionalism*

Overview

Maintaining a commitment to professionalism means:

- Continually assessing your own performance
- Continuing to learn about caring for children
- Applying professional ethics at all times

A professional is a person who uses specialized knowledge and skills to do a job or provide a service. As an early childhood teacher, you are a member of an important profession. You work with children during a time when they are developing more quickly than they will at any other period in their lives. You help shape children's views about learning and the world around them. By providing an appropriate early childhood program, you help children learn to see themselves as competent individuals. This self-confidence will help children make good decisions and lead satisfying and fulfilling lives.

Your professional skills also help families. By building a partnership with each child's parents, you give parents confidence in the reliable, high-quality care you and your colleagues provide. Often as a result, parents' own performance improves. They can concentrate on work rather than being distracted by concerns about their children's care.

In the early childhood field, professionalism means planning and implementing a program that is based on knowledge of children's individual and developmental characteristics and needs. It also means taking advantage of opportunities to learn more about children and to develop and continually improve new skills.

When you need a service such as medical or legal advice, or electrical repairs, you look for a professional business or individual who can meet your needs. You choose professionals because you want:

- the needed service;

- specialized knowledge;

- a commitment to quality;

- dependability; and

- effectiveness.

Early childhood teachers are members of an important profession.

Professionals are always open to learning and gaining new skills.

Early childhood professionals meet the needs of children and families when they provide:

- the needed service—a high-quality early childhood program;

- specialized knowledge—an understanding of how children grow and develop and of how to meet their needs appropriately;

- a commitment to quality—a developmentally appropriate program in a safe and healthy environment;

- dependability—service on a regular basis; and

- effectiveness—a program that helps children develop physically, cognitively, socially, and emotionally.

Lilian Katz, an early childhood educator, has studied how teachers grow professionally. Her research suggests that teachers pass through four different stages of professional development: survival, consolidation, renewal, and maturity. These stages are described in the following paragraphs.[1]

1. Survival

Teachers at the Survival Stage are new to the field and are often insecure. They devote most of their attention to learning the center's routines and performing tasks as assigned. This stage is called *survival* in part because of the concentrated focus on immediate needs rather than long-range planning. If you are at this stage, you will benefit from a comprehensive orientation to the job and shadowing or observing an experienced teacher. You may want to join a professional association such as the National Association for the Education of Young Children (NAEYC). Continued training and experience will help you move to the next stage, Consolidation.

2. Consolidation

When teachers reach this stage, they are more confident and begin to look beyond simply completing the daily routines. They seek new ways to accomplish routine tasks and to handle problems. If you are at this stage, you will find it useful to exchange ideas with other teachers and become actively involved in a professional association. Informal conversations, group meetings, training sessions, and open discussions will help you grow and move to the next stage, Renewal.

[1] Lilian G. Katz, "Teacher's Developmental Stages," in *Talking with Teachers: Reflections on Early Childhood Education* (Washington, DC: National Association for the Education of Young Children, 1977), pp. 7-13.

3. Renewal

During the third or fourth year on the job, teachers may begin to be bored with the day's routines. Often their interest drops and enthusiasm falls. Teachers in this stage need renewal—new challenges to rekindle their excitement and commitment to caring for young children. If you are at this stage, try to attend conferences and workshops, take on a leadership role in a professional organization, or pursue a special interest. These professional activities will provide needed stimulation and help you move to the fourth stage, Maturity.

4. Maturity

Teachers at this stage are committed professionals. They understand the need to seek new ideas and skills and continue to grow professionally. If you are a mature teacher you can be a mentor for new teachers. You might also gain the skills needed to assume new challenges as a supervisor, trainer, or center administrator.

Maintaining a commitment to professionalism has several positive results. First, learning new skills, acquiring knowledge, and becoming more competent all build your self-esteem. As you become a competent teacher, the sense of success you experience is very rewarding.

Second, when you provide professional care, you are helping children grow, learn, and develop to their full potential. Third, your professional behavior contributes to the field of early childhood education. As you and others provide high-quality programs for children, you build respect for the profession, which can result in more recognition for the important service you provide.

Teaching is not just a job—it's a profession. While you help children to grow and develop, you can enjoy your work, do the best job you can, and continue to advance as a teacher and as a person.

Listed on the following pages are three sets of examples showing how teachers demonstrate a commitment to professionalism. Following each set of examples is a short reading and two questions to answer. When you have finished this section, compare your answers with those on the answer sheet at the end of the module. If your answers are different, discuss them with your trainer. There can be more than one good answer.

Continually Assessing Your Own Performance

Analyze your skills to identify areas in need of improvement.	"I need some new strategies for helping John learn to use his words instead of hitting other children. Perhaps this article on positive guidance will help me."
Ask colleagues to observe you and provide objective feedback.	"Could you observe me reading to the children so I can learn more about how I respond to children's interruptions and questions?"
Use professional standards as guidelines for providing high-quality care.	"This checklist will help us evaluate the safety and quality of our outdoor area."
Review your performance against written procedures and guidelines.	"Even though the children are napping, it's not safe to leave them unsupervised. I'll wait until Ms. Kim returns before going to the supply room."
Accept and address feedback and criticism from parents, colleagues, and supervisors.	"Mr. Drake complained because Jill wasn't ready to go home. I will remind Jill to collect her belongings before choosing a quiet activity."

Ms. Kim sinks down in her chair to think at the end of a long day. The morning started out smoothly, but by late afternoon, when parents began picking up their children, the room was in chaos. A basket of crackers sat upside down on the floor, several children chased each other around the room, and clothes and other belongings covered the floor in front of the cubbies. She groans to herself as she recalls that several parents had complained to Ms. Richards earlier in the week that their children had come home wearing someone else's clothes. When Joseph's mother arrived, Ms. Kim had to help her find Joseph's hat and gloves. They found the gloves with Matthew's coat. The hat was near the block corner, where Joseph had left it when he came in from outdoor play. "This cannot go on," she says to herself. "Ms. Richards and I need to make some changes. Mr. Lopez and Ms. Thomas seem so organized. Maybe they can give us some pointers. Our supervisor can give us some suggestions, too."

1. **How did Ms. Kim assess her own performance?**

2. **What did she do with the results of her self-assessment?**

Continuing to Learn About Caring for Children

Participate in professional organizations and training opportunities.

"I'm going to attend the upcoming state conference to learn more about advocacy."

Keep up-to-date about appropriate practices for encouraging young children's growth and development.

"I'll review the new book on prop boxes and dramatic play this weekend. Then, I can share the information at our next staff meeting."

Talk with and observe colleagues to learn more about caring for young children.

"I'll try to take my break with Ms. Williams today. Maybe she has some suggestions on preparing the children for the field trip."

Use parents as resources for responding to children's skills, interests, and needs.

"Mr. Carter, what kinds of books does Brady enjoy hearing at home?"

Develop and follow short-and long-range plans for professional development.

"I'm planning to finish this module by the end of the month. I'll finish all thirteen by the end of the year."

During his break, Mr. Lopez sits in the staff lounge thumbing through a journal for early childhood teachers. An article on using portfolios to document and assess children's progress catches his eye. "This looks really interesting," he says. "I'd like to learn more about how to begin using portfolios." Before returning to the classroom, he signs out the journal so he can read the article at home. During the next day's planning meeting, he shares what he has learned with Ms. Thomas and asks her to read the article, too. "I've heard about portfolios," she says, "but I don't understand how they are different from what we already do. Perhaps this article will answer my questions." After reading the article, Ms. Thomas is as enthusiastic about portfolios as Mr. Lopez. They decide to ask their supervisor to help them locate other resources so they can learn more about portfolios and begin using them for the children in their classroom.

1. **How did Mr. Lopez and Ms. Thomas choose a topic to learn more about?**

2. **How did they plan to expand their knowledge and skills?**

Applying Professional Ethics at All Times

Keep information about children and their families confidential.

"Children's files are confidential, Ms. Robinson. Only the center staff and you and her father may read her file."

Behave in an honest, reliable, and dependable manner in performing duties.

"Boy, I'm tired this morning, but I won't call in sick, because I know the children need me."

Treat each child as an individual and show no bias because of culture, background, abilities, or gender.

"Jamal, both boys and girls can use the woodworking area. There's room for Marcia to join you and Derek."

Stand up for practices that are developmentally appropriate and speak out against those that are not.

"Make-believe play helps children make sense of the world, Ms. Gwynn. Judson knows the difference between make-believe and fibbing."

Support the center director and other administrative staff by avoiding gossip.

"I know you're upset, Ms. Frilles, but it's best to discuss your performance appraisal directly with the center director."

Support other teachers when they need assistance.

"I'll help you rearrange your room, Mr. Lopez. Let me know when you're ready."

Take care of your personal physical, emotional, social, and intellectual needs.

"Tonight I'm having dinner with a close friend. I always feel energized after being with her."

Ms. Jones arrives to pick up her child, Dora, at the end of the day. As she walks in, she glances disapprovingly at Joshua, who is about to jump off a table. Ms. Williams says, "Hello, Ms. Jones. Dora's in the block area making a sign to protect her building. Excuse me a moment." She immediately turns to Joshua and says, "I know you like to climb and jump, Joshua, but it is not safe to jump off the table. Let me help you down. You can jump on the pillows where it is safe." When she comes back, Ms. Jones says, "Boy, he's a wild one. He must drive you crazy. Ms. Williams responds, "Joshua really likes climbing and facing new challenges. Now, let me tell you about Dora's day."

1. How did Ms. Williams use professional ethics while talking to Ms. Jones?

2. How did Ms. Williams interact with Joshua in a professional manner?

The Early Childhood Profession and You

Each early childhood teacher, just like each child, is a unique person with special interests and strengths. You bring your own interests and skills to your profession, and you share them with the children in your class. Whether a person shares a love of music or a love of the outdoors, the children pick up on his or her enthusiasm and learn to appreciate something new. By using special interests on the job, you can make your work more satisfying and fun.

You also bring your own personal style to your work. Some teachers have boundless physical energy; others are calm and easygoing. Both styles are valuable. The important thing is to look at your own personal style and consider how it affects your interactions with children.

What are your special abilities and interests? What do you most enjoy? Which personal qualities enhance your work as an early childhood professional? Which ones sometimes make your work more difficult? What do you like best about your job? What would you like to change? These are questions early childhood professionals can ask themselves to identify what makes them unique and what special qualities they bring to the profession.

The reading that follows will help you think about yourself and the reasons why you became an early childhood professional.

Each person has special interests and abilities.

Carol Hillman: Gardener, Naturalist, Teacher[2]

I believe deeply that what you are outside of school affects what you are in school. I have a farm in Massachusetts that has for many years been a resource to me and to the children in my classroom. On my farm I grow things, looking after the whole process myself. I like knowing that I can grow vegetables or flowers without relying on chemicals. The flowers are just as important as the edible things. I pick and dry many of them, making everlasting bouquets. The whole process gives me a feeling of self-sufficiency and a kind of calmness.

Those feelings translate to the classroom in unexpected ways. There, as on the farm, I take great pleasure in making do with what we have. I try to show the children those same pleasures. They make bird feeders from cups and chenille-wrapped wire, then take the feeders home and have a season's worth of birds coming and going.

Growing things takes attention—constantly watching what needs water, thinning, or to be picked. I want to communicate that awareness to children. Every morning when we meet, I ask them what they notice that is different. Almost every

---

[2] Adapted with permission from Carol Hillman, "Teachers and Then Some: Profiles of Three Teachers," *Beginnings* (Redmond, WA: Exchange Press, 1986), pp. 21-22.

day we go outdoors, not just to a playground, but to the surrounding woods. I want the children to be investigators in the natural world—curious about the stream, the trees, and the leaves on the ground.

My aesthetic sense—a love for beautiful arrangements, shapes, and colors—is also fed by growing things. On my first job after college, I worked for an art gallery and learned how to hang an exhibition. Since then, I have known the importance of placement, whether placing blocks on a shelf or plants in a garden. The blocks, the baskets of parquetry blocks, the puzzles and pegboards must each stand apart to command their own space and importance. This creates a sense of order, not a strict cleanliness. Children need messiness, too.

But beyond that sense of order, my experiences in gardens and the wider outdoors have given me a taste for naturally beautiful things. Rather than stickers or predrawn forms, the children in my classes make collages from shells and sand, sweetgum pods, the bright orange berries of bittersweet vines, acorns, and pine cones.

Outside my garden, my most important role as a part-time naturalist is raising monarch butterflies. For a number of years, I've worked with Dr. Fred Urquart of Toronto, who was looking for the hidden spot where monarchs migrate during the winter. I've been a part of that search by raising, tagging, and releasing butterflies. Only a few years ago, after a lifetime of tracking the butterflies marked by many people such as myself, Urquart was able to locate the monarch's wintering spot high in the mountains near Mexico City.

One part of my garden is devoted to milkweed—the sole food source for monarchs. I find the small caterpillars on the plants and take them to school. During the first few weeks of the school year, we watch the metamorphosis—from caterpillar, through chrysalis, to full butterfly. We keep the monarchs in a huge case for a few days after they emerge. Then, on warm, blue sky days, children take turns holding and releasing the monarchs into the air. It is probably a moment they won't forget.

Taking a Look at Yourself

Reflection is an important part of being a professional. Take time to think about how you feel about your work. Then, answer the questions that follow.

I think I'm really good at:

I really enjoy:

I can share my interests and skills with children in the following ways:

What I find most difficult about my work is:

I would like to be better at:

I would like to know more about:

Discuss your responses with two colleagues. Have they learned anything new about you? Do they see things you did not see? Use the space below to summarize what you learned from reflecting on your role as an early childhood professional.

When you have finished this overview section, you should complete the pre-training assessment. Refer to the glossary at the end of the module if you need definitions for the terms used.

Pre-Training Assessment

Listed below are the skills that teachers use to enhance their professionalism. Think about whether you do these things regularly, sometimes, or not enough. Place a check in one of the boxes on the right for each skill listed. Then discuss your answers with your trainer.

Continually Assessing Your Own Performance

I Do This:	Regularly	Sometimes	Not Enough
1. Analyze my skills to identify areas in need of improvement.	☐	☐	☐
2. Ask colleagues to observe me and provide objective feedback on my performance.	☐	☐	☐
3. Use professional standards as guidelines for providing high-quality care.	☐	☐	☐
4. Review my performance against written procedures and guidelines.	☐	☐	☐
5. Accept and address feedback and criticism from parents, colleagues, and supervisors.	☐	☐	☐

Continuing to Learn About Caring for Children

	Regularly	Sometimes	Not Enough
6. Participate in professional organizations and training opportunities.	☐	☐	☐
7. Keep up-to-date about appropriate practices for encouraging young children's growth and development.	☐	☐	☐

Continuing to Learn About Caring for Children
(continued)

	I Do This:	Regularly	Sometimes	Not Enough
8. Talk with and observe colleagues to learn more about caring for young children.		☐	☐	☐
9. Use parents as resources for responding to children's skills, interests, and needs.		☐	☐	☐
10. Develop and follow short- and long-range plans for professional development.		☐	☐	☐

Applying Professional Ethics at All Times

	Regularly	Sometimes	Not Enough
11. Keep information about children and their families confidential.	☐	☐	☐
12. Behave in an honest, reliable, and dependable manner in performing duties.	☐	☐	☐
13. Treat each child as an individual and show no bias because of culture, background, abilities, or gender.	☐	☐	☐
14. Stand up for practices that are developmentally appropriate and speak out against those that are not.	☐	☐	☐
15. Support the center director and other administrative staff by avoiding gossip.	☐	☐	☐

Applying Professional Ethics at All Times

(continued)

	I Do This:	Regularly	Sometimes	Not Enough
16. Support other teachers when they need assistance.		☐	☐	☐
17. Take care of my personal physical, emotional, social, and intellectual needs.		☐	☐	☐

Review your responses, then list three to five skills you would like to improve or topics you would like to learn more about. When you finish this module you will list examples of your new or improved knowledge and skills.

Begin the learning activities for Module 13, Professionalism.

Learning Activities

I. Assessing Yourself

In this activity you will learn to:

- Recognize your own skills and abilities
- Use the profession's standards to assess your own competence

---

Every profession sets standards for performance. These standards are not meant to restrict you, but rather to serve as guides. In using them, you, your colleagues, and parents can confirm you are providing high-quality care.

A number of professional associations and groups concerned with the quality of early childhood education have established standards for performance. These standards recommend a child-centered approach that allows children to learn through exploration and hands-on activities. They agree on the importance of basing program practices on child development and building partnerships with families. The standards are listed below. Your supervisor may have copies of these documents. If not, you can order your own copies from the associations identified.

National Association for the Education of Young Children (NAEYC)
1509 16th Street, NW
Washington, DC 20036-1426
800-424-2460 or 202-232-8777

Several NAEYC publications describe standards and positions on key early childhood issues.

- *Developmentally Appropriate Practice in Early Childhood Programs Serving Children from Birth through Age Eight* offers guidance on meeting individual and developmental needs of children from infancy through age eight. Appropriate activities and teaching practices for children at particular ages and stages of development are described.

- *The NAEYC Statement on Standardized Testing of Young Children 3 Through 8 Years of Age and Testing of Young Children: Concerns and Cautions* addresses standards for screening and assessment.

Caring for Preschool Children

- *NAEYC Position Statement on Violence in the Lives of Children* discusses the impact of violence on children and how early childhood educators can advocate for public policies and actions that prevent violence, help children cope with violence, and promote non-violent behavior.

- *Guidelines for Appropriate Curriculum Content and Assessment in Programs Serving Children Ages 3 Through 8* is a position statement that guides professionals through selecting and implementing a curriculum and using appropriate assessment techniques to observe, document, and otherwise record children's work.

- *Responding to Linguistic and Cultural Diversity—Recommendations for Effective Early Childhood Education,* is a position statement that assists professionals in working with families to meet the needs of children who speak languages other than English.

- *Accreditation Criteria and Procedures of the National Academy of Early Childhood Programs* describes standards for quality in centers serving children from birth through age 8. The National Academy of Early Childhood Programs, a division of NAEYC, applies the standards as criteria for accrediting centers through the Center Accreditation Program (CAP). The accreditation process involves self-study, a validation visit, and a final team review. Many early childhood programs voluntarily elect to take part in the CAP.

The Council for Early Childhood Professional Recognition (The Council)
2460 16th Street, NW
Washington, DC 20009
202-265-9090 or 800-424-4310

The Council operates a national credentialing program for early childhood educators. The Council awards the Child Development Associate (CDA) credential, which is the nationally recognized credential for early childhood professionals. The CDA *Competency Standards* define 13 functional areas in which early childhood teachers must demonstrate competence. The competency standards also serve as guidelines for teachers who are not seeking a CDA credential but want to improve their child care skills. The functional areas serve as the framework for the 13 modules in *Caring for Preschool Children*. The Council publishes guides to the assessment system and competency standards, as well as a newsletter.

National Association of State Boards of Education (NASBE)
1012 Cameron Street
Alexandria, VA 22314
703-684-4000

Right From the Start, available through NAEYC, describes how schools can implement developmentally appropriate early childhood units and create partnerships with child development programs. *Caring Communities: Supporting*

Young Children and Families encourages communities to create, review, and extend programs for children and families.

National Association of Elementary School Principals (NAESP)
1615 Duke Street
Alexandria, VA 22314-3483
703-684-3345

The NAESP presents its standards for quality in *Standards for Quality Programs for Young Children: Early Childhood Education and the Elementary School Principal.* This document is particularly useful as early childhood programs forge relationships with public schools.

National Education Association (NEA)
1201 16th Street, NW
Washington, DC 20036-1426
202-833-4000

The NEA presents its views on standards for quality in *Early Childhood Education and the Public Schools.*

The Carnegie Foundation for the Advancement of Teaching
order publications from:
Princeton University Press
3175 Princeton, Pike
Lawrenceville, NJ 08648
609-896-1344

The Carnegie Foundation has issued its recommendations for meeting the readiness goal to prepare children for school in *Ready to Learn: A Mandate for the Nation,* by Ernest L. Boyer.

Reviewing these documents and completing the pre-training assessments for each of the modules in *Caring for Preschool Children* should provide a comprehensive picture of your skills and capabilities. This review will also identify areas you need to know more about and skills you need to develop or improve.

Applying Your Knowledge

In this learning activity you select one part of your program on which to focus. You compare and contrast this part with guidelines in two documents that define standards for quality. Next, you discuss with a colleague how the standards apply to your program and to your roles as early childhood professionals.

Standards for Quality

Select one part of your program on which to focus. For example, you might choose the outdoor environment, teacher-child interactions, assessment, curriculum, or guidance.

I will focus on this part of our program: _____

Next, select two documents that define standards for quality. If they are not available in your center or local library, order copies from the addresses provided in this learning activity. Record the titles of the selected documents at the top of the columns and summarize how each one defines quality. Then, answer the questions that follow.

Title:	Title:
Summary:	**Summary:**

How are these standards similar to each other?

How are these standards different from each other?

Which standards are met by your program?

Which standards are not met by your program?

Discuss with a colleague how these standards apply to your program and to your roles as early childhood professionals. Together, answer the following question.

What can you do to improve this part of your program?

Meet with your trainer to discuss ways to implement the suggestions developed by you and your colleague.

II. Continuing to Learn About Caring for Children

In this activity you will learn to:

- Expand your knowledge and skills
- Make short- and long-range professional development plans

Continual learning has many benefits.

No matter how many years you've been a teacher or how much you already know, it is important to continue to learn more about your profession. This is true for a number of reasons.

- There is always new information to be learned. All professionals need to keep up with the latest developments in their fields. Research and experience often lead to more effective strategies for working with children. Learning is ongoing for the early childhood professional.

- Continual learning makes you an active, thinking person. Teachers who are always learning are more interesting people. They have new ideas to bring to the program to inspire children. If you enjoy learning, you probably help children enjoy learning, too.

- You care about children. Each article or book you read, every discussion you participate in, and every conference you attend, can give you new insights or help you resolve problems. Because you care about children, you are always alert for new and helpful information relating to their development. For example, when a child with a disability joins your group, you can try to learn new ways to include this child in the program's activities.

- You want to grow professionally. A commitment to continue learning can lead to improved performance. Learning can result in greater confidence, more responsibility, a promotion, and may lead to a salary increase.

- Continual learning is affirming. The process of learning tends to affirm the good work you've been doing and the knowledge you already have. You may rediscover ideas you haven't thought about in a while.

How can teachers continue growing and learning? In addition to participating in this training program, there are many other ways you can continue learning. Some suggestions are described in the following paragraphs.

Join a professional organization.

Professional organizations help you keep up-to-date on the latest information and current issues in the profession. Many have local affiliates that meet regularly. These organizations offer newsletters, books, videotapes, brochures, and other publications with useful information and helpful tips. Attending professional conferences is a way to meet other teachers with similar interests and concerns.

Early Childhood Professional Organizations

Organization	Services
Association for Childhood Education International (ACEI) 11501 Georgia Avenue, Suite 315 Wheaton, MD 20902 301-942-2443 800-423-3563	Resources and support for meeting the developmental needs of children from birth through early adolescence Journals: *Childhood Education* and *Journal for Research in Childhood Education* Membership divisions for infancy, early childhood, and later childhood/early adolescence Holds annual conference Represented in all 50 states and many nations abroad
Ecumenical Child Care Network 1580 N. Northwest Highway, Suite 115 Park Ridge, IL 60068-1456 708-298-1612	Advocates for high quality, equitable, and affordable child care and education in churches and other religious organizations National, interdenominational membership Committed to applying anti-bias and anti-racist principles in work with children and families
National Association for the Education of Young Children (NAEYC) 1509 16th Street, NW Washington, DC 20036 800-424-2460 202-232-8777 World Wide Web: http://www.naeyc.org/naeyc/	Print and video resources and support for meeting the needs of children from birth through age eight Journal: *Young Children* Holds annual conference Has 360 affiliates at local, state, and regional levels
National Black Child Development Institute (NBCDI) 1023 15th Street, NW Suite 600 Washington, DC 20005 202-387-1281	Advocates on behalf of the growth and development of African-American children Focuses on critical issues in early childhood education, child welfare, and health care Quarterly newsletter, *Black Child Advocate* Quarterly publication, *Child Health Talk* Annual conference
National Center for the Early Childhood Work Force 733 15th Street, NW, Suite 1037 Washington, DC 20005 202-737-7700 800-U-R-WORTHY (879-6784)	Works to improve wages, status, and working conditions of early childhood professionals Quarterly newsletter and other resource materials

Organization	Services
National Head Start Association (NHSA) 201 N. Union Street Suite 320 Alexandria, VA 22314 703-739-0875 World Wide Web: http://www.nhsa.org/	Represents Head Start children, families, staff, and programs nationwide Agency and individual memberships Annual training conference Training conferences for Head Start community (e.g., parents, policy council) Quarterly journal: *NHSA Journal* Networks with state and regional associations for Head Start directors, staff, and parents
National Indian Child Care Association 279 East 137th Street Glenpool, OK 74033 918-756-2112	Advocates for quality child care for Native American children Represents Tribal needs by communicating unified voice to government of United States
Southern Early Childhood Association (SECA) P. O. Box 56130 Little Rock, AR 72215-6130 501-663-0353	Provides a voice on local, state, and federal issues affecting young children Quarterly journal: *Dimensions* and other resource materials Holds annual conference Has 13 state groups

Books and articles help you expand your knowledge and skills. The following are good sources of books on working with young children:

Gryphon House
P. O. Box 207
Beltsville, MD 20704-0207
800-638-0928

Kaplan Companies
1310 Lewis Clemmons Road
Lewisville, NC 27023
800-4-KAPLAN

Redleaf Press
450 North Syndicate, Suite 5
St. Paul, MN 55104-4125
800-423-8309

Some of the professional organizations listed previously publish journals with articles of interest to early childhood teachers. The bibliography in the Orientation to this training program lists many helpful resources. Look in both the adult and children's collections of your public library for these and other titles.

Networking is spending time and sharing ideas, information, and experiences with people who perform tasks similar to yours. It is a good way to find solutions to problems, gain new knowledge, or help colleagues cope with difficult situations. You can network with one other person or with a group. Group networks can include other early childhood professionals in your community or at the state level. Meetings can be very informal, perhaps after work or on a Saturday. They can also be formal, with speakers and a detailed agenda. What is important is that teachers have opportunities to meet, share ideas, and get support in coping with the demands of their jobs.

The international communication network known as the Internet provides access to data bases, discussion groups, and files on early childhood education. To take advantage of this resource you will need a computer, modem, communications software program. You access the Internet through an Internet Service Provider (ISP), such as America Online, CompuServe, or other local service. The Internet has dozens of organized discussion groups, called LISTSERVS, that are concerned with children's issues. To learn more about using the Internet, refer to *A to Z: The Early Childhood Educator's Guide to the Internet*, from the ERIC Clearinghouse on Elementary and Early Childhood Education, which is listed in the Bibliography in Volume I.

You can learn a lot by observing colleagues, a supervisor, or a teacher in another program. Because each person has a personal style, you can study new approaches to solving discipline problems, managing transitions, or providing a variety of activities outdoors. Seeing how someone else handles situations similar to the ones you experience can offer new insights and expand your repertoire of successful strategies.

Read books and articles.

Networking is a way to share ideas and get support.

Use the Internet.

Observe teachers in action to gain new perspectives.

Participate in training on topics related to your job.

Attending training is a good way to keep up to date and develop new skills. As you complete each module in this training program, your knowledge of the characteristics of preschoolers and how to support their development will grow.

In addition, training workshops or conferences may be offered in your area. Often these training programs are administered by the Department of Social Services, the public school adult education program, an Office on Child Care Services, a County Extension Office, or other government agencies. In many areas, community colleges offer courses leading to state certification or a CDA credential. Individual courses at colleges and universities may also be an option.

Teach something you have learned to someone else.

After attending a conference or workshop, you can use your knowledge and skills to lead a training session for your peers. This reinforces your learning and contributes to program improvement.

Keep a journal.

Everyone needs to take time to reflect and evaluate, and, if necessary, change the environment, interactions, or routines to make them more appropriate for children. A journal can provide a written record of what you do and what happens as a result of your efforts. Journals also record your successes and help you feel competent.

Ask a colleague to help you assess your performance.

If you are concerned about your skills in a certain area, ask a colleague to conduct an objective, focused observation. Afterwards, meet to discuss the observation notes. If the notes identify problems, plan ways to improve your Skills. Alternatively, you can assess your skills by setting up a video camera in the classroom to record what you say and do and how the children respond. Then view and discuss the tape with a colleague. Identify the skills you want to improve, and plan ways to meet your training needs.

Develop plans for continued learning.

In addition to identifying resources to help you learn more about young children, it helps to have a plan for using those resources. If you know where you're going and how you're going to get there it is easier to take each step and to recognize your goal when you reach it. As you take each step and check it off on your plan, you will see yourself moving closer to your goal.

Applying Your Knowledge

There are two parts to this learning activity. Begin by reviewing your answers to "Taking a Look at Yourself" in the overview section of this module. Pick one item from your responses to "I would like to be better at" or "I would like to know more about." Consider the sources of assistance available to you: the public library, workshops, professional organizations, your supervisor, and other colleagues. Identify specific resources to help you with the task or topic you selected. List what you find on the chart that follows.

Taking Another Look at Yourself

I want to improve or learn more about:

Resources I can use:

Source	Contact Person
Public library	
Workshops	
Professional organizations	
Trainer/colleagues	
Other	

Completing this chart has probably helped you think about readily available resources. Next, use this information to develop a professional development plan. Set short- and long-range goals for professional development, identify possible barriers to reaching your goals, and plan ways to overcome them. For the short term, you might focus on areas you think most need improving. For the long term, you could build on an area of strength, adding to or improving your skills. Read the example on the following page, and complete the form that follows.

Professional Development Plan
(Example)

Short-Range Goals

1. **What short-range goals would you like to pursue?**

    Take a course on guiding children's behavior and complete Module 8, Self

2. **What resources can you use to achieve these goals?**

    The center library

    My trainer and supervisor and other teachers who have expertise in guiding children's behavior

3. **What barriers might hinder you from completing these goals?**

    It's hard to find time to complete learning activities and still care for children.

    I might not find anything in the center library on the reasons for children's behavior.

4. **What can you do to overcome these barriers?**

    I can identify some time-wasting activities that I could do more efficiently.

    Send for the NAEYC brochures: "Helping Children Learn Self-Control" and "Love and Learn: Discipline for Young Children"

5. **Accomplish your goal, congratulate yourself, then set a new one.**

Long-Range Goals

1. **Set a long-range goal to pursue and a time line for achieving it.**

    I will get a degree in early childhood education.

2. **What resources can you use to achieve this goal?**

    I can attend classes at the local community college.

3. **What barriers might hinder you from completing this goal?**

    I have no time to attend school and I can't afford to pay tuition.

4. **What can you do to overcome these barriers?**

    I can take one or two courses at a time rather than a full load.

    I can find out about student loans and scholarships, and other ways to take for-credit courses.

5. **Accomplish your goal, congratulate yourself, then set a new one.**

Professional Development Plan

Short-Range Goals

1. What short-range goals would you like to pursue?

2. What resources can you use to achieve these goals?

3. What barriers might hinder you from completing these goals?

4. What can you do to overcome these barriers?

5. Accomplish your goals, congratulate yourself, then set new ones.

Long-Range Goals

1. Set a long-range goal to pursue and a time-line for achieving it.

2. What resources can you use to achieve this goal?

3. What barriers might hinder you from completing this goal?

4. What can you do to overcome these barriers?

5. Accomplish your goal, congratulate yourself, then set a new one.

Discuss your professional development plan with your trainer. Agree on an overall plan to achieve your short- and long-range goals.

III. Applying Professional Ethics at All Times

In this activity you will learn to:
• Recognize professional and unprofessional behavior
• Follow the standards of ethical behavior in the early childhood profession

Ethics are the principles, standards, or guidelines that identify acceptable behavior. Professionals are people who follow the ethical standards of their profession. Early childhood professionals are committed to doing what is best for all children in their care at all times.

The chart below identifies ethical standards for teaching young children and provides several examples of professional and unprofessional behaviors related to each standard.

Ethics of Teaching Young Children	Professional Behavior	Unprofessional Behavior
Maintain confidentiality about children and their families.	Discussing a child's problem confidentially with another teacher or the supervisor and trying to identify ways to help the child. "Ms. Kim, Max often comes to the center in dirty clothes. We need to discuss the situation with our supervisor."	Talking about a particular child in front of the child or with a parent other than the child's. "Did you see that child's clothes? I'm glad you don't dress your child like that."
Be honest, dependable, reliable, and regular in attendance.	Arriving at work every day on time and ready to perform your assigned duties. "I'll be ready to go home after I finish wiping these tables."	Talking with colleagues rather than paying attention to children. Calling in sick unnecessarily, arriving late, or not doing assigned duties. "You'll have to watch these kids yourself. I have to call my girlfriend to make plans for tonight."

Ethics of Teaching Young Children	Professional Behavior	Unprofessional Behavior
Treat parents with respect, even during difficult situations.	Talking privately to a parent who always comes late about the problems this causes and discussing possible solutions. "Ms. Lowell. Our center closes at 6:30. If you can't get here by that time, could someone else pick up Jan?"	Getting angry at a parent who is late and demanding he or she do better. Talking to other parents or acquaintances about parents. "This is the third time you've been late this week. I need to go home too, you know!"
Treat each child as an individual, avoid comparisons, and show no bias because of culture, background, abilities, or gender.	Comforting a child who is hurt or upset. Including materials and activities that reflect the cultures and backgrounds of all children. "It's okay to cry if you hurt. Do you want to tell me about it?"	Teasing children if they cry. Comparing one child to another. "Why can't you play nicely like Timothy does?"
Make sure materials, activities, practices, and routines are developmentally appropriate.	Allowing children to participate in routines according to their personal schedules. "Sure, Randy, you can have a snack now. I'll help you get out the crackers and peanut butter."	Making all children do the same activities or follow the same strict schedule for meeting their needs. "Wake up Damian, it's time to eat snack. You've slept long enough."
Be a positive model for learning and language skills. Never use profanities in front of children.	Giving children clear directions that show respect for their work and play. "In 10 minutes, it will be time to pick up and get ready to go outside."	Speaking rudely to children, using harsh words, and a negative tone. "How many times do I have to tell you to clean up? Get busy. Now!!"

Ethics of Teaching Young Children	Professional Behavior	Unprofessional Behavior
Wear clothes appropriate to job. Pay attention to dress, grooming, and hygiene.	Wearing comfortable, clean clothes suitable for playing with and caring for children, bending and lifting, sitting on the floor, and moving quickly, when necessary. "I'm most comfortable in wide skirts or slacks so I can sit on the floor with the children."	Wearing clothes that hinder movement and are inappropriate for a child care setting. "Ask Ms. Peterson to help you. I can't walk on the grass in these shoes."
Maintain accurate, timely, and appropriate records.	Completing an accident report immediately after the incident. "Lori's mother took time to read the accident report on Lori's fall before she went home."	Failing to record information about an accident. "No one ever reads these accident reports. I'm not wasting my time filling one out.
Advocate on behalf of children, families, self, and others. Let others know the importance of quality early childhood programs.	Joining a professional organization. "I'm really glad I joined NAEYC. Their journal articles are filled with information I can use."	Belittling child care work as "only babysitting." "As soon as I can, I'm going to get a real job."

Applying Your Knowledge

In this activity you list examples of ways that your behavior conforms to ethics of teaching young children. Then you read several case studies and decide what an early childhood professional should do in each situation.

Applying Professional Ethics

Ethics of Teaching Young Children	Examples of Your Own Professional Behavior
Maintain confidentiality about children and their families.	
Be honest, dependable, reliable, and regular in attendance.	
Treat parents with respect, even during difficult situations.	
Treat each child as an individual, avoid comparisons, and show no bias because of culture, background, abilities, or gender.	
Make sure materials, activities, practices, and routines are developmentally appropriate.	
Be a positive model for learning and language skills. Never use profanities in front of children.	
Wear clothes appropriate to job. Pay attention to dress, grooming, and hygiene.	
Maintain accurate, timely, and appropriate records.	
Advocate on behalf of children, families, self, and others. Let others know the importance of quality early childhood programs.	

Ethics Case Studies[3]

The following situations were developed by NAEYC. After reading each one, answer the question: What should an early childhood professional do? These are difficult issues to resolve. You may want to discuss your ideas with others. There can be more than one ethical response to each case study.

1. The Abused Child

Mary Lou, a three-year-old in your center, is showing several signs of possible abuse: multiple bruises, frequent black eyes, and psychological withdrawal. Her mother, a high-strung woman, says Mary Lou falls a lot, but nobody at the center has seen the child do this. On two occasions, the child's father appeared to be drunk when he picked her up. The law says you are a mandated reporter who must report suspicions of abuse to Child Protective Services. But in your experience, when the authorities get involved they are usually unable to remove the child from the home or improve the family's behavior. Sometimes the families simply disappear, or things become worse for the children.

What should an early childhood professional do?

2. The Working Mother

Timothy's mother has asked you not to allow her four-year-old son to nap in the afternoon. She says, "Whenever he naps he stays up until 10:00 at night. I have to get up at 5:00 in the morning to go to work. I am not getting enough sleep." Along with the rest of the children, Timothy takes a one-hour nap almost every day. He seems to need it in order to stay in good spirits in the afternoon.

What should an early childhood professional do?

[3] Adapted with permission from Stephanie Feeney, "Ethical Case Studies for NAEYC Reader Response," *Young Children* (Washington, DC: National Association for the Education of Young Children, May 1987), pp. 24-25.

3. Case Study: The Aggressive Child

Eric is a large and extremely active four-year-old who often frightens and hurts other children. You have discussed this repeatedly with the director, who is sympathetic but unable to help. Eric's parents listen but they think his behavior is typical for boys his age. They ignore your referrals to a counselor. A preschool specialist from the Department of Mental Health has observed Eric, but her recommendations have not helped either. Meanwhile, Eric terrorizes other children and as a result, parents are starting to complain. You are becoming stressed and tired, and your patience is wearing thin. You and your co-teacher are spending so much time dealing with Eric that you are worried the other children are not getting the attention they need.

What should an early childhood professional do?

4. The "Academic" Preschool

Heather just went back to college to get her CDA credential. She has been assigned as your trainee. She has taught at a preschool center for several years, is happy there, and receives a good salary. During your observations, you saw three- and four-year-olds using workbooks for long periods of time. The daily program included repetitious drill on letters, numbers, shapes, and colors. Children were regularly "taught" the alphabet and rote counting to 100. You also noticed that most interactions were initiated by adults and that children had few opportunities to interact with materials.

You mention to Heather that you do not think the center's curriculum is appropriate for preschool children. She replies that she had a similar reaction when she began working there, but the director and other teachers assured her there was no problem with the curriculum. They told her that this is the way they have always taught at the school. The parents are very satisfied with it.

What should an early childhood professional do?

When you have completed these case studies, plan a time to discuss your responses with your trainer and other teachers.

IV. Becoming an Advocate for Children and Families

In this activity you will learn to:

- Recognize the importance of being an advocate for children and families
- Become involved in advocacy efforts

Advocacy is working for change. Early childhood advocates speak out on issues that may affect children and families or on issues related to their own working conditions. Often, decisionmakers aren't aware of the problems and issues related to providing quality child development programs for preschool children. Without awareness and understanding, change is not possible. As an early childhood professional you are in a good position to help others understand important issues and concerns.

Becoming an Advocate[4]

A first step in becoming an early childhood advocate is to understand the importance of advocacy. This means recognizing how public and private policies affect children's lives and accepting that children need a strong voice to ensure that the programs they attend support their development. Advocates must ask themselves, "What can I do to ensure that policymakers, elected officials, administrators, schools, businesses, and other groups pay adequate attention to children's needs?"

Advocates try to improve the circumstances of children's lives. Early childhood professionals are especially well-informed on this issue in terms of both theory and practice. Advocates commit themselves to sharing their knowledge with others. Because they realize the problems faced by children and families are a collective responsibility, they are willing to become involved and act on their concerns.

You and your colleagues can become effective advocates for children, families, and the early childhood profession in at least six ways, as described in the following paragraphs.

Your professional beliefs and knowledge are based on an understanding of child development, the practice of early childhood education, and relationships with parents. This is your professional knowledge base. Therefore, you can help parents, policymakers, and other decision makers understand children's developmental needs and the characteristics of safe and nurturing early childhood environments. You can clarify the link between policy and positive outcomes for children. As an advocate, you can be a catalyst for change.

Share your knowledge.

---

[4] Adapted with permission from Stacie G. Goffin and Joan Lombardi, *Speaking Out: Early Childhood Advocacy* (Washington, DC: National Association for the Education of Young Children, 1988), pp. 2-5.

Share your professional experiences.

Through your day-to-day interactions with children and families, you are all too familiar with the causes of extreme stress—unemployment, lack of child care, drug and alcohol abuse, chronic illnesses, homelessness, and conflicts between work and family responsibility. You see how children and families are affected by high levels of stress. Your daily work gives you firsthand knowledge of the effectiveness of services community agencies are providing to children and families. You know which needs are being met, and which are not. As a result, you have an opportunity—and a professional responsibility—to share the personal stories that give meaning to group statistics. Without revealing confidential information, you can describe the real impact of policies that affect children and families.

Redefine the "bottom line" for children.

The debate about programs for young children is often tied to other policy issues such as welfare reform, job training, substance abuse, and teenage pregnancy. Funding for children's programs is "sold" as an investment in the nation's future productivity. Joining children's issues with broader political issues and social concerns is an effective political technique. It can expand the base of support and help frame children's issues in ways consistent with accepted social values.

Your ongoing work with children makes you an effective advocate for children's inherent "worth." You understand that childhood is a crucial time for development. If policies for children and families are devised solely on the basis of "return on investment," children will suffer when investors seek a higher return or decide to pull out of the "market." We all must remember that these strategies are simply means to achieve a desired end. They must not undermine the "bottom line" of advocacy—encouraging policies that promote children's healthy development.

Stand up for the early childhood profession.

Early childhood education is a growing profession that provides essential services to children and families. Therefore, teachers must speak out on behalf of the profession—and for the specialized skills and knowledge required of those who care for and support the development of young children.

Many people don't know that early childhood education has a distinctive, professional knowledge base or that program quality is closely tied to staff training and compensation. Many teachers have experienced the impact of low wages, high staff turnover, burnout, and inadequately trained staff and administrators. They are obligated to share these stories, too.

Advocacy efforts on behalf of child development programs are most effective when professionals emphasize how their work benefits children and families. Teachers must begin to exercise their power to speak out on issues that affect the profession.

Involve parents.

Your daily interactions with parents provide many opportunities to share your common concerns and goals for children's well being. You can help parents recognize their power as primary advocates—for their own children as well as for all children.

Parents can be especially effective advocates on behalf of their children. They represent a critical consumer voice. By involving parents, you can dramatically expand the group of people speaking out for children.

Early childhood professionals may have ongoing relationships with other individuals and agencies that provide services for children and families: public school administrators and teachers, health care providers, religious organizations, and many professional and volunteer groups. These interactions offer natural opportunities to inform others about children's developmental needs, appropriate teaching practices, and the support services families need.

Expand the constituency for children.

You can choose from many courses of action once you make a commitment to become an advocate for children, families, and your profession. Here are a few choices.[5]

Choose a course of action.

- Share ideas for appropriate practice with other teachers and parents (instead of just observing disapprovingly).

- Explain to administrators why dittos are inappropriate learning tools for young children (rather than using them, while resenting that you must use practices that are inconsistent with your profession's knowledge base).

- Explain to parents why children learn best through play (instead of bemoaning that parents are pushing their children or giving in yourself and using inappropriate methods and materials).

- Write a letter to the editor of a newspaper or magazine to respond to an article or letter (instead of complaining about how other people don't understand the needs of children, families, or early childhood professionals).

- Write to your state or federal legislators about a pending issue and share your experiences as a way to point out needs (rather than just assuming someone else will write).

- Meet someone new who is interested in early childhood education and ask her or him to join a professional group such as NAEYC, NBCDI, SECA, or ACEI (instead of just wondering why the person isn't involved).

- Ask a friend to go with you to community meetings where issues of concern to children and families will be discussed (instead of staying home because you don't want to go alone).

- Volunteer to represent your professional group in a coalition to speak out on the developmental needs of young children (instead of waiting to be asked or declining because you've never done it before).

- Agree to serve on a legislative telephone tree (rather than refusing because "my phone call won't matter anyway").

[5] Adapted with permission from Stacie G. Goffin and Joan Lombardi, *Speaking Out: Early Childhood Advocacy* (Washington, DC: National Association for the Education of Young Children, 1988), pp. 14-15.

- Work and learn with others to develop a position statement on a critical issue (instead of saying, "I don't really know much about this topic.").

- Volunteer to speak at a school board meeting about professional standards for early childhood education set by groups such as NAEYC, NASBE, NAESP, or Head Start (instead of resigning yourself to the fact that your school system doesn't understand much about early childhood education).

- Conduct a local or state survey of salaries in early childhood programs (instead of ignoring the issue because no one has the facts).

- Persuade colleagues that it is important to work toward accreditation from the National Academy of Early Childhood Programs (rather than just assuming no one wants to improve the program).

Applying Your Knowledge

In this activity you consider your own feelings about advocacy and develop a plan for becoming an advocate. Review the suggestions in this learning activity, then answer the following questions.

Becoming an Advocate

What contributions would you like to make as an advocate for children, families, and your profession?

What obstacles might prevent you from being an advocate, and how can you overcome them?

What is one advocacy step you can take this month?

What is one advocacy step you can take within six months?

What is one advocacy step you can take within a year?

Discuss your responses with your trainer.

V. Taking Care of Yourself

In this activity you will learn to:

- Recognize the importance of taking care of yourself
- Take care of your physical, emotional, social, and intellectual well-being

Early childhood teachers need to consider their own well-being.

Although your first responsibility as a teacher is to take care of the needs of children, you also have a responsibility to take care of yourself. All you have to give is yourself—your energy, your ideas, and your commitment. You cannot do this when you are not at your best. To work successfully with young children, you have to be in good physical and emotional health. You also need to feel you are appreciated, meaningfully connected to others, intellectually stimulated, and performing a job worth doing. Taking care of yourself means considering your needs and well-being in four areas: physical, emotional, social, and intellectual.

Physical well-being is very important to a person who works with preschoolers. Without physical stamina and good health, you are not prepared to work with young children every day. Three key factors in achieving physical well-being are: eating a healthy diet, getting enough sleep, and exercising regularly.

Emotional well-being—the way you feel about yourself, your work, and the world—affects how you interact with the children and adults around you. The more positive you feel about yourself, the better you will be able to care for children. If you start to feel worried or depressed, it is good to talk with family and friends about your concerns.

Social well-being is essential for survival. Having a trusted friend with whom to share your joys and successes, frustrations, concerns, and ideas, can be very important in determining how you feel about yourself as a person and as a professional. The person may be a colleague, spouse, relative, or friend. What is important is that you have someone (at least one, but preferably several people) with whom you can exchange ideas, feelings, resources, and moral support.

Intellectual well-being comes from the joy of learning something new and feeling challenged. Like children, adults learn from ongoing exploration, experimentation, and problem solving. The more you learn about working with preschoolers, the more satisfying your work will become. This is what professionalism is all about.

Stress is a part of our daily lives.

In Module 2: Healthy, we discussed how stress affects children and what you and your colleagues can do to reduce children's stress and help them cope in positive ways. Most adults also find that stress—at work and in their personal lives—is part of their daily routines.

The sources of stress in your life may differ from those in your colleagues' lives. A situation one person finds stressful may not be for another. For example, you may feel very anxious when you get caught in traffic on your way to an appointment; a colleague might accept the fact that there is nothing to do but sit back, review his plans for the day, and enjoy listening to a new tape. Stress on the job may also affect you and your colleagues. Work-related stress might be due to situations such as:

- disagreeing with a colleague or supervisor;

- getting caught in a rain storm while on a neighborhood walk;

- working with children who have many problems in their lives; or

- supporting a parent whose problems are overwhelming.

Some work-related stress can be alleviated through effective communication, improved adult-child ratios, or revised management practices ("From now on, we'll make sure we check the weather report and bring coats and umbrellas on cloudy days."). Other stressful situations are "part of the job." Working with young children is challenging. Even the most qualified and highly-skilled teachers experience days when their jobs seem overwhelming.

How we respond to stress can affect our physical, emotional, social, and intellectual well-being. Some examples follow:

Our responses to stress can affect our well-being.

- Responses affecting your **physical well-being** might include:

  increased pulse, racing heart

  increased or decreased appetite

  excitability, hyperactivity

  always feeling tired

  difficulty relaxing, trouble sleeping

  difficulty staying awake

- Responses affecting your **emotional well-being** might include:

  feelings of inadequacy

  lowered self-esteem

  sadness, mild depression

  fear of losing control

- Responses affecting your **social well-being** might include:

  clinging to others

  withdrawing from others

  feeling angry with yourself and/or others

  being unusually impatient

  experiencing mood swings

- Responses affecting your **intellectual well-being** might include:

  racing from one thought to another

  forgetting how to solve simple problems

  thinking about performing routine tasks (e.g., getting ready for work in the morning) rather than doing them automatically

  forgetting important events or responsibilities

  being easily distracted

Taking care of yourself helps you cope with stress.

It's almost impossible to eliminate all of the sources of stress in our lives. Instead, we need to cope in healthy ways so the stress does not lead to burn-out. The responses listed above are messages that tell us we need to take better care of ourselves. The suggestions for helping children handle stress that appear in Module 2: Healthy, may also be useful for adults. Many people find eating a healthy diet, getting regular exercise, spending time with friends, and taking time to meet their own needs, can help them manage their stress.

When people don't cope with their stress, these responses may continue for a long time. For example, if a person is forgetful for a few days while handling a difficult situation, there is no cause for alarm. If the forgetfulness continues for weeks or months, the individual may need professional assistance. A mental health counselor can help the individual talk about the situation and learn to cope with stress in healthy and positive ways.

Applying Your Knowledge

In this learning activity you assess how well you are taking care of yourself. Record your activities for two days. For Day 1 record your activities for today. Then, review your answers, consider areas where you could take better care of yourself, and try to be better to yourself tomorrow. Record your improved activities under Day 2.

Taking Care of Myself

	Day 1		Day 2	
	yes	no	yes	no
Physical Well-Being				
Did I eat three balanced meals?	☐	☐	☐	☐
Did I get enough sleep?	☐	☐	☐	☐
Did I get any exercise?	☐	☐	☐	☐
Emotional Well-Being				
Did I have a generally positive outlook?	☐	☐	☐	☐
Did I take a few moments to relax after a stressful situation?	☐	☐	☐	☐
Social Well-Being				
Did I spend time with someone I care about?	☐	☐	☐	☐
Did I talk through a problem with a friend or colleague?	☐	☐	☐	☐
Intellectual Well-Being				
Did I read anything for information or interest—a book, an article, the newspaper?	☐	☐	☐	☐
Did I learn something new?	☐	☐	☐	☐

Discuss this activity with your trainer and make a commitment to take good care of yourself. Use the space below to note what actions you will take.

I will do the following to take care of myself:

Summarizing Your Progress

You have now completed all of the learning activities for this module. Whether you are an experienced teacher or new to the profession, this module has probably helped you to learn about maintaining a commitment to professionalism.

Before you go on, review your responses to the pre-training assessment for this module. Write a summary of what you learned and list the skills you developed or improved.

If there are topics you would like to know more about, you will find recommended readings listed in the Orientation in Volume I.

Your final step in this module is to complete the knowledge and competency assessments. Let your trainer know when you are ready to schedule the assessments. If this is your last module, you have successfully completed the training program. Congratulations on a job well done.

Answer Sheet

Overview
(pp. 308-310)

1. **How did Ms. Kim assess her own performance?**
   a. *She thought about the day's events.*

   b. *She considered feedback from parents.*

2. **What did she do with the results of her self-assessment?**
   a. *She decided that she and Ms. Richards need to make some changes in their classroom.*

   b. *She planned to talk to Mr. Lopez and Ms. Thomas, two teachers who seem well-organized, to get some pointers.*

   c. *She planned to talk to her supervisor to get some suggestions.*

Continuing to Learn About Caring for Children

1. **How did Mr. Lopez and Ms. Thomas choose a topic to learn more about?**
   a. *Mr. Lopez read an article on portfolios and shared it with Ms. Thomas.*

   b. *They discussed the article and agreed to ask their supervisor for more resources on portfolios.*

2. **How did they plan to expand their knowledge and skills?**
   a. *They planned to ask their supervisor for additional resources on portfolios.*

   b. *They planned to begin using portfolios for the children in their classroom.*

Applying Professional Ethics at All Times

1. **How did Ms. Williams use professional ethics while talking to Mrs. Jones?**
   a. *She greeted Mrs. Jones politely when she arrived.*

   b. *She responded to Mrs. Johnson's comments in a positive way.*

   c. *She maintained confidentiality by not discussing Joshua's behavior with another parent.*

2. **How did Ms. Williams interact with Joshua in a professional manner?**
   a. *She acted quickly to ensure Joshua's safety.*

   b. *She used positive guidance techniques to redirect Joshua to a safe place for jumping.*

Glossary

Competence

A skill or ability to do something well.

Ethics

A set of principles, standards, or guidelines that direct acceptable behavior—what is right or good rather than what is quickest or easiest.

Maintaining confidentiality

Sharing information only with people who have a need to know.

Networking

Spending time with people who perform similar tasks to share ideas, information, and experiences.

Professionalism

A commitment to gaining and maintaining knowledge and skills in a particular field, and to using that knowledge and those skills to provide the highest-quality services possible.

Professional behavior

The consistent, complete application of knowledge, skills, and ethics.

Notes

Notes

Notes

Notes

Notes